SINGLES GUIDE

to the

SAN FRANCISCO

BAY AREA

Where & How to Meet
a Romantic Partner
and New Friends

RICHARD GOSSE

Dedicated to Jeff Mulanax & Dorothy Schad

Published by
Marin Publications
4 Highland Avenue
San Rafael, CA 94901
(415) 459-3817

ISBN 0-934377-08-1

CONTENTS

Part One

BEING SINGLE

in the

SAN FRANCISCO

BAY AREA

THE BAY AREA SINGLES SCENE

Congratulations for choosing to live in the San Francisco Bay Area! You've chosen the best region in the country to be single. That's because the Bay Area has the highest per capita singles population in the United States. A majority of the adults are single.

That's not true of other areas of the country where singles are often a minority looked upon with scorn or pity. Isn't it great to be part of the majority?

Over a million single adults in the Bay Area just like you are hoping to meet the right person for a lasting relationship. And we all have one thing in common. We all need love.

The tragedy is that most of us are too embarrassed to admit it. And we're too scared of rejection to reach out to each other. So we stay home and feel lonely. And complain about how hard it is to meet people.

Single women are particularly pessimistic. Many complain that "all the men in San Francisco are either married, gay, or dead." That's simply not true. Noreen Goldman & Charles F. Westoff did a study of eligible men in the top 38 metropolitan areas of America (Money Magazine, December, 1984). They only counted eligible bachelors (men who were

The Bay Area Singles Scene

10

not gay and were open to marriage) and still concluded that
San Francisco is the third best major city in the country to
meet a husband!

I teach classes for singles at 30 colleges throughout
California. Wherever I go I hear amazing statistics from
women about the shortage of men. Some single women
actually believe that there are eight women for every man in
their county!

The fact of the matter is that there is a tiny surplus of
women in most counties and there actually is a surplus of
men in Solano County! Let's look at the actual numbers.
Here are the estimated populations of San Francisco and ten
nearby counties, as of January 1, 1985, together with the
male-female ratio:

Alameda County - Population 1,174,800; 51.4% women;
    48.6% men
Contra Costa County - 703,400; 51.2% women; 48.8% men
Marin County - 223,200; 50.9% women; 49.1% men
Monterey County - 48.8% women; 51.2% men
Napa County - 102,200; 50.9% women; 49.1% men
San Francisco - 719,200; 50.2% women; 49.8% men
San Mateo County - 606,200; 51.3% women; 48.7% men
Santa Clara County - 1,376,900; 50.5% women; 49.5% men
Santa Cruz County - 51.1% women; 48.9% men
Solano County - 269,100; 49.3% women; 50.7% men
Sonoma County - 330,000; 51.6% women; 48.4% men
    (Source: California Almanac, 1986-87, James S. Fay, et. al.,
    which may be obtained from Presidio Press, 31 Pamaron
    Way, Novato, CA 94947).

Clearly there are literally hundreds of thousands of living,
breathing, single men in the Bay Area who want to meet a
special woman for a loving relationship.

Sometimes, of course, statistics can lie. These figures are
misleading because they aren't broken down by age bracket.
While there is a surplus of single women in most age
brackets, there's actually a shortage of single women in San

The Bay Area Singles Scene

Francisco in the 20-29 age bracket. According to Goldman & Westoff, there are 136 eligible bachelors for every 100 single women in the 20-24 age bracket and 104 single men for every 100 single women in the 25-29 age bracket. This is despite the fact that an estimated 24% of men in San Francisco are gay.

Here are the statistics for the number of single men in their 20s and 30s per 100 single women. Salinas/Monterey - 166; San Francisco/Oakland -115; San Jose -122; Santa Rosa-Petaluma -110; Vallejo/Fairfield/Napa -141. (For an 18" x 24" Singles Map of the best cities in America to meet single men send $9.95 to Map Makers, Box 97, Kenmore, NY 14217 or call (800) 388-6277).

Where does this surplus come from? Partly it's because of the fact that there are more boys born each year than girls (a surplus of 1% more male babies). Since men tend to marry women 2 - 3 years younger than they, there is a shortage of eligible women in their twenties.

Eventually, however, another factor moves in to reverse the imbalance: men tend to die seven years younger than women. At age 35, for example, enough men have died that there is an equal number of men and women in the United States. By age 60 there are 3 and 1/2 single women for every single man in the U.S. The odds are even worse than this statistic suggest because men 50 years old and over marry women an average of eight years younger than they. If you're a middle-aged woman, however, don't panic. The surplus of single women of your age isn't an insurmountable problem because most of these women aren't really much competition. The overwhelming majority of them either stay home almost all the time or don't have a clue as to where to meet single men. That's where you have the advantage. By following the simple suggestions in this book you can beat the odds and find the right man for a happy, loving relationship.

As for men, the odds get better each year. In San Francisco there are 91 eligible bachelors for every 100 single women in the 30-34 age bracket; 73 men, 100 women, ages

35-39; 58 men, 100 women, ages 40-44; 47 men, 100 women, ages 45-49; 41 men, 100 women, ages 50-54 bracket; 36 men, 100 women, ages 55-59.

Here are the figures for San Jose: 142 eligible bachelors for every 100 single women, ages 20-24; 100 men, 100 women, ages 25-29; 81 men, 100 women, ages 30-34; 63 men, 100 women, ages 35-39; 51 men, 100 women, ages 40-44; 42 men, 100 women, ages 45-49; 36 men, 100 women, ages 50-54; 31 men, 100 women, ages 55-59.

But enough of statistics. Regardless of how many single men or women there are to meet, Mr. or Ms. Right isn't going to knock on your door. You've got to go out of your way to find them.

This Guide has all the information you'll need. But there's one missing ingredient. And that's you. You've got to be committed to implementing the suggestions in this Guide. That means hard work. And a lot of frustration. But in the end it will all be worth it. Because the pay-off will be a loving relationship that brings great joy to your life.

HOW TO BE HAPPILY SINGLE

Most singles approach the single state as a cross to bear. They see bachelorhood as a way station between marriages. It's inconceivable to them that they could ever be happy as a single. Society reinforces this belief. It teaches us that happiness lies in the nuclear family. Singles are often dismissed as "old maids" or suspected of being gay. No wonder it's tough to be single in America!

The fact of the matter, however, is that single people are often far happier than couples. You can be happily single also. The first step is to get rid of the "grass is greener on the other side syndrome". You have to realize that being married isn't all it's cracked up to be. There are 3 ways to accomplish this.

1. **Make a List of All the Unhappy Couples You Know**. We all know couples that are continually fighting or ignoring each other. If you know a reasonable number of married people you should be able to write up a long list of unhappily married couples. That should help dispel the "grass is greener on the other side syndrome."
2. **Double Your List**. We all know that many people are phony. That holds true for a surprising number of

How to Be Happily Single

14

supposedly happy couples. Secretly they hate each others guts, but publicly they put on a show of matrimonial bliss. We have all seen married couples who appear to be perfectly suited to one another. They make "a lovely couple" and are always kissing and hugging in public. A week later you read in the Society page that they're getting a divorce. You can safely assume that for every obviously unhappy couple you know there is another that is secretly unhappy.

3. **Count Your Blessings.** Make a list of all the advantages of being single. Think of all the things you are free to do that would be forbidden if you were coupled. Think of all the rotten habits you don't have to tolerate. Be imaginative. You should be able to come up with a long list of blessings that are associated with your single lifestyle.

Once you get over the "grass is greener on the other side syndrome" you're ready to make the most of being single. There are three keys to being happily single.

Key #1: Accepting Yourself

Several years ago I had the good fortune of spending a weekend at the Esalen Institute in Big Sur, California. I was with a group of about 20 people in an encounter group. There was one middle-aged gentleman who impressed me deeply. He appeared to be very happy and seemed to have a genuinely high opinion of himself. Believing that self-esteem was the most important key to happiness, I asked him for his secret.

His answer astounded me. He said, "I don't have high self-esteem. I know my limitations and I accept them. That's the key to my happiness."

Unfortunately society teaches that you should "live up to expectations—your own and those of others. That's great if you can live up to all of them. But what happens if you have contradictory expectations? Or what if you fail to meet some of them? Often the result is low self-esteem and misery for the rest of your life.

Think back to your childhood. Your parents always insisted that you be a good little boy or girl. You were taught that if you didn't meet those standards you were a rotten person. You were rejected and/or punished by your parents for being yourself and not being the person they wanted you to be.

When you went to school the same process continued. Your teachers rewarded you with compliments, smiles, gold stars, and good grades when you were "good". But if you were a lousy speller, couldn't memorize your times tables, or were noisy you were rejected and labeled as a "slow learner" or "discipline problem".

Likewise your peer group damaged your self concept. If you couldn't hit the ball as far as your friends or didn't have as pretty a dress you were shunned. You learned that you were an unattractive or bad person.

The process continues throughout life. Bosses, co-workers, employees, customers, clients, friends, lovers, spouses, children. All of them are in a position to do damage to your self-concept by insisting that you be something you aren't.

You can spend your entire life striving to meet those expectations. But that's not the road to happiness. The key to happiness is to dump all the expectations and give yourself permission to be yourself.

Key #2: Changing Yourself

Most people will agree that accepting yourself is a key to happiness. But shouldn't you also strive to be the best person you can possibly be? Certainly there's nothing wrong with trying to change yourself for the better. Be careful to consider two points, however, before deciding to change yourself.

1. Will changing yourself make YOU happy or simply meet someone else's expectations? If it isn't going to make you

happy, then why change just to appease someone else? You are under no obligation to meet their expectations. If you find yourself in a relationship with someone who won't be satisfied with you unless you change, wouldn't you be better off finding someone who likes you as you are?

2. Are you willing to pay the price to change? Change requires effort and often involves a great deal of pain. As a human being you are a creature of habit. The vast percentage of your actions and qualities are habitual. And habits are extremely difficult to change. If you don't believe this, ask smokers why they keep smoking despite the fact that they are slowly killing themselves.

Unless you are motivated to pay the price you're kidding yourself if you expect to change. As an example let's look at obesity. In our society women in particular are trained to be ashamed of their bodies because they're too fat. Hundreds of thousands of teenage girls are anorexic or bulemic (they starve themselves or throw up continuously) because of this neurotic American obsession with slimness. If you don't have the figure of a model you probably chastise yourself continuously.

Most American women (and many men) go from one crash diet to the next. This is despite the fact that 98% of the time they either don't lose a significant amount of weight or regain it all within 6 months.

Why is it so hard to lose weight and keep it off, despite the intense pressure placed on you to do so? Because being slim, for most people, involves paying a very high price—pain every day of your life. You can't be "good" every other day or every other week. You have to diet 7 days a week, 52 weeks a year—forever. Not many people are willing to pay this price.

So what do you do? You go on crash diets, lose weight, and then eventually get tired of the price and go back to being fat. Then you beat yourself up psychologically and the cycle resumes with another crash diet. The result: you

How to Be Happily Single

wind up being as fat or fatter than before and your self-concept goes down the drain.

What's the solution? Ask yourself, "Am I willing to suffer every day for the rest of my life in order to be thin? Or will I be happier being fat?" If you aren't willing to pay the price for slimness the only rational alternative is to give yourself permission to be fat and abandon all dieting. Eat to your heart's content and become a happy fat person.

The same holds true for any other negative quality or habit. Be honest with yourself and ask whether you are willing to pay the price to rid yourself of your habits. If you aren't, then try to make the most of your life in spite of these qualities.

On the other hand, suppose you have a positive goal. For example, you may have a desire to become wealthy. If you're like most people you'll never achieve wealth—because you aren't willing to pay the price. You'll fantasize about great wealth. Or you'll wait for a miracle to happen—e.g. winning the Irish sweepstakes or marrying a millionaire. In the meantime you remain impoverished.

If you want to make a great deal of money you have to do it "the old-fashioned way", as the commercial goes. "You have to earn it". That means long, hard, tedious hours. It involves working when you'd rather play. It means taking chances. You'll have to live a frugal lifestyle so you can save the nest egg you need for starting a business or investing in real estate.

If you're not willing to pay the price to achieve wealth, give up the fantasy. Be realistic and face the fact that you have chosen to live comfortably now rather than sacrifice for the future. There's nothing wrong with a modest standard of living—as long as you have rationally decided that it's preferable to working to achieve great wealth.

Key #3: Controlling Negative Emotions

One of the cardinal tenets of pop psychology is to "let it all hang out". You're supposed to unleash all of your anger, frustration, bitterness, and repression. That's supposed to be the key to emotional health.

There's an element of truth to this. If you keep your negative emotions locked up there is the danger that one day you'll explode. Ulcers and other negative symptoms may also result from keeping a lid on your emotions.

But there is a better way to deal with your negative feelings. You can take charge and control them, rather than sit back passively and allow them to control your life.

Your negative emotions don't just happen. They are the results of statements you make to yourself. Let's take jealousy as an example. Your sweetheart is flirting at a party. You react by saying to yourself: "My lover has no right to flirt with someone else. My lover should only flirt with me. This is unfair and cruel. I don't have to take this." Needless to say, if you make these statements you will feel jealous and miserable. You may wind up making a nasty scene, leaving in a huff, and refusing to have sex with your partner for a week as punishment for lack of fidelity. You suffer, your partner suffers, and the relationship deteriorates.

Sound familiar? The tragedy of this scene is that it didn't have to happen. You could have said to yourself, "My lover has a right to live his/her life as s/he wishes. That includes flirting." If you say this to yourself (and believe it) you won't feel upset at innocent flirting at a party.

Another negative emotion you can control is guilt. Beating yourself up psychologically over a past indiscretion serves no useful purpose. You can make yourself feel miserable for the rest of your life over past mistakes if you aren't careful. The solution is to control your guilt by changing the statements you make to yourself.

Let's take an extreme example. Suppose you murder someone. You go to prison and, like most murderers, you eventually are released. It would be easy to say to yourself, "I'm a rotten, disgusting human being. I don't deserve to live. What I did was horrible. I hate myself."

The only problem with these statements and the resulting

guilt is that they serve no useful purpose. The person you murdered is dead. No amount of guilt will ever make up for your dastardly deed. The important thing now is to make sure that you never repeat your mistake and to try to make your life the best life possible.

Maybe you can help the family of your victim. Perhaps you will choose to devote some of your time to charitable endeavors. Whatever you do, don't wallow in guilt. Try to make the most of the rest of your life by saying, "I did something terribly wrong and will do everything I can to avoid repeating my mistake. In the meantime I will do my best to bring happiness into my life and the lives of others."

Worry is another negative emotion that must not be indulged. As an example, supposed you fear your lover will dump you. Every time your lover comes home late, ignores you, or says something angry you conclude that the relationship is about to end. You spend a considerable amount of time each day worrying about being dumped. You probably drive your lover up the wall by neurotically demanding attention and reassurance. Meantime your constant worrying serves no purpose other than to make your life miserable. No amount of worrying will increase the chances of survival of your relationship.

The wise course would be to change your statements to yourself. Don't say, "My lover is going to leave me and my life will be ruined. I'm going to be miserable for the rest of my life." Instead say, "Maybe my relationship will end and I'll be miserable for a while. But millions of other people have been dumped and have gone on to happy relationships. I can also. Besides, I don't know for sure my relationship will end. Maybe if I sit down with my lover and share honestly we can work things out."

What do you do if you find that you can't stop making statements that cause negative emotions? You may wish to employ the thought-stopping techniques recommended in **Thoughts & Feelings** (Oakland, CA: New Harbinger Publications, 1981.) One easy technique is yelling "Stop!" at the top of your lungs. For example, every time you worry about losing your job, shout "Stop!". Obviously you won't feel comfortable doing this publicly. There are other techniques you can employ. For example, wear a rubber band around your wrist. Whenever you make negative statements to yourself that make you miserable, snap the rubber band. These techniques are so simple they may appear silly. They aren't. They are effective ways of avoiding a lifetime of misery.

Changing or stopping the statements you make to yourself aren't the only methods for controlling your negative emotions. There are many others. Relaxation techniques are an effective way of overcoming negative emotions such as anger or anxiety. When you feel under stress the first thing to is to concentrate on your breathing. You will find that you are breathing faster and less deeply than normal. Hopefully your breathing will slow down and become deeper just in the process of monitoring your breath. If not, concentrate on achieving this.

The interesting thing about negative emotions is that they are usually associated with a tense body. If you can relax your body you will often find that your negative emotions dissipate.

There are many other relaxation techniques that are taught in books and cassette tapes. A good book to read is **The Relaxation & Stress Reduction Workbook** (Oakland, CA: New Harbinger Publications, 1980). You will learn new breathing techniques and ways of relaxing your body.

Conclusion

If you're like most people, you bought this book because you wanted to meet someone special for a lasting, loving relationship. The information and techniques in this book will help you achieve that goal. But it's hard work. So before you get your hopes up, ask yorself if you're willing to pay the price for finding love.

In the meantime, don't put your life on hold. Make the most out of being single. Strive to be the happiest person you can possibly be. That way if someday you do choose to commit yourself to someone, it won't be out of desperation. It will be because you have met someone wonderful and have succeeded in creating a beautiful relationship. Good luck!

TEN RULES
FOR DATING

If you're like most singles you work 40 or more hours a week at a job you don't particularly enjoy. The reason is that you value money very highly.

How many hours a week do you spend looking for love? Probably zero. And that's the problem. Here in America our value system is twisted. We're taught to value money a lot more highly than we do love. The result is millions of single people in America who have money but not happiness.

This Guide is based on a different value system. One that holds love to be the most precious thing in life. One that says that good friends are worth their weight in gold.

You can sit back and patiently wait for romantic partners and intimate friends to come your way. Or you can take the initiative and make things happen!

This Guide does the easy part. It tells you where to go to meet people. The hard part, however, is up to you. You've got to implement the suggestions in this Guide. And that takes hard work.

So before we talk about the hundreds of places to meet people in your area let's get to the unpleasant part. There

24

are 10 rules for meeting someone special for a lasting, loving relationship. They aren't pleasant rules. And they aren't easy. But they work. If you're willing to follow these rules, you'll leave the ranks of those who are waiting for love and join those who have found love.

Rule #1: Have Realistic Expectations

Have you ever noticed that 95% of us seem to be chasing after the same 5%. I call them the "lucky 5%". They have no trouble meeting someone for a romantic relationship. They are blessed with physical beauty or money or status or all three. Relationships come to them rather than the other way around. Looking at things logically, if 95% of us are chasing after the same 5%, each of them has to date 19 of us simultaneously in order to keep all of us happy. And that's not going to happen.

How realistic are your expectations? Take a good, long, honest look at yourself.

"I've got a great personality and a heart of gold", you say. That's great, except that you live in a world in which people judge you initially by superficial things like the beauty of your face, the slimness of your body, the clothes you wear, the car you drive, and the job you hold.

So if people find your exterior to be unattractive, you've got a tough road ahead of you. For example, if you're a 3 on a scale of 10 in terms of initial attractiveness to the opposite sex, don't expect to attract a 9 or 10. If you're a woman, forget about Tom Selleck or a millionaire. If you're a man, forget about meeting a Playboy bunny. Settle for someone nice who finds you attractive.

"Does that mean I have to lower my standards?"

Sadly the answer is yes. I know it's hard to give up fantasies of Prince Charming or the beauty queen. Just remember that it's even harder to go through life without romantic love.

Newsweek Magazine's cover story for June 2, 1986 demoralized single women throughout the nation. The

10 Rules for Dating

article claimed that if you are 30 years old, college-educated, and never been married, that you only have a 20% chance of ever finding a husband. If you reach age 35 without a spouse, your chances drop to 5%. And if you have the misfortune of being single at 40, according to Newsweek you have a greater chance of "being killed by terrorists" than finding a husband.

The Newsweek article was based on a study by two professors at Harvard and Yale Universities. Fortunately the figures have been discredited by the U.S. Census Bureau. For one thing, the Harvard-Yale Study was based on a relatively small sample. More importantly, it was based on a critical assumption: that single women in the United States would continue to follow three patterns in selecting a mate as they have in the past:

1. Marrying a man who is older than she. The average woman in America chooses a man two to four years older than she. Since men live seven years less than the average woman, this means that the older a woman becomes the fewer men are still left that are older than she. At birth there are more boy babies than girls (a 1% surplus of boys). This continues until age 35 where there is an equal ratio of single men to single women. From that point on the men start dying off so that at age 60 there are three and one half single women for every single man in the United States. This statistic becomes even more grim when you consider that many of these scarce 60 year single men are dating women in their forties and fifties! Obviously if single women continue to prefer older men their chances of finding a husband will diminish.
2. Marrying a man who is taller than she. Women who are tall (over 5'6") and like to wear high heels have a problem in meeting suitable men. I have spoken to many women who insist that a man be over 6 feet tall. That eliminates 90% of the single men in this country!
3. Marrying a man who earns more money than she. Even though women in this country still only earn 62 cents on

the dollar in comparison to men, this doesn't apply to successful professional women, who have literally priced themselves out of the market! They have a very tough time finding a man who is older, taller, and wealthier than they.

The main flaw in the Harvard-Yale Study is that there's no reason why you can't adjust to these realities. Why not choose a man who is younger, shorter, or less prosperous? For years women have been complaining about how superficial men are. They chastise men for overlooking inner beauty, intimacy, and communication. Perhaps single women need to look at their own superficial prejudices regarding age, height, and money.

Single men have their own set of unrealistic expectations. They tend to prefer young, slim, pretty women. These women are at a tremendous premium. They have men standing in line for them. Unless you're rich and handsome, what are the chances that you'll attract one of these beauties?

The reality is that few women in this country have the slim figure of a model. Women begin with one third more fat than men. That is nature's way of preparing them for pregnancy. Otherwise our species might not be around today. The old adage that "beauty is only skin deep" may sound corny, but it's true. So don't worry if she is a few pounds overweight. Find yourself a loving woman with whom you can share a happy life.

Rule #2: Take Advantage of Your Friends

"Oh no, don't tell me I have to go on blind dates. You only get to meet losers."

The number one method for meeting people in this country is through mutual friends. Spread the word to your friends that you'd like to meet more people. Be sure to share with them exactly the qualities you are looking for. Ask them to include you on their guest list for dinners and parties. Have them introduce you to their friends, relatives, and co-workers as well.

Don't be afraid of blind dates. They are still a very common way of meeting people. Just don't expect too much. The likelihood is that on any particular blind date either you or the other person won't find the other to be attractive. So be patient.

Rule #3: Exploit Your Job

"Hey, wait a second. I'm not going to choose a job on the basis of whether it's a good place to meet people. I've got to put food on my table."

Most people choose a job on the basis of such things as money, status, enjoyment, and proximity to their homes. There's nothing wrong with that, but think about adding one more criterion: likelihood of meeting new friends. 10% of all romantic relationships begin between people who meet each other on the job, according to a study of 3000 singles. (Simenauer, J. and Carroll, D., Singles: The New Americans, N.Y., Simon & Schuster: 1982). Furthermore, according to a survey of 1,800 professional women between the ages of 21-45, "a romance between coworkers is four times more likely to last than one between a couple who met elsewhere.... About 20% of on-the-job romances lead to marriage." (Marin Independent-Journal, March, 25, 1986.)

What about the risks involved? Will you have to find another job if your office romance doesn't work out? According to the survey of professional women cited above, "only 5.3% of the women said they felt their relationship had hurt their career. Only 1 in 400 reported losing her job."

If possible choose a job where you are dealing with the public on a daily basis. Unfortunately these are often low-paying jobs (e.g., waiters and waitresses, bank tellers and cashiers.) The pay-off is that you meet lots of new people. Another option is to choose an office where there are plenty of attractive single people of the opposite sex.

What if you don't work and don't need the money? Consider a volunteer job. There are all kinds of interesting opportunities to help others and make your community a better place to live. Call up your local volunteer bureau to find out how. Along with "contributing to society" you'll also increase your visibility in the community and meet new friends. See the chapter on Volunteer Work.

Rule #4: Get Out of the House

Staying home is natural. It's comfortable. It's safe. It's inexpensive. There's only one problem. You'll never meet anybody by staying at home. Most singles spend almost all of their free time at home. Then they wonder why they never meet anybody!

How often should you get out of the house to meet people? That depends on how soon you want to meet someone special. If you're willing to wait 20 years, then don't sweat about it. Once a month is fine. On the other hand, if you want to meet someone soon, remember that every night you go out looking hastens the day when you succeed.

Rule #5: Hang Around Strangers Alone

When we're kids our parents warn us to stay away from strangers. That's good advice at the time. Strangers are dangerous. What's also true, however, is that the love of your life is probably a stranger to you right now. So if you want to meet that person you're going to have to forget what your parents taught you about strangers. A good example of the problem is the following conversation:

Julie: "Are you going to the party Saturday night?
Sally: "No, I don't think so."
Julie: "Why not?"
Sally: "I won't know anyone there."

10 Rules for Dating

Sally's attitude is typical. She's afraid to go to a party full of strangers. But that's exactly the party she should go to. She'll have the greatest chance of meeting someone special if she knows few of the guests. In fact, the ideal party would be one where you knew absolutely no one, not even the host. In other words, a party you crashed.

The hardest part of Rule #5 is the word "alone". If you're like most single people, when you go to social functions you usually drag along your friends. I call them bodyguards. Their purpose is to insure that you won't meet anyone new. As long as you have your friends to engage in conversation, you won't have the motivation to meet new people.

Hanging around your friends is a particularly serious problem if you are a single woman, because your bodyguards make you unapproachable. Most men are scared to approach you if you're alone, due to fear of rejection. Think of how much more intimidating it is for a single man to approach you if you are part of a group! A man will wait patiently for the magic moment that never comes—the time when the women stop talking so he can introduce himself.

Rule #6: Hang Around the Opposite Sex

"Don't insult my intelligence. Of course I know that I've got to hang around people of the opposite sex in order to find a romantic partner."

It sounds a little ridiculous to make something so obvious into a rule. Unfortunately what is obvious isn't always followed. Most people feel most comfortable hanging around their own sex. Don't believe what you read about women's liberation or men's liberation. The fact of the matter is that men and women are very different. Men usually prefer to do "masculine" things and women like to do "feminine" things. As a result, more times than not the sexes don't mingle.

If you want to meet a man, ask yourself this question: "What do women hate to do that men love to do?" If you're a man ask yourself, "What do men hate to do that women love to do?" Whatever it is, do it. You'll find that there will be very little competition. You'll have all those attractive men or women to yourself. For example, if you're a woman, the best place to meet men is at a basketball gym.

"Are you crazy? I'm only 5 foot 2 and I have long nails. How am I going to play basketball?"

Who said anything about playing basketball? What's to prevent you from going down to the gym to watch?

"But what if a guy comes up to me and asks what I'm doing there?

You have two options: you can tell the truth or you can lie. If you have the courage, by all means tell the truth: "I'm here to meet men." If you haven't the guts to be honest, then lie: "I thought the NBA game was on tonight and was dying to see some good basketball." All's fair in love and war. If you have to tell a lie that hurts no one in order to find someone for a loving relationship, isn't it worth it?

So rush down to the gym. If nothing else you'll get to see a bunch of good looking hunks all night running around in their underwear!

In general just about any sport is a good place to meet single men. Some sports, of course, have a greater surplus of men than others. The rule of thumb is "the bloodier, more violent, more dangerous, more demanding the sport, the greater the surplus of men". Boxing, martial arts, wrestling, and hockey have a greater surplus of men than tennis or bowling, which are quite popular among women. See the chapter on **Sports** for specific places to watch or participate in individual sports.

"Enough of this advice for women. What about us guys? Where are all the women hanging out?"

Try an aerobics class. The ratio is usually 10 women for every man! Or try folk dancing. Here the ratio is usually three to one. In fact you'll usually find more women than men in any kind of event that features dancing (other than singles bars). Women are also more likely to attend classes, seminars, pot luck dinners, and singles clubs in general.

10 Rules for Dating

Where else can single men and women go to meet new friends?   Your local chamber of commerce probably sponsors a monthly mixer which is ideal for meeting new friends and potential business contacts. Health clubs are becoming the "singles bars of the 80s", for people who don't like booze and tobacco.

The most obvious place to meet is at the non-profit singles clubs, which are the topic of a future chapter. Other chapters that give information on where to meet singles are:
Dating Services
Long Distance Romance
Love in the Classroom
Singles Bars
Advertising for Love

Rule #7: Initiate Contact

"Oh, oh. I knew there was a catch. I'm willing to lower my expectations, get out of the house, and hang around strangers of the opposite sex. But don't ask me to put my ego on the line and initiate contact. I might get rejected!"

When you get right down to it, it's the fear of rejection that causes millions of singles to remain single. We're all just plain chicken.

"All right, I'll admit it. I'm chicken. So what's the solution? How do I overcome the fear of rejection?"

There's only one way: go out and get rejected. Each time you get rejected you build up scar tissue. You'll find it a little easier to approach someone the next time. Pretty soon you'll be desensitized to the pain of rejection to the point where your fear is manageable.

But don't expect to ever get rid of the pain of rejection. That will always remain. I've been rejected many, many times, but it still hurts. It's just that the pain has subsided to the point where I don't have a nervous breakdown each time I get turned down. So go out there and make contact!

"Hold it a second. Men don't like women who initiate contact."

This is pure b.s. I've asked hundreds of men in my classes this question and over 90% of them answer that they love women to take the initiative. If you're a woman, put yourself in the shoes of single men. All your life the pressure has been on you to initiate contact. You've been rejected countless times. Wouldn't you love to reverse the tables?

Where does this myth come from that men don't like forward women? I think it has to do with the **Law of Rejection:** Unless you're one of the lucky 5%, most single people will not find you attractive. In other words, most men are going to reject you. It has nothing to do with them not liking women who take the initiative. They just don't like you. "O.k., you've talked me into it. But how should I initiate contact?"

The first thing is to make eye contact with someone you find attractive and smile. If they return the smile, you're in! If they turn away or fail to smile, things get riskier. If you approach them you know there's a high probability they're going to reject you. On the other hand, they may just be shy. There's only one way to find out. Take the plunge.

Most singles procrastinate for an hour before making their move. They keep waiting for an opening where they can come over comfortably and initiate contact. Before that happens usually one of two things occurs: the person leaves before you meet them or someone else beats you to the punch. In either case you lose out because you waited for the perfect opportunity.

The secret to initiating contact is to do it right away before you have time to talk yourself out of it.

"But what do I say? Give me a sure-fire opening line."

Sorry, there's isn't one guaranteed to work with everyone. You've just got to come up with the best line you can and hope for the best. If you try a funny line you may impress someone with your sense of humor or you may just end up with egg on your face.

If you try the straightforward approach, "Hi, I'm Charlie", they may dismiss you as a nerd. So you can't win all the

10 Rules for Dating

time. But that's not the point. Nobody's keeping score! You only have to win once. Then you're set for the rest of your life. So don't worry about the flops. "Damn the torpedoes; full speed ahead!"

Rule #8: Get Involved in Superficial Conversations

"Wait a second, did I read that right? Get involved in superficial conversations? That's the whole problem with meeting people, you wind up talking about Reagan, the weather, or the latest sports scores. BORING!"

Do you expect people to spill their guts the first five minutes they meet you? If so, you're very unrealistic. People usually want to feel you out before they open up. They want to make sure it's safe.

Every intimate conversation with a stranger begins on a superficial level. You have to kiss a lot of frogs to find one prince. A dozen phony, boring conversations may be the price you pay for one sincere conversation with someone special.

Rule #9: Pin Down Your Next Contact

Does this situation sound familiar? You meet someone special. You get involved in a superficial conversation. Before you know it, both of you start opening up with private things and feelings. You start laughing. You almost feel like you've known each other all your lives. Could this be the big one? After all the searching, is this it?

But then the moment of truth arrives. If you meet at the beach, eventually the sun's gonna set. If it's at a bar, at 2 a.m. it's closing time. Sooner or later, wherever you met, the party's over. Before you leave, one of you has to end the conversation. So the two of you stand up and stare at each other, nervous and hesitant. Finally you break the silence. "I had a real nice time talking to you. Hope to see you again." Your new friend replies, "Yeah, catch you next time.

Disaster can strike so quickly at the moment of truth. Let's look at things logically. If you've seen this person once in forty years, what's the likelihood that you'll ever see each other again? Both of you have blown it. It's back to the drawing board.

This kind of tragedy happens all the time. Two people meet, obviously are attracted to each other, but then fail to follow through. And so all is for nought.

"But wait. I'd never be so dumb as to say 'catch you next time'. I'd exchange phone numbers."

That's a little better, but not much. Think of all the times you've exchanged phone numbers in the past. How many times did you actually get to see the other person again. Probably less than 50%.

People always are puzzled about this. The women all ask, "How come I meet this guy, we have a great conversation, he asks for my number, I give it to him, and then he never calls? What's wrong with men?"

Many women are quite bitter about this. They feel betrayed. Often they rush home from work the next three nights expecting him to call. The silence is deafening. What's going on here? There are many reasons why a man doesn't call after asking for your phone number:

1. He lost it.
2. He forgot who you were. This is common in situations where a great deal of drinking has gone on.
3. He remembered who you were, but forgot what a great time he had with you.
4. He fantasized that you might reject him and therefore chickened out.
5. He called a few times, nobody answered, so he gave up.

"But wait a second, I have an answering machine. Why didn't the jerk leave a message?"

Many people hate or fear answering machines. Just count the number of times people call and fail to leave a message.

10 Rules for Dating

In a stressful situation like calling someone for a date, is it that surprising that he might hang up?

Of course the guys have their version of the story. "How come I run into women all the time who give me their number and then come up with a song and dance about how busy they are each time I call to ask them out?"

There are many reasons why a woman might not respond positively to your telephone call:

1. She forgot who you were.
2. She lost interest once she sobered up.
3. She is genuinely very busy.
4. She's afraid of dating.
5. She never intended to go out with you in the first place.

The last reason is the hardest for men to deal with. "If she didn't want to go out with me then why did she give me her damn number?" The best way to answer that question is to pretend you're an attractive woman. All your life men have come on to you and asked you out or for your telephone number. It's hard to say to someone, "I find you unattractive" or "I don't want to go out with you" or "No, you can't have my telephone number". So what do you do? You give up your telephone number, hoping he'll never call. If he does call, you lie. You say that you're busy Saturday night or you have a boyfriend.

It would be great if we lived in a world where people were honest and didn't play these games. Unfortunately, such is not the case. The price you pay for flirting with women and asking them out on dates is that a certain percentage will lie and pretend to want to go out with you. If you were a woman you'd probably do the same thing.

One piece of advice that is critical for both men and women is to always confirm a date ahead of time. Occasionally you will find that the phone number that was given to you is a phony or that the person has no intention of meeting with you. You can avoid the pain, frustration, and anger of being stood up by taking this simple precaution.

10 Rules for Dating

Rule #10: Don't Fall in Love With the Wrong Person

The great American fantasy is to fall in love and live happily ever after. Unfortunately your heart is a poor judge of character. Many single people fall in love with the wrong person and live miserably ever after. Following your feelings can be a recipe for disaster unless they are based on sound information about this person. How do you get the facts about a potential spouse? The answer is you ask.

Unfortunately most singles are afraid to getting personal for fear of scaring off a potential loving partner. So they "play it cool" at the beginning of a relationship. They especially avoid "heavy" subjects like sex.

That's fine as long as your feelings towards each other are casual. But what happens when you fall in love? All of a sudden you panic and realize that you know very little about this special person. So now you start with the personal questions. Then disaster strikes. You discover a fatal flaw. For example, you want to have children and they don't. You want marriage and they don't. They want to move to Denver and you love the San Francisco Bay Area.

Now you're on the horns of a terrible dilemma. You can drop the person and go through the agony of a broken relationship. Or you can do what most people do: marry them and hope to change them. Fat chance! You'll probably end up being married to someone inappropriate and resent them for not changing. The way to avoid disastrous relationships is to get personal early in a relationship.

"Hold it a minute. Get personal with a stranger? That's too risky. They're going to think I'm nosy if I ask intimate questions.

There's no doubt that it's risky to get personal. Some people can't handle intimacy. They are closed and feel uncomfortable being around someone who wants to share secrets and intimate feelings. But don't you want to find that out as soon as possible? Or would you rather date a guy for 6 months before discovering that he's an emotional cripple?

Of course there's nothing wrong with playing it cool for a while. At some point, however, you're going to have to bite the bullet. You're going to have to do two things: pry and reveal. When you pry you ask personal questions. When you reveal you let the other person learn personal things about you. That's all there is to it.

If you want to play it safe, pry and reveal simultaneously. For example, suppose you're talking to someone who mentions that they were recently living with someone but moved out. Here's your chance to get personal and raise your superficial conversation to an intimate level. You could ask, "Were you dumped or did you do the dumping?" That's getting personal, but there's a good chance you're going to offend the other person with such a heavy-handed question. An alternative is to say, "I was in a relationship until three months ago, but it broke up very painfully for me. How did yours end?"

"How soon should I get personal?"

That depends on how long you're willing to wait before falling in love. If you want to chitchat for six months before getting serious about someone, that's o.k. Just remember that you are not allowed to fall in love unless you have the answers to your critical questions. I call them **killer questions**. If any of them are answered incorrectly the relationship is dead. You drop the person immediately.

1. Are you single? Pretty obvious, isn't it? You'd be surprised how many people assume that someone by themselves at a party or a dance is single. Always ask. In addition, it makes particular sense for women to ask a man for his home telephone number. If he hands you a business card ask him to write his home number down as well. And be sure to call that number to make sure he isn't married or living with a woman. Be careful with people who answer that they are separated. "Have you moved out?" and "Have you filed for divorce?" are indispensable killer questions. If they are still living with their spouse or haven't yet filed for divorce, it's best you pass and move on

to greener pastures.

2. Are you involved with someone romantically? Here's where you avoid someone who already loves someone else.

3. Why didn't your other romantic relationships last? Find out as much as you can about their marriage(s) or past relationships. Hopefully you'll find out their negative qualities. Then you can decide whether you can live with that flaw or should move on to someone different. You can also find out if they are incompatible with a certain kind of person. For example, maybe they can't stand being with someone who is possessive and is always checking up on them. If you are that kind of person, you can move on to someone compatible with your flaws.

4. How do you deal with conflict and problems in relationships? If their preference is to sweep problems under the rug or to fall into a rage, they are not good relationship material.

5. Do you have children? How many? Do you want children? How many? How soon do you want to have children? I have dated two women in the past who wanted to have children. By terrible coincidence both wound up falling in love with men who had had vasectomies. Talk about falling in love with the wrong person! Ask questions first; fall in love later.

6. What are your long term goals? Do you want to get married? Do you want to change careers? Do you plan to go back to school? Are you happy in this area or would you prefer moving elsewhere?

7. What do you like to do sexually? What are your sexual fantasies? Most singles are squeamish when it comes to asking these questions. The result is marriages that are unfulfilling sexually for one or both partners. Another potential result is your partner fulfilling their fantasies with others rather than you. Sexual questions are particularly important if you don't believe in pre-marital sex. In that case there's only one way to find out their sexual preferences—ask.

10 Rules for Dating

8. Do you have any contagious diseases? Have you engaged in high risk behavior (intravenous drugs or sex with bisexual or homosexual males)? These are literally killer questions. Falling in love with the wrong person can kill you.
9. How much do you drink? Which drugs do you do, and how often?

Here's a homework assignment. Develop your own list of killer questions. The way to do it is to analyze your previous love relationships. What character trait or behavior pattern of a romantic partner destroyed the relationship? Formulate a question to find out whether a prospect has this trait.

"How do I know that my prospective romantic partner is answering my killer questions honestly?"

Unfortunately you can't always trust people. They're going to be tempted to tell you what you want to hear rather than the truth. One way of getting around this is to quiz their parents, relatives, and friends. The ideal person to ask, of course, is their ex-spouse. Find out the "dirt" about a prospective romantic partner before you fall in love. This advice is decidedly unromantic, but it sure beats finding out disastrous information after you fall in love.

"If my partner finds out I've been snooping around their private life, there's going to be hell to pay!"

That's true, so you have to be very subtle.

DATING ETIQUETTE

There was a time when dating was simple. Men were expected to be gentlemen and women were expected to be ladies. Their roles were clear-cut. Today single people are often mixed up about proper dating etiquette. This is particularly true if you are re-entering the singles scene after years of being half of a married couple. It can be quite traumatic to play the "dating game" without knowing the rules.

Singles often feel in a "damned if I do, damned if I don't" situation. For example, if you're a man and automatically pick up the check at a restaurant, you may gain points with one woman but antagonize another. If you're a woman and prefer to pay your own way you'll find that some men love it and others hate it. So what are the rules for dating in America in the Eighties?

There are none. What works with some singles, doesn't work with others. It may be helpful therefore, to do 2 things:

1. Communicate with your dating partners. Let them know your preferences in terms of male/female roles, and find

out theirs. For example, if you are a man who enjoys opening the door for a woman, ask her if she's comfortable with that or prefers to open her own door. If you're a woman who likes to pay her own way, check that out with your partner before the date.

2. Be tolerant of your date's desires. Again using the example above, if she says she doesn't want you to open her door, then don't. Don't get upset or try to persuade your date to give in your expectations.

There are 3 issues that come up most often during dates.

Issue #1: Who Initiates the Date?

Despite what you hear about women's liberation, the man usually initiates dates in America. But it also is socially acceptable for a woman to initiate a date. So do what feels comfortable.

Issue #2: Who Controls the Date?

Some men enjoy the "masculine" role of deciding where to go on a date. Many women feel quite comfortable with this. In that case, there's nothing wrong with an "old-fashioned date" with the man making the decisions. Many men and women, however, want a more equal relationship where both share in the decisions. It's important, therefore, to communicate your preferences and try to come to an accommodation with your partner.

Issue #3: Who Pays?

Here again you can't believe all you read and hear about women's liberation. The fact of the matter is that most women in California expect the man to pick up the check at restaurants, bars, etc. If you're a man, therefore, expect to pay most of the time.

Dating Etiquette

Some men feel uncomfortable with picking up the bill. They prefer a "Dutch treat" where the bill is split. That's fine, as long as you have discussed this earlier with your date and she has agreed to it. Otherwise, it is quite rude to ask a woman out to a movie, for example, and announce to her at the ticket window that she has to pay for her own ticket.

Men who would prefer that the woman "pay her fair share" often feel uncomfortable about discussing these matters. They are afraid that the woman will consider him to be cheap. This is indeed a possibility. Many women expect to be treated generously by a man. Some want to be taken to expensive restaurants, night clubs, etc. They may expect the man to bring flowers, a bottle of wine, or candy on a date when he comes to pick her up.

What do you do if you're a man and feel uncomfortable with all this? Don't date that kind of woman. There are plenty of women who are willing to pay their own way. They are the minority, but still a sizable one.

Some men feel quite bitter about society's expectation that they pick up the tab on dates. They can't understand why women are so "unfair". The most obvious reason is tradition. Throughout history men have been the "providers" and women have been the "homemakers". Today, with a significant percentage of the American work force composed of women, this is no longer always the case. But old traditions die slowly.

Another explanation is the fact that women only earn 59% of what men do in our society. For this reason many women feel that it is quite fair that the man pay for activities on dates.

One way the issue of equity is often settled is by the man paying for out-of-pocket expenses and the woman repaying him by having him over for dinner. This is a very fair way of handling the issue since most single men don't eat very good meals and really appreciate a home-cooked meal.

If you are a woman, you may have a problem adjusting to the expectations of different men on this issue. One man

Dating Etiquette

may be offended if you offer to pay your half. The next may be delighted. Again communication and tolerance are the keys. Normally it's assumed that the man will pay, but if you prefer to pay your own way you should discuss this ahead of time, preferably on the phone before your first date. Come to an agreement on who is to pay.

What do you do if the man insists on paying? You can call him a male chauvinist pig and refuse to go out with him again. Or you can accede to his wishes and let him pay. This has obvious financial advantages. There often is a disadvantage, however. Some men believe that if they spend money on a woman this entitles them to sexual favors. Don't allow yourself to fall into this trap. If you're going to feel pressured to give in sexually to a man who spends a lot of money on you in an evening then insist on paying your own way. If he won't agree to this, then cancel the date.

In other words, stick up for your rights. Try to be accommodating to the needs of your date, but not at the cost of sacrificing your own values or comfort.

The most difficult issues of all often pertain to sex. They are discussed in the chapter on **Sex and the Single Person**.

SEX AND THE SINGLE PERSON

One of the myths in our society is that the difference between men and women is that men want sex more. The fact of the matter is that women want sex and enjoy sex just as much as men. So what's the difference between the sexes?

The difference is that men want sex today. And that's where the conflict arises. As a general rule women want emotional intimacy before physical intimacy. They don't feel comfortable sleeping with a man they hardly know. Men tend to be the opposite. They've been conditioned by our society to seek sex immediately and with as many different partners as possible, regardless of how emotionally close or distant they may be.

Of course these ideas are generalizations. There are many men who feel uncomfortable with casual sex, just as there are many women who love it. But as a general rule men want sex earlier in a relationship than women do.

The result is what I call the natural incompatibility of the sexes. Men and women are in a constant struggle whereby the men try to seduce every woman they find attractive while the women fight to maintain their "virtue". The result is a great deal of frustration and bitterness. And the death of many a promising relationship.

Both men and women often find themselves in uncomfortable positions regarding sex. The man often wants to sleep with a woman but is afraid of making a move for fear that she will be insulted or angered. The woman wants to postpone sexual intimacy until after emotional closeness, but she's afraid to say no for fear that the man will lose interest and move on to another woman who says yes.

And so both walk a tightrope between asserting their needs and acceding to those of their partners. Often neither feels very good about it all.

In order to get along with the opposite sex it is important to understand them. Below is information about the opposite sex together with suggestions on how to get along.

What Men Need to Know About Women

Are you often puzzled by women's sexual behavior? For example, you meet a woman at a party. While slow dancing she rubs your hand and appears to be very comfortable in your tight embrace. Later in the evening she invites you into her home for some coffee. She responds positively to touching and hugging and kissing. But just as you try to escalate physical intimacy, all of a sudden she pulls back and says "not tonight". What's going on here? Why do women appear to be ready for sex and suddenly "chicken out"? There are many reasons:

1. She sees sex as inextricably entwined with love. Since she doesn't love you, she doesn't feel comfortable having sex with you.
2. She is afraid that if she has sex with you early in a relationship that you'll think she's "cheap" and promiscuous and therefore drop her.
3. She's afraid of pregnancy or disease.
4. She is having her menstrual period.

Sex & the Single Person

5. She finds that when she engages in casual sex she usually feels empty or ashamed the next morning. In other words, she enjoys the casual sex as it happens but regrets it the next morning.

Whatever the reason, the fact is that most women don't want to engage in casual sex. They want to get to know you first. How do you deal with this? One way is to be patient and wait for when she's ready for more physical intimacy. Another option is to try to persuade her to become more intimate with you sexually, but respect her right to say no.

What if you get tired of waiting? At some point you might frankly tell her, in a non-demanding tone of voice that you aren't getting your needs met in the relationship. At that point she has the choice of compromising with you or sticking to her guns. If she isn't willing to compromise then you have a choice. You can continue the relationship or move on to greener pastures.

What Women Need to Know About Men

How could a man want to sleep with a complete stranger? Wouldn't he feel uncomfortable? Wouldn't he feel empty? Why doesn't he go slow, get to know a woman, and then move on to sexual contact? These are questions that boggle most women's minds.

The answer is that men have been conditioned to sleep with every attractive woman they meet. They are taught that they are more masculine and have greater value if they sleep with many women. The old "notch in the belt" analogy that women hate so much is sadly appropriate in many cases. Some men do indeed count their "conquests". They achieve self-esteem by seducing women.

The other thing you need to know about men is that often they find it very difficult to achieve emotional intimacy. Men are taught to hide their feelings. It's difficult for them to open up and share their inner selves. Most men seek intimacy but are frightened by emotions. Therefore they attempt to gain the intimacy they need in what to them is a safer means—through sex.

Whatever the reason, the fact is that often a man will try to seduce you. He will use all kinds of tricks to try to accomplish this objective:

1. He will play caveman and attempt to physically overwhelm your defenses.
2. He will try to get you drunk. He knows that this greatly increases his chances of seducing you.
3. He will lie to you and tell you that he loves you. Some women are dumb enough to fall for that kind of line.
4. He will accuse you of hating sex or being frigid.
5. He will threaten to drop you if you don't have sex with him.

How do you handle all this? There are several options. One is to hate men and dismiss them as insensitive, selfish brutes. Many women choose this course. They become quite bitter about men and often refuse to date. This is obviously a foolish choice.

A second option is give in. This is also a foolish strategy if you're going to regret it the next morning.

A third option is to insist that he respect your needs. If he is unwilling to do so, he's probably not the man for you. Find one who is.

The important thing is to accept the facts of life. Many men like to seduce women. You don't have to like it. Just accept it and learn to deal with it.

How do you avoid having casual sex?

1. Don't drink. The more alcohol you consume the less resistance you will have to his sexual advances.
2. Don't invite him into your home after a date. Most men will interpret your invitation to come in for a cup of coffee or a drink as a invitation to have sex as well.

Sex & the Single Person

3. Let him know that you don't want to have sex with him tonight.
4. Don't hug and kiss all night long and then think you can cut him off anytime you please without suffering certain negative consequences. Some men will either attempt to physically overpower you or get angry that you are a "tease".

Sexual Morality

All your life people have been telling you how you should behave sexually.   Parents, siblings, teachers, clergymen, friends, and potential romantic partners all have advice on what is best for you. I don't choose to join these unsolicited counselors. Instead my suggestion is that you think things through yourself and develop a moral system that works for you.

How do you go about doing this? The first step is to throw out all the conditioning from the past. That's not easy to do, but the key is to realize that the advice you have been getting from others is hopelessly contradictory. One person advises you to avoid all sexual contact outside marriage. The next person suggests that you "loosen up" and enjoy yourself. You can't follow everyone's advice, so why not chuck it all and start from scratch?

What sexual code will make you happy? That's the place to start.   Consider your physical and emotional needs. Develop a moral code that you can live with. Otherwise you're going to violate it anyway and wind up feeling guilty. Better to be realistic and develope a code of conduct that works for you.

What about your moral responsibility to others?   It would be great if what made you happy also made others happy. Unfortunately that's not always true. Occasionally you will be faced with sexual dilemmas. Do you make yourself happy or someone else happy? That's for you to decide.

Sex & the Single Person

A.I.D.S.

Once upon a time sexual promiscuity was the "in thing to do" in the American singles scene. That's no longer true. First there was herpes. Now there's Acquired Immune Deficiency Syndrome (AIDS). Estimates are that most if not all people who carry the virus will eventually die from it.

Before you panic, however, it's important to realize some important facts. First, AIDS is extremely difficult to catch. You have to go out of your way to get it. You cannot be infected through normal, everyday contact. Second, the vast majority of cases have been limited to a few high-risk groups: homosexual and bisexual men; intravenous drug users; hemophiliacs. Finally, AIDS is easily prevented. Here's how to do it:

1. Avoid sexual contact with the high risk groups listed above.
2. Don't be promiscuous. The more people you sleep with the greater the likelihood that you will catch AIDS. One of the reasons that so many members of the gay community became infected is because they tended to be far more promiscuous than heterosexuals.
3. Avoid sexual contact with promiscuous people (for the reasons given above).
4. Avoid anal intercourse.
5. Use a condom with new sexual partners or partners who may be promiscuous.

Of course the surest way to avoid AIDS is to refrain from sex altogether. After all, you can never be 100% certain that even a spouse isn't secretly consorting with someone who has AIDS. Obviously this is carrying things to an extreme. There's a difference between being reasonably cautious and being paranoid. Only a tiny percentage of the heterosexual population of the United States is carrying the AIDS virus. If you follow the suggestions above the chances of catching AIDS are minuscule.

Sex & the Single Person

Even if you fail to follow the recommended precautions, a study at the University of California at San Francisco concluded that there is only one chance in five million that you will catch AIDS if you have sexual intercourse with someone who does not belong to a high risk group. This "is about the same as the risk of being killed in a traffic accident while driving 10 miles to that encounter." (San Francisco Chronicle, April 22, 1988, p. A2.)

Remember that life involves a certain amount of risk. Every time you get on the highway you are risking being crippled or killed. That doesn't mean you stay off the freeway. It just means that you have to be careful. So too with AIDS. Don't let fear dominate your life to the point that you don't get your needs met for physical intimacy.

Herpes

Before the AIDS epidemic herpes was the main cause of paranoia in the singles community. Today many singles are still scared to death of herpes. Which is quite foolish. The facts about herpes are as follows:

1. Many people with herpes never have a recurrence. In other words, it was an unpleasant one-time illness. They won't ever infect anyone.
2. Those who do have recurrences usually have them infrequently (a few times a year at most). The chances of infecting someone are small.
3. The vast majority of herpes attacks are mild (ranging from itching to flu symptoms.

In view of these three facts, isn't it amazing how frightened people are of herpes? People don't dread catching the flu. So why are they so afraid of herpes? The main reason is that it is a sexually transmitted illness. In our society anything dealing with sex becomes magnified. That's because here in America we have an unhealthy attitude about sex. If we regarded it as other physical

Sex & the Single Person

functions like eating and sleeping, there wouldn't be any emotional charge associated with sexually transmitted illnesses.

What should you do if you are infected with herpes at one time or another?

1. Don't be ashamed. You don't feel guilty when you catch the flu. Why should you feel any differently about herpes?
2. Accept the moral responsibility to avoid infecting others. That involves examining yourself frequently and avoiding sex when it appears that you are experiencing a flare-up.

Of course the big moral dilemma is "Should I tell a new romantic partner that I have had herpes?" That's a tough one. There's no right or wrong answer. Some people will be very grateful that you told them. Their esteem for you will increase because you were honest. Others may reject you, however, if they find out you have had herpes. In the worst case, they may share your secret with other people.

In weighing this decision it might be wise to try to calculate the chances that you might inadvertently transmit herpes to someone new. If the chances of transmitting the illness are slim, you may decide to keep your past experience to yourself and just be very careful.

On the other hand, if you have frequent recurrences there is a much larger chance that you will infect someone. If you do, they will be extremely angry and bitter. This will put a tremendous strain on your relationship with them.

So think carefully about this dilemma. Consider the happiness of others. But also don't lose sight of your responsibility to do what makes YOU happy.

For some people, herpes is far worse than the flu. Some people have severe attacks. Others chronically experience recurrences. So avoiding herpes is certainly a prudent policy. Many of the steps for preventing herpes are the same as those for AIDS:

Sex & the Single Person

1. Don't be promiscuous. The more people you sleep with the greater the likelihood that you will catch herpes.
2. Avoid sexual contact with promiscuous people, since they are more likely to be infected.
3. Use a condom with new sexual partners or partners who may be promiscuous.

MARRIAGE

85% of singles in this country want to happily married. The problem is that close to half of all marriages in this country end in divorce. Why? The primary cause is that most singles get married for the wrong reasons. For example:

1. A high percentage of brides are pregnant on their wedding day. Many of them get married to avoid having an illegitimate child.
2. Many singles are lonely and unhappy. They get married out of desperation.
3. Many people get married because they are madly in love.
4. Some singles get married because "it's the thing to do". Their parents, friends, or society in general expect it of them.
5. Women over 30 worry about the biological clock. They see time running out and the day approaching when they will be too old to have children.

With reasons like this it's no wonder that a third of all marriages in America end tragically. How can you avoid divorce?

1. Don't get pregnant. With Planned Parenthood and other organizations to assist you, there's no excuse for unwanted pregnancy.

2. Don't turn to marriage as a lifeboat that will rescue you from your unhappiness. Unhappy singles usually become unhappy couples. Become a happy single and then become married.

3. Don't get married because you're madly in love. The word "madly" should tip you off. You want to make an intelligent, rational decision to get married. Erich Fromm, in The Art of Loving, differentiates between "falling" in love and "standing" in love. When you fall in love you are not in contact with reality. You are idealizing your partner and blind to their shortcomings. After you get through the honeymoon stage you'll discover all of their negative qualities. Then it will be too late to decide intelligently about whether or not to get married.

4. Don't succumb to pressure from outside. The people who are advising you to get married aren't going to have to live with your spouse. You are. Being single is more socially acceptable today than ever before. So don't worry about what others think. Do what's right for you.

5. Don't get married because you want to have a child. You'll wind up raising your child in an unhappy marriage or broken home.

6. Don't expect to change your partner. People are remarkably resistant to change. If you can barely tolerate your partner during the engagement period you'll hate them later.

But enough of the "don't"s. What positive things can you do to increase your chances for a happy marriage?

1. Be patient. Don't marry the first decent person that comes along. Wait for someone right for you.

2. Play the numbers game. The more singles you meet the more choices you'll have.

3. Get to know someone well and make sure they know you well. Let them see your "worst foot" instead of always putting your best foot forward. Insist that they do the same. If you've never had a fight, if all is sweetness and light, don't get married! Sooner or later you're going to discover areas of incompatibility. It's wise to do so before the marital vows.

Marriage

4. Make sure that there's more than just sexual attraction binding you together. It is very difficult to sustain a passionate relationship over the years. What usually holds marriages together is friendship and intimacy. If you don't truly like each other and enjoy each others company your marriage will not be a happy one.

The best way to insure a happy marriage is to be happily single first! How do you do that? The most important thing is to realize how lucky you are to be single. Instead of being in a rotten marriage like so many people in America, you have the freedom to remain single or marry someone special. That's quite a luxury.

Of course the grass always looks greener on the other side. You see married couples all the time who appear to be experiencing unlimited bliss. What you don't see are all the arguments and unmet needs. People have an uncanny knack for putting a good face on an unhappy marriage. So don't take the marriages around you at face value. Unless they're newly-weds, they all have their secret problems.

On the other hand, avoid becoming so bitter and disillusioned with your past relationships that you decide to remain single for the rest of your life. The fact of the matter is that there are millions of happy marriages in America. Yours can be one of them.

Marriage

Part Two

SINGLES

RESOURCE

DIRECTORY

LOVE
IN THE CLASSROOM

Classes are a great place to meet singles. Almost every city in the Bay Area has a recreation department that offers non-credit classes. The same holds true for most community colleges. In addition, some of the school districts also offer adult classes. Finally, organizations such as The Learning Annex also sponsor these "personal enrichment" classes.

These classes usually meet in the evenings and Saturdays. You will find that a large percentage of the people attending these classes are singles, since married people usually stay home with their families. A national survey that the number one reason people take "lifelong learning" classes is not to learn anything! 40% stated that their motivation was "to meet new friends". In other words, a high percentage of people who take adult education classes are singles hoping to meet other singles. Some classes are aimed exclusively at singles. They concentrate on such topics as how and where to meet other singles or how to be happily single.

Call up the listings below that are in your area and ask for a current catalog of courses. If you want to save yourself a lot of time why not ask the person in charge to recommend the class that has the most single men or the most single

Love in the Classroom

women? Whatever the class is, be it body-building, karate, or macrame, take it!

The point isn't to learn something, it's to meet someone for a romantic relationship!

Classes that tend to attract men deal with such "masculine" subjects as sports, building things, automotive repair, and investments. Women tend to take classes dealing with arts and crafts, relationships, self-improvement, and psychology.

The following publications list classes and seminars throughout the Bay Area:

Bay Guardian, 2700 19th St., San Francisco 94110, (415) 824-7660.

Common Ground, 9 Mono Ave., Fairfax 94930, (415) 459-4900.

Lifestyle, 419 W. MacArthur Blvd., Oakland 94609, (415) 420-1381.

Open Exchange, Box 5905, Berkeley, 94705, (415) 526-7190/527-4273.

You may also wish to consult the calendar sections of your local newspapers and magazines for class listings.

CLASS DIRECTORY

ALAMEDA COUNTY

Alameda Recreation Dept., City Hall, Rm. 201, Santa Clara Ave. & Oak, Alameda 94501, (415) 522-4100.

Albany Recreation Dept., 1100 San Pablo Ave., Albany, (415) 528-5740.

Dublin Recreation Dept., Box 2340, Dublin 94568, (415) 829-4932.

Fremont Community Services, Box 5006, Fremont 94537, (415) 791-4320.

Fremont Adult School, 4700 Calaveras Ave., Fremont 94538, (415) 793-6465.

Hayward Adult School, 2652 Vergil Ct., Hayward 94546, (415) 537-4203.

Hayward Area Recreation District, 1099 E St., Hayward 94541, (415) 881-6735.

Livermore Area Recreation & Park Dept., 71 Trevarno Rd., Livermore 94550, (415) 447-7300.

Love in the Classroom

ALAMEDA COUNTY (continued)

Oakland Recreational Services Dept., 1520 Lakeside Dr., Oakland, (415) 339-8919.
Ohlone College, Community Services, 43600 Mission Blvd., Box 3909, Fremont 94537, (415) 659-6215.
Piedmont Recreation Dept., 358 Hillside Ave., Piedmont, (415) 420-3070.
Pleasanton Recreation Dept., 200 Old Bernal Ave., Pleasanton 94566, (415) 484-8160.
San Leandro Recreation Dept., 835 14th St., San Leandro, (415) 577-3462.
Separation & Divorce Workshop, Marilyn G. Denn, Ph.D., Berkeley and Alameda, (415) 644-0124.
Union City, Holly Community Center, 31600 Alvarado Blvd., Union City, (415) 471-6877; or Charles Kennedy Community Center, 1333 Decoto Rd., Union City, (415) 489-0360.

CONTRA COSTA COUNTY

Acalanes Adult Center, Walnut Creek, (415) 935-0170.
Antioch Leisure Services, 213 F St., Antioch 94509, (415) 757- 0900.
Brentwood Recreation Dept., 724 3rd St., Brentwood 94513, 634-1044.
Concord Leisure Services, 2885 Concord Blvd., Concord 94519, 671-3270.
Contra Costa College, Community Services Dept., 2600 Mission Bell Dr., San Pablo 94806, (415) 235-7800 x3303.
Diablo Valley College, Community Services, 321 Golf Club Rd., Pleasant Hill 94523, (415) 685-1230.
El Cerrito Community Services, 10890 San Pablo Ave., El Cerrito 94530, (415) 234-7445.
Hercules Community Services, 111 Civic Dr., Hercules, (415) 799-8230.
Jessica Mercure, M.F.C.C., (415) 232-8499, teaches classes on how to prepare yourself emotionally for better relationships.
Lafayette Recreation Dept., 500 St. Mary's Rd., Lafayette 94549, (415) 284-2232.
Martinez Adult School, 600 F St., Martinez, (415) 228-3276. Sponsors classes that are predominantly attended by singles.
Martinez Leisure Services, 525 Henrietta, Martinez 94553, (415) 372-3510.
Moraga Recreation Dept., 2100 Donald Dr., Moraga 94556, 376-2520.
Pinole Recreation Dept., 2131 Pear, Pinole 94564, (415) 724-9004.
Pittsburg Leisure Services, 340 Black Diamond, Pittsburg 94565. (415) 439-3440.
Pleasant Hill Adult School, Pleasant Hill, (415) 937-1530. Sponsors classes that are predominantly attended by singles.
Pleasant Hill Recreation Dept., 320 Civic Dr., P.H. 94523, (415) 676-5200.
Richmond Recreation Dept., (415) 620-6792.
San Pablo Community Services, (415) 236-7373.

Love in the Classroom

64

CONTRA COSTA COUNTY (continued)

San Ramon Recreation Dept., 2222 Camino Ramon, San Ramon 94583, 275-2300.
San Ramon Valley Community Services Group, 545 Sycamore Valley Rd. W., Danville 94526, (415) 837-8235.
Walnut Creek Leisure Services, Box 8039, W.C. 94596, (415) 943-5858.

MARIN COUNTY

Corte Madera Recreation Dept., 498 Tamalpais Dr., Corte Madera 94925, (415) 924-2901.
Fairfax Recreation Dept., 142 Bolinas Rd., Fairfax, 94930, (415) 453-1584.
Larkspur Recreation Dept., 400 Magnolia Ave., Larkspur 94939, (415) 924-4777.
Marin Community College, Community Education Dept., Kentfield 94904, (415) 485-9657.
Marin County Recreation Dept., Marin County Civic Center, San Rafael 94903, (415) 499-6387.
Mill Valley Recreation Dept., 180 Camino Alto, Mill Valley 94941, (415) 383-1370.
Novato Recreation Dept., 917 Sherman Ave., Novato 94947, (415) 897-4323.
Ross Recreation Dept., Lagunitas Rd., Ross, (415) 453-6020.
San Anselmo Recreation Dept., 1000 Sir Francis Drake Blvd., San Anselmo 94960, (415) 453-9055.
San Rafael Recreation Dept., 1400 5th Ave., San Rafael 94901, (415) 485-3333.
Sausalito Recreation Dept., 420 Litho, Sausalito 94965, (415) 332-4520.
Tiburon Recreation Dept., 1155 Tiburon Blvd., Tiburon 94920, (415) 435-4355.

MONTEREY COUNTY

Carmel Recreation, 15th Ave. & Monte Verde Blvd., Carmel 93923, (408) 625-2252.
Hartnell College, 156 Homestead Ave., Salinas 93901, (408) 755-6700.
King City Recreation, 411 Division, King City 93930, (408) 385-3575.
Marina Recreation, 211 Hillcrest Ave., Marina 93933, (408) 384-3715.
Monterey Peninsula College, Community Services, 980 Fremont Blvd., Monterey 93940, (408) 646-4051.
Monterey Recreation, 546 Dutra, Monterey 93940, (408) 646-3866.
Pacific Grove Recreation, 515 Junipero Ave., P.G. 93950, (408) 372-2809.
Salinas Recreation, 200 Lincoln Ave., Salinas, (408) 758-7306.
Seaside Recreation, 986 Hilby Ave., Seaside 93955, (408) 899-6270.

Love in the Classroom

NAPA COUNTY

Calistoga Recreation Dept., 1232 Washington, Calistoga 94515, (707) 942-5188.
Napa College, Community Education Dept., 2277 Napa-Vallejo Hwy., Napa 94558, (707) 253-3095.
Napa Recreation Dept., 1100 West, Napa, (707) 252-7800.
St. Helena Recreation Dept., 1360 Oak Ave., St. Helena 94574, (707) 963-5706.

SAN FRANCISCO

A Good Relationship Class, Isadora Alman, M.F.C.C., (415) 386-5090.
Ft. Mason Art Center, Building B, Laguna & Marina Blvd., San Francisco 94123, (415) 776-8247.
The Learning Annex, 2500 Clay St., San Francisco 94115, (415) 922-9900.
San Francisco Community College, Adult Learning Center, 33 Gough St., San Francisco, (415) 239-3070.
San Francisco Recreation Dept., McLaren Lodge, Golden Gate Park, San Francisco 94117.

SAN MATEO COUNTY

Belmont Recreation Dept., 1225 Ralston Ave., Belmont 94002, (415) 573-3561.
Burlingame Recreation Dept., 850 Burlingame Ave., Burlingame 94010, (415) 344-6386.
Canada College, Community Education, 4200 Farm Hill Blvd., Redwood City 94061, (415) 364-1221.
College of San Mateo, Community Education, 3401 College of San Mateo Dr., San Mateo 94402, (415) 574-6563.
Daly City Recreation Dept., 111 Lake Merced Blvd., Daly City, (415) 991-8004.
East Palo Alto Community Services, 2415 University Ave., East Palo Alto, (415) 853-3144.
Foster City Recreation Dept., 650 Shell Blvd., Foster City, (415) 345-5731.
Half Moon Bay Recreation Dept., 501 Main, Half Moon Bay, (415) 726-1617.
Menlo Park Recreation Dept., 700 Alma, Menlo Park 94025, (415) 858-3470.
Millbrae Recreation Dept., 477 Lincoln Circle, Millbrae 94030, (415) 697-7426.
Pacifica Recreation Dept., 170 Santa Maria Ave., Pacifica 94044, (415) 875-7380.

Love in the Classroom

SAN MATEO COUNTY (continued)

Redwood City Recreation Dept., 1400 Roosevelt Ave., Redwood City, (415) 780-7251.
San Bruno Recreation Dept., 567 El Camino Real, San Bruno 94066, (415) 877-8863.
San Carlos Recreation Dept., 666 Elm St., San Carlos 94070, (415) 593-8011.
San Mateo Recreation Dept., 330 W. 20th Ave., S.M. 94403, (415) 377-4700.
Skyline College, 3300 College Dr., San Bruno 94066, (415) 574-6563.
South San Francisco Recreation Dept., 33 Arroyo Dr., South San Francisco 94080, (415) 877-8560.

SANTA CLARA COUNTY

Campbell Recreation Dept., 70 N. 1st St., Campbell 95008, (408) 866-2105.
Cupertino Recreation Dept., 22221 McClellan Rd., Cupertino 95014, (408) 253-2060.
De Anza College, Community Education Dept., 21250 Stevens Creek Blvd., Cupertino 95014, (408) 996-4966.
Evergreen Valley College, Community Education & Services, 3095 Yerba Buena Rd., San Jose 95135, (408) 288-3720.
Foothill College, Community Services Dept., Los Altos Hills 94022, (415) 948-2588.
Gavilan College, 5055 Santa Teresa Blvd., Gilroy, 95020, (408) 848-4771.
Gilroy Recreation Dept., 7351 Rosanna St., Gilroy 95020, (408) 842-0221.
Los Altos Recreation Dept., 97 Hillview Ave., Los Altos 94022, (408) 941-0950.
Los Gatos Recreation Dept., 123 E. Main, Los Gatos, (408) 354-8700.
Mission College Community Education, 3000 Mission College Blvd., Santa Clara 95054, (408) 727-7584.
Milpitas Community Services, (408) 942-2470.
Morgan Hill Recreation Dept., 17666 Crest Ave., Morgan Hill 95037, (408) 779-7283.
Mt. View-Los Altos Adult Education, 415 E. Middlefield, M.V. 94043, (415) 967-7986.
Mountain View Recreation Dept., Box 7540, M.V. 94039, (415) 966-6331.
    Palo Alto, Mitchell Park Center, 3800 Middlefield Rd., Palo Alto, 329-2487; Lucie Stern Center, 1305 Middlefield Rd., 329-2261.
San Jose City College, Community Education & Services, 2100 Moorpark Ave., San Jose 95128, (408) 288-3720, 288-3755.
San Jose Recreation Dept., 151 W. Mission, San Jose, (408) 277-4000.
Santa Clara Recreation Dept., 1500 Warburton Ave., Santa Clara, (408) 984-3223.

Love in the Classroom

SANTA CLARA COUNTY (continued)

Saratoga Community Center, 19655 Allendale Ave., Saratoga 95070, (408) 867-3438.
Sunnyvale Recreation Dept., 550 E. Remington Dr., Sunnyvale 94087, (408) 730-7350.
West Valley College, Community Development Dept., 14000 Fruitvale Ave., Saratoga 95070, (408) 867-0440.

SANTA CRUZ COUNTY

Cabrillo College Community Education, 6500 Soquel, Aptos 95003, (408) 479-6229.
Capitola Recreation, 4400 Jade, Capitola 95010, (408) 475-5935.
Santa Cruz County Cultural Services, 701 Ocean, Santa Cruz, (408) 425-2079.
Santa Cruz Recreation, 307 Church, Santa Cruz, (408) 429-3663.
Watsonville Recreation, 20 Maple, Watsonville 95076, (408) 728-6081.

SOLANO COUNTY

Benicia Recreation Dept., 250 E. L St., Benicia 94519, (707) 746-4285.
Fairfield Civic Arts, 1000 Webster, Fairfield 94533, (707) 428-7465.
Solano Community College, Community Services Dept., 4000 Suisun Valley Rd., Suisun City 94585, (707) 864-7115.
Vacaville Recreation Dept., 1100 Alamo Dr., Vacaville 95688, (707) 449-1830.
Vallejo Recreation Dept., 395 Amador, Vallejo 94590, (707) 648-4600.

SONOMA COUNTY

Healdsburg Recreation Dept., 126 Matheson, Healdsburg 95448.
Petaluma Recreation Dept., Box 61, Petaluma 94953, (707) 778-4380.
Rohnert Park Recreation Dept., 5401 Snyder Ln., Rohnert Park 94928.
Santa Rosa Junior College, Office of Community Services, 1501 Mendocino Ave., Santa Rosa 95401, (707) 527-4371.
Santa Rosa Recreation Dept., 415 Steele Ln., S.R. 95401, (707) 576-5116.
Sebastopol Recreation Dept., 7120 Bodega Ave., Sebastopol 95472, (707) 823-1511.

MISCELLANEOUS

Improvisational Theater Classes for Singles, (415) 626-4229 (Rita Shimmin) or 420-1230 (Merry Ross).

Love in the Classroom

VOLUNTEER WORK

10% of all romantic relationships start on the job. But what do you do if you have the kind of job situation where no one is appropriate for you? Or what if you're unemployed? One alternative is to take on a volunteer job. There are thousands of non-profit organizations throughout the Bay Area that need help. You'll be donating your time in a good cause, meeting new friends, and possibly find a romantic partner.

Some of the volunteer jobs involve working with the public. Others allow you to serve on a board of directors. In each case you'll be meeting new friends. In addition, non-profit organizations often throw staff parties, particularly during the holiday season. As an example, Big Brothers/Big Sisters pair up adults with boys and girls who need a father/mother figure. Big Brothers/Big Sisters frequently throw joint parties, so you'll be able to meet adult singles of the opposite sex.

Another good way to meet people of both sexes is to volunteer to be a docent for one of the museums. You'll be able to meet your fellow docents as well as the general public.

In choosing from so many volunteer opportunities, it makes sense to choose a job where you are likely to meet the kind of person you seek. If, as an example, you want to meet single mothers, join the P.T.A. or volunteer to help at school fundraising activities.

Call up your local Volunteer Center listed below. They'll be glad to meet with you personally and match you up with a job suitable to your talents and that you will enjoy. Don't be afraid to be honest and say that you're hoping to meet new friends. They'll be glad to suggest a volunteer position where you'll be likely to find the kind of person you seek.

ALAMEDA COUNTY VOLUNTEER CENTERS

477 15th St., Oakland, (415) 893-6239.
21455 Birch St., Hayward, (415) 538-0554.
333 Division, Pleasanton, (415) 462-3570

CONTRA COSTA COUNTY VOLUNTEER CENTERS

3905 MacDonald Ave., Richmond, (415) 233-5558.
213 G St., Antioch, (415) 778-3308.

MARIN COUNTY VOLUNTEER CENTER

70 Skyview Terrace, San Rafael 94903, (415) 479-5660.

MONTEREY COUNTY VOLUNTEER CENTERS

444 Pearl, Monterey 93940, (408) 373-6177.
971 N. Main, Salinas, (408) 758-8488.

NAPA COUNTY VOLUNTEER CENTER

1700 2nd, Napa, (707) 252-6222.

SAN FRANCISCO VOLUNTEER CENTER

1090 Sansome, San Francisco, (415) 982-8999.

SAN MATEO COUNTY VOLUNTEER CENTERS

450 Peninsula Ave., San Mateo, (415) 342-0801.
940 Douglas Ave., Redwood City, (415) 364-7770.

Volunteer Work

SANTA CLARA COUNTY VOLUNTEER CENTER

110 E. Gish Rd., San Jose, (408) 288-6868.

SANTA CRUZ COUNTY VOLUNTEER CENTERS

1100 Emeline Ave., Santa Cruz, (408) 423-0554.
15 Madison, Watsonville 95076, (408) 722-6708.
8500 Hwy. 9, Ben Lomond 95005, (408) 336-2257.

SONOMA COUNTY VOLUNTEER CENTER

7 4th Ave., Petaluma 94952, (707) 762-0111.

Volunteer Work

MIXING BUSINESS WITH PLEASURE

Why not mix business with pleasure? Most cities in the Bay Area have Chambers of Commerce that sponsor mixers, networking parties, and educational events that are ideal for meeting new friends as well as potential customers. Most of the members are married, but there still are plenty of single people to meet.

Chamber of Commerce Directory

ALAMEDA COUNTY

Alameda Chamber of Commerce, City Hall, Alameda 94501, 522-0414.
Albany Chamber of Commerce, 1108 Solano Ave., (415) 525-1771.
Berkeley Chamber of Commerce, 1834 University Ave., (415) 845-1212.
California Hispanic Chambers of Commerce, 4580 Central Ave., Fremont, (415) 797-0844.
Castro Valley Chamber of Commerce, 21096 Redwood, (415) 537-5300.
Fremont Chamber of Commerce, 39650 Liberty, Fremont, 657-1355.
Hayward Chamber of Commerce, 22300 Foothill Blvd., (415) 351-8292.
Union City Chamber of Commerce, 33484 Alvarado-Niles Rd., (415) 471-3115.
Oakland Chamber of Commerce, 1939 Harrison, (415) 451-7800.
San Leandro Chamber of Commerce, 262 Davis, (415) 351-1482.

CONTRA COSTA COUNTY

Antioch Chamber of Commerce, 212 H St., (415) 757-1800.
Brentwood Chamber of Commerce, (415) 634-3344.
Concord Chamber of Commerce, 1982 Concord Ave., (415) 685-1181.
Dublin Chamber of Commerce, 7986 Amador Valley, (415) 828-6200.
El Cerrito Chamber of Commerce, 10506 San Pablo, (415) 527-5333.
Lafayette Chamber of Commerce, 1003 Oak Hill Rd., (415) 284-7404.
Martinez Chamber of Commerce, 620 Las Juntas, (415) 228-2345.
Moraga Chamber of Commerce, 1450 Moraga Rd., (415) 376-0150.
Oakley Chamber of Commerce, Hwy. 4, (415) 625-1035.
Orinda Chamber of Commerce, 70 Moraga Way, (415) 254-3909.
Pittsburg Chamber of Commerce, 2010 Railroad, (415) 432-7301.
Pleasant Hill Chamber of Commerce, 1881 Contra Costa, (415) 671-0700.
San Ramon Chamber of Commerce, 2333 San Ramon Valley, 831-9500.
Valley Chamber of Commerce, 274 S. Hartz, Danville, (415) 837-4400.
Walnut Creek Chamber of Commerce, 1501 N. Broadway, 934-2007.

MARIN COUNTY

Corte Madera Chamber of Commerce, 498 Tamalpais, (415) 924-4888.
Larkspur Chamber of Commerce, (415) 924-3330.
Marin County C. of C., 30 N. San Pedro, San Rafael 94903, 472-7470.
Mill Valley Chamber of Commerce, 38 Miller Ave., (415) 388-9700.
Novato Chamber of Commerce, 807 DeLong, (415) 897-1164.
San Anselmo Chamber of Commerce, 1000 Sir Francis Drake, 454-2510.
San Rafael Chamber of Commerce, 1030 B St., (415) 454-4163.
Sausalito Chamber of Commerce, 333 Caledonia, (415) 332-0505.
Tiburon Chamber of Commerce, 96 Main St., (415) 435-5633.

MONTEREY COUNTY

Carmel Business Association, San Carlos & 7th, Carmel, 625-2212.
Marina Chamber of Commerce, 3200 Del Monte, (408) 384-9155.
Monterey Peninsula Chamber of Commerce, 380 Alvarado, Monterey
   93940, (408) 649-1770.
Pacific Grove Chamber of Commerce, Forest & Central Ave., 373-3304.
Salinas Chamber of Commerce, 119 E. Alisal, (408) 424-7611.
Seaside Chamber of Commerce, 505 Broadway Ave., (408) 394-6501.

NAPA COUNTY

Calistoga Chamber of Commerce, 1458 Lincoln Ave., (707) 942-6333.
Napa Chamber of Commerce, 1900 Jefferson, (707) 226-7455.
Yountville Chamber of Commerce, Box 2064, (707) 944-0334.

Mixing Business With Pleasure

SAN FRANCISCO

British-American Chamber of Commerce, 3150 California, 392-4511.
French-American Chamber of Commerce, 312 Sutter, (415) 398-2449.
German-American Chamber of Commerce, 465 California, 392-2262.
San Francisco Black Chamber of Commerce, 111 New Montgomery,
   (415) 777-0944.
San Francisco Chamber of Commerce, 465 California, (415) 392-4511.
San Francisco Junior Chamber of Commerce, 251 Kearney, 398-0444.
Southeast Asian-American Chamber of Commerce, 775 Commercial,
   (415) 781-6160.
Soviet-American Chamber of Commerce, 317 12th Ave., 752-4093.
Swedish-American Chamber of Commerce, World Trade Ctr, 781-4188.
U.S.-Arab Chamber of Commerce, 1231 Market, (415) 552-8202.

SAN MATEO COUNTY

Belmont Chamber of Commerce, 1365 5th Ave., (415) 595-8696.
Brisbane Chamber of Commerce, 42 Visitacion Ave., (415) 467-7283.
Burlingame Chamber of Commerce, 306 Lorton, (415) 344-1735.
Daly City Chamber of Commerce, 244 92nd St., (415) 755-8526.
Foster City Chamber of Commerce, 1125 E. Hillside Blvd., (415) 573-7600.
Half Moon Bay Chamber of Commerce, 225 S. Cabrillo Hwy., 726-5202.
Menlo Park Chamber of Commerce, 1100 Merrill, (415) 325-2818.
Millbrae Chamber of Commerce, 316 Broadway, (415) 697-7324.
Redwood City Chamber of Commerce, Jefferson & Middlefield, 364-1722.
San Bruno Chamber of Commerce, 668 San Mateo Ave., (415) 588-0180.
San Carlos Chamber of Commerce, 1250 San Carlos Ave., (415) 593-1068.
San Mateo Chamber of Commerce, 2031 Pioneer Ct., (415) 341-5679.
South San Francisco Chamber of Commerce, 226 Miller, (415) 588-1911.

SANTA CLARA COUNTY

Campbell Chamber of Commerce, 328 E. Campbell Ave., (408) 378-6252.
Cupertino Chamber of Commerce, 20455 Silverado, (408) 252-7054.
East Palo Alto Chamber of Commerce, 1475 E. Bayshore, (415) 328-5769.
Gilroy Chamber of Commerce, 7780 Monterey, Gilroy, (408) 842-6437.
Gilroy Hispanic Chamber of Commerce, 7365 Monterey, Gilroy, (408)
   848-5780.
Los Gatos Chamber of Commerce, 5 Montebello Way, Los Gatos, (408)
   354-9300.
Milpitas Chamber of Commerce, 75 S. Milpitas Blvd., Milpitas, (408)
   262-2613.
San Jose Chamber of Commerce, 180 S. Market, (408) 998-7000.

Mixing Business With Pleasure

Santa Clara Chamber of Commerce, 4699 Old Ironsides Dr., Santa Clara, (408) 296-6863.

Saratoga Chamber of Commerce, 20460 Saratoga-Los Gatos Rd., Saratoga, (408) 867-0753.

SANTA CRUZ COUNTY

Santa Cruz Chamber of Commerce, 105 Cooper, Santa Cruz, (408) 423-1111.

SOLANO COUNTY

Benicia Chamber of Commerce, 831 1st St., Benicia 94519, (707) 745-2120.

Dixon Chamber of Commerce, 201 S. 1st St., Dixon 95620, (707) 678-2650.

Fairfield-Suisun Chamber of Commerce, 1111 Webster, Fairfield 94533, (707) 425-4625.

Vacaville Chamber of Commerce, 400 E. Monte Vista Ave., Vacaville 95688, (707) 448-6424.

Vallejo Chamber of Commerce, 2 Florida, Vallejo 94590, (707) 644-5551.

SONOMA COUNTY

Cotati Chamber of Commerce, 8000 Old Redwood Hwy, (707) 795-5508.

Cloverdale Chamber of Commerce, Box 476, (707) 894-2862.

Healdsburg Chamber of Commerce, 217 Healdsburg Ave., (707) 433-6935.

Petaluma Chamber of Commerce, 314 Western Ave., (707) 762-2785.

Rohnert Park Chamber of Commerce, 6050 Commerce Blvd., (707) 584-1415.

Russian River Chamber of Commerce, Box 331, (707) 869-9009.

Santa Rosa Chamber of Commerce, 637 1st St., (707) 545-1414.

Santa Rosa Christian Businessmen's Committee, (707) 887-1448.

Other Business Organizations

There are many business service clubs, such as Rotary, Kiwanis, Lions, and Elks, that are ideal for meeting new friends and making business connections. As a member you would also be supporting many charitable activities. Until recently these clubs were limited to men, but recent court decisions require them to open up membership to women. If you are hoping to meet single professional men, one of these organizations would be great. Most of the members

Mixing Business With Pleasure

are married, but a reasonable percentage will be single.

Other business groups that provide social as well as financial opportunities are listed below.

Business Executives Association of Marin, 24 Marsh, Mill Valley 94941, (415) 381-3816. Weekly breakfast in San Rafael. Networking.

Community Entrepreneurs Organization (CEO), Box 2781, San Rafael 94912, (415) 435-4461. Brainstorming, lectures, and networking for current and aspiring entrepreneurs. Typical donation is $5 per meeting. Games Chapter, for people who want to invent or play newly invented games, meets in San Francisco. Other chapters are in San Jose, San Francisco, Novato and the East Bay.

Connections, 479-4509 (Margaret). Lunch & networking, Tuesdays, La Toscana Restaurant, San Rafael.

Leads Club, 388-7179 (Vera).

Marin Professional Women's Network, Diana Good, Western Federal Savings, (415) 383-6110. Breakfast & networking, Tuesdays, 7:30am.

North Bay Ad Club, (415) 492-9226.

OZ, St. Francis Hotel, San Francisco, (415) 774-0235, sponsors elegant business networking parties.

The Professional Association of Secretarial/Word Processing Services (PASS), (415) 655-4296 has members who are owners of word processors. This would be a particularly good organization if you wanted to meet single professional women.

LOVE
AMONGST
THE NERDS

The San Francisco Bay Area is the computer capital of the world. There are vast numbers of singles who use computers almost daily. Many of them are computer fanatics who actually think that computers are fun! They are likely to join User Groups, which are listed below.

Computer User Groups specializing in business computers and software are excellent places to meet single men, since most women find computers to be boring. Unfortunately, many women think that computer buffs are all nerds. As a person who spends a great deal of time in front of a computer terminal, I resent this stereotype. Most of us are fun to be with, as well as intelligent and well-educated. Computer buffs also tend to have good incomes.

In addition to being fertile meeting grounds for singles, Computer User Groups usually have a public domain software library that enables you to get free or almost free software. Assistance and classes are often available to help you use the software.

The clubs are listed below according to the type of computer hardware or software they use. For a current and complete listing of Computer User Groups, meeting times and sites, read MicroTimes, 5951 Canning St., Oakland 94609, (415) 652-3810 or Bay Area Computer Currents, 5720 Hollis St., Emeryville 94608, (415) 547-6800. Both magazines are free.

BERKELEY

Amiga East Bay User Group, (415) 845-4814. 2nd Wednesdays, 7pm, 2618 Telegraph.

Apple East Bay Users, (415) 845-4814. 1st Tuesdays, 7pm, 2618 Telegraph Ave.

Bay Area Design & Graphics Group (Desktop Publishing with MAC), (415) 849-9114. Mondays, 8pm, 2150 Kittredge.

Berkeley PC Compatibles User Group, (415) 526-4033 (Mel). 2nd Mondays, 7pm, Winners Circle, 2618 Telegraph.

East Bay MacIntosh User Group, (415) 486-0147 (Terry). 3rd Tuesdays, 7:30pm, 724 Allston.

PC Desktop Publishing User Group, (415) 848-8200 (Dr. Wallia). Thursdays, 7pm, 2601 College Ave.

CONCORD

Diablo Valley Apple Users, (415) 672-7596 (Merle). Odd Fridays, 7pm, Willow Creek Ctr, Mohr Lane.

CUPERTINO

Apple II Programming & Interfacing Enthusiasts, (408) 258-0284 (Fred). 4th Thursdays, 7:30pm, Lynbrook High.

64/More Commodore User Group, (408) 945-4327. 3rd Sundays.

Ventura Publisher User Group, (408) 227-5030. 3rd Wednesdays, 6-9pm, Hewlett-Packard, Oak Room, Wolfe Rd at Pruneridge.

DIABLO VALLEY

Amiga Addicts Anonymous, (415) 689-3453.

EAST BAY

DBASE Users, (415) 641-9704 (Darrell) or 893-7637 (Alexandra). 3rd Sundays, 1pm.

Diablo Valley PC User Group, (415) 943-1367. 1st Wednesdays, 7:30pm.

FREMONT

FUNHUG-PC, (415) 797-5433 (Russ). 3rd Wednesdays, 7:30pm, Fremont Main Library, 39770 Paseo Padre Pkwy.

Society for the Prevention of Cruelty to Apples, (415) 537-3439.

HAYWARD

PC Clubhouse, (415) 538-2449. 1st Fridays, 8pm, Cal State Univ., Meiklejohn Hall.

South County PC Users Group, (415) 537-9899 (Bob). 2nd Thursdays, 7pm, Round Table Pizza, 22457 Foothill Blvd.

Love Amongst the Nerds

LIVERMORE
    ACCESS(Amiga-CommodoreComputerEnthusiasts),(415)829-6053 (Paul). 2nd Thursdays, Livermore Muni Airport.
MARIN
    Amiga Users of Marin, (415) 924-5384. 3rd Wednesdays, 7:30pm, College of Marin, Science Ctr 190.
    DBASE Users Group, (415) 488-0342 (John).
    Hellman's MacIntosh User Group, 814 E St., (415) 453-7924. Odd Tuesdays, 7pm.
    Macs of Marin (MOM), (415) 459-5707 (Steve). 2nd Thursdays, 7pm, Redwood High, 395 Doherty, Larkspur.
    MarinCommodoreComputerClub,(415)883-7748.2ndWednesdays, 7:30pm, Redwood High, Larkspur.
    Marin/Sonoma PC User Group, (415) 491-4295. 4th Mondays, San Rafael Community Center, B St. near 3rd St.
MILPITAS
    64/More Commodore User Group, (408) 945-4327. 2nd Saturdays.
MONTEREY COUNTY
    Epson Monterey Bay Area User Group, (408) 375-6667 (Eddie).
    Plus/4 User Group (PLUG), Box 1001, Monterey 93942.
    Salinas-Monterey Amiga User Group, (408) 678-2518 (Richard). 3rd Tuesdays, 7pm.
OAKLAND
    Amiga Users Oakland, (415) 652-4746. 3rd Wednesdays.
    Professional Association of Secretarial Services (PASS), (415) 655-4293. 2ndSaturdays,11:30am,Scott'sSeafood.DesktopPublishing.
    VideoShow Graphics Users Group, Executive Solutions, 333 Hegenberger Rd. #601, (415) 562-4801.
PALO ALTO
    Macintosh Users of ComputerWare, 490 California, (415) 496-1068. 3rd Tuesdays, 7pm.
PENINSULA
    KAYFUN, Peninsula Computer Club (IBM), (415) 593-9981 (Larry).
    Peninsula Apple Users, (415) 591-9124 (Les).
PLEASANTON
    Tri-Valley Apple II User Group, (415) 929-3672 (Esther) or 828-6237 (Dan). 1st Thursdays, 6:30pm.
    Tri-Valley Macintosh User Group, (415) 426-8756. 1st Thursdays, 7pm, 4695 Chabot Dr #114, Hacienda Business Park.
REDWOOD CITY
    Bay Area Epson Salts, (415) 364-0232 (Joe) or 992-5475 (Tom). 1st Tuesdays, 7:30pm, 2611 Broadway.
    Ventura Desktop Publishing User Group, (415) 726-3181 (Elenor Church). 2nd Mondays, 7pm, 619 Bradford.

Love Amongst the Nerds

ROHNERT PARK
>   Amstrad Word Processing User Group, 1269 SW Blvd., R.P. 94928, (707) 795-8548.

SAN BRUNO
>   Commodore Owner's Workshop (COW). 3rd Thursdays, San Bruno Park & Rec. Bldg.
>
>   San Bruno Apple Core, (415) 952-9309.

SAN FRANCISCO
>   AT/XT Clone User Group, (415) 861-9321. 2nd Mondays, 7-9pm, Ft. Mason Bldg E, Rm 287.
>
>   Bay Area Commodore User Group, Box 146731, S.F. 94114.
>
>   Bay Area MacForum, Box 281797, S.F. 94128, (415) 771-5830. 3rd Tuesdays, 7pm, Ft. Mason.
>
>   Christian MacIntosh User Group, (408) 437-1913 (Rick). 2nd Thursdays.
>
>   Computer Associates User Group, (415) 864-6770 (Beth). 3rd Wednesdays, 6:30pm, 1500 Van Ness.
>
>   dBASE User Group, (415) 474-6693 (Frank).
>
>   Epson QX/PX, (415) 956-7911. 1st Thursdays, 7pm, Ft. Mason.
>
>   S.F. Apple Core, Box 281797, S.F. 94128, (415) 771-5830, 771-5830 or 398-2335. 3rd Tuesdays, 7pm, Fort Mason.
>
>   S.F. Commodore Users, (415) 832-1539 (Malcolm). 3rd Fridays, 7:30pm, Log Cabin, Storey at Ralston.
>
>   S.F. Computer Society, (415) 929-0252 (Ralph). 1st Mondays, 7pm, Homestead Savings, 5757 Geary Blvd.
>
>   S.F. PC Jr User Group, (415) 472-7035. 1st Sundays, 7:30pm, Ft. Mason, Rm C205.
>
>   S.F. PC User Group, (415) 221-9166. 3rd Mondays, 7:30pm, UCSF Auditorium, 3333 California.

SAN JOSE
>   Christian MacIntosh User Group, (408) 437-1913 (Rick). 1st Thursdays.
>
>   Commodore Computer Generated People User Group, (408) 226-9225 (Tom).
>
>   IBM & Compatibles Programming & Interfacing Enthusiasts, (408) 736-7704 (Clay). 3rd Wednesdays, 7:30pm, General Disk Corporation.
>
>   Silicon Valley dBASE User Group, (408) 723-3471 (Michael) or (415) 846-1814 (Karl).
>
>   64/More Commodore User Group, (408) 945-4327. 1st Sundays.

SAN LEANDRO
>   S.L. Apple Eaters Users Group, (415) 887-7499. 1st Thursdays, San Leandro High School, Rm 213, 2200 Bancroft.

Love Amongst the Nerds

SAN RAMON

MacDiablo User Group, (415) 828-4995. 3rd Tuesdays, Glendale Federal Savings, 3101 Crow Canyon Rd.

SANTA CLARA

Apple IIGS Programming & Interfacing Enthusiasts, (415) 322-7867 (David). 2nd Tuesdays, 7:30pm, Wilcox High.

Appleworks Programming & Interfacing Enthusiasts, (408) 356-2660 (Egon). 4th Tuesdays, 7pm, Wilcox High.

SANTA CRUZ

MUSC (Apple Computers), (408) 476-0504 (Barney). 2nd Tuesdays, Green Acres School, 966 Bostwick Ln.

Santa Cruz Computer Society, (408) 479-1180. 3rd Thursdays, 7pm, Santa Cruz County Office of Education, 809 Bay Ave #H, Capitola.

SANTA ROSA

Applepickers of the Redwood Empire, (707) 763-8322. 2nd Saturdays, 10am, Santa Rosa Junior College, Shuhaw 1735.

IBM PC User Group of the Redwoods, (707) 527-USER. 2nd Thursdays, Vets Memorial Bldg, East Dining Room.

SARATOGA

Apple IIIrs Unanimous, 4th Tuesdays, 7:30pm, 12604 Wardell Ct.

SCOTTS VALLEY

Scotts Valley Amiga User Group, (408) 438-5001 (Rudy).

SILICON VALLEY

Amiga Users Group of Silicon Valley, (415) 651-1160. 2nd Fridays.

Bay Area TimeStar User Group, (408) 983-4930. 2nd Thursdays, 7:30pm.

Bay Talk PC User Group, (415) 486-6411 (DON).

Silicon Valley Commodore Computer Club, (408) 942-1679 (Brian).

Silicon Valley Computer Society, (408) 286-1271. 2nd Wednesdays, 7:30pm, Tech Mart.

STANFORD UNIVERSITY

Bay Area Amiga Developers Group (BADGE), (415) 723-1646. 3rd Thursdays, 8pm, Turing Auditorium.

Stanford MacIntosh Users Group, (415) 723-SMUG.

Stanford/Palo Alto PC User Group, (415) 322-3850 (Louise). Last Wednesdays, 8pm, Stanford Polya Hall, Turing Aud., Rm 11.

SUNNYVALE

Amiga Science & Technology Users Group, (408) 742-8817. 2nd Thursdays, 5-7pm, Lockheed, Bldg 157, Rm 4C.

Interex Hewlett-Packard Computer Users Group, 585 Maude Ct, Sunnyvale 94086, (408) 738-4848 (Maria).

PC UNIX Group, (408) 432-1300. 1st Wednesdays, 7pm, AT&T Training Ctr,f 1090 E. Duane Ave.

Love Amongst the Nerds

VALLEJO
  Vallejo Amiga People (VAMP), (707) 554-0263 (Bill). 2nd Tuesdays, 6:15pm, Software 1st, Vallejo Corners.
MISCELLANEOUS
  The Amiga Class, (415) 949-4864 (Patrick).
  Amiga Desktop Video User Grp, (415) 543-8282. 3rd Mondays, 6pm.
  Bay Hewlett-Packard Laptops & Handhelds Group, (707) 794-3130 (Jim) or (415) 564-8279 (Michael).
  dBASE III Prog. Developers, (415) 931-0377 (Gil) or 923-0659 (Bruce).
  1st Amiga User Group, (415) 595-5452. 1st Tuesdays.
  FOG International MS-DOS Group, (415) 755-2000.
  Freelance & Freelance Plus Users Group (Graphics), (415) 882-7344.
  IBM & Compatibles User Group, D. Tuma, 30 Arjang Ct., Alamo 94507.
  PC Publishers of N. California, (415) 635-0159. 3rd Thursdays, 6pm.

Love Amongst the Nerds

NON-PROFIT ORGANIZATIONS

What do you like to do in your leisure time? Are you interested in civic affairs? Do you have any hobbies? If you do, there are thousands of singles in the Bay Area to share these interests with you. Join one of the many non-profit organizations listed below. Many of their members will be single also.

Animals

Bay Area Amphibian & Reptile Society, Palo Alto Jr. Museum, 1451 Middlefield Rd., Palo Alto 94301.
Diablo Valley German Shepard Dog Club, (415) 935-7719.
East of Eden Cat Fanciers, Box 783, Pacific Grove 93950, (408) 372-7018.
Fremont Dog Training Club, 45581 Industrial, Fremont, (415) 490-9887.
Fund for animals, (415) 474-4020.
Martinez Homing Pigeon Club, The Embarcadero, Martinez, 228-8222.
Oceanic Society, (415) 441-5970.
San Francisco Aquarium Society, 2029 Palmetto, Pacifica, (415) 359-7916.
Santa Cruz Kennel Club, (408) 438-3647.
Society for the Prevention of Cruelty to Animals, 2500 16th St., San Francisco, (415) 621-1700.
Whale Center, (415) 654-6621.

Architecture

American Institute of Architects, (707) 576-7799. Contests, picnics.

Art

Artist's Round Table, Santa Rosa, (707) 539-4170.
Palo Alto Art Club, 668 Ramona, Palo Alto, (415) 853-9608.
San Francisco Museum of Modern Art, Van Ness at McAllister, 863-8800.
San Ramon Arts Council, (415) 829-4562.
Sunnyvale Art Club, (408) 736-3056 (Virginia Miller). 3rd Mondays, 7pm, Senior Center.

Autos

Car enthusiasts are likely to be prosperous men. Single women would be wise to attend car-related events. Read the San Francisco Chronicle's Sports section for lists of races and shows for cars and motorcycles.

Cabrillo Region Antique Auto Club of America, Box 2755, Santa Cruz, (408) 475-7256.
Sports Car Club of America, San Francisco Chapter, 1610 Pacific, (415) 775-1010. Sponsors shows, races, and road rallies.

Books

The Book Club of California, 312 Sutter, San Francisco 94108, (415) 781-7532.
Friends of the San Francisco Public Library, Main Library, Civic Center, S.F. 94102, (415) 558-3770. Sponsors book sales, films, volunteering, parties, exhibits, outings.

Bridge

Cavendish Bridge Club, 1100 Gough, San Francisco 94109, (415)776-7080.
Bridge Club of San Francisco, 777 Jones, (415) 776-6949.
San Francisco Bridge Center, 256 Laguna Honda Blvd., (415) 681-4688.
Chess Club, 57 Post St., San Francisco, (415) 421-2258.
Chess Friends of Northern California, 2460 21st Ave., San Francisco 94116, (415) 731-6851.
Monterey Chess Center, 430 Alvarado, Monterey 93940, (408) 372-9790.
Sonoma County Chess Information, (707) 795-9377.

Non-Profit Organizations

Coin Collecting

Northern California Numismatic Association, Box 5075, San Jose 95150.
San Francisco Coin Club, Box 27006, San Francisco 94127, (415) 697-2096.

Cultural Activities

American Conservatory Theatre (A.C.T.), 450 Geary St., San Francisco
   94102, (415) 771-3880.
California Academy of Sciences, Golden Gate Park, (415) 752-8268.
Exploratorium, 3601 Lyon St., (415) 563-3200.
Museum Society, De Young Museum, Golden Gate Park, San Francisco.
Oakland Museum Association, 1000 Oak St., Oakland 94607, (415)
   893-4257.   Quarterly exhibition tours and receptions, catering to
   singles 21-60s.
San Francisco Ballet Association, (415) 861-1177
San Francisco Conservatory of Ballet & Theater Arts, 347 Dolores,
San Francisco, (415) 626-1001.
Sonoma County Yiddish Cultural Society, (707) 584-5612.
Sunnyvale Community Players, (408) 732-2497 (Carmen Stone).

Discussions

Brain Exchange, 826-8248.

Engineering

Engineers Club of San Francisco, 169 Sansome, (415) 421-3184.

Ethnic Organizations

Alianza Argentina, 464 Reynolds Circle, San Jose, (408) 436-0748.
Alliance Francaise, 414 Mason, San Francisco 94102, (415) 781-8755.
Alliance Francaise of the East Bay, (415) 548-1520.
Argentina Circulo de San Jose, 824 N. 12th, San Jose, (408) 998-3123.
Arribas/Juntos/Obeca, 2017, Mission, 2nd Floor, San Francisco 94110,
   (415) 863-9307.
Australian-American Association, 400 California, 13th Floor, San
   Francisco 94104, (415) 772-9229.
British American Club of Northern California, 4255 Williams Rd., San
   Jose 95129, (408) 257-2221 or 948-9784.
British American Club of Northern California, 3 W. 37th Ave., San
   Mateo, (415) 573-6440.
Caledonian Club, 1310 Mercer St., Richmond 94804.

Non-Profit Organizations

Ethinic Organizations (continued)

Caledonian Club (Scottish) of San Francisco, (415) 897-4442.
Canadian American Society, Box 2931, San Francisco 94126.
Cercle de L'Union, 414 Mason St., San Francisco 94102, (415) 362-5956.
Chinese American Citizens Alliance, 414 Mason, San Francisco 94102, (415) 362-5956.
Croatian-American Social Club, 415 Grand Ave., South San Francisco, (415) 952-3830.
Diablo Japanese American Club, 3165 Treat, Concord, (415) 680-9768.
Diablo Valley Japanese American Citizens League, (415) 838-9148.
Filipino American Senior Citizen Center, 3483 Mission, San Francisco, (415) 285-2076.
Filipino Community Center, 3361 Fulton Rd., Fulton, (707) 546-2795.
Filipino Community of San Francisco, 2970 California, San Francisco 94115, (415) 346-7252.
Filipino Senior Citizens Club, 83 6th St., San Francisco, (415) 974-5871.
Goethe Institute, 530 Bush, San Francisco, (415) 391-0370, promotes German culture through films, concerts, art exhibits, classes, books, and parties.
German-American Society of Marin, Box 1276, Novato 94948, (415) 897-7985. Activities include dances and parties.
Italian American Club, 747 Black Diamond, Pittsburg, (415) 439-9977.
Italian American Social Club, 958 Oak Ln., Menlo Pk, (415) 322-8933.
Irish Center, Inc., 2123 Market, San Francisco 94114, (415) 621-2200.
Irish Social Club, (408) 265-7512.
Japanese-American Philatelic Society, Box 1049, El Cerrito 94530, (415) 529-1045.
Japan Society of San Francisco, 312 Sutter, San Francisco 94108, (415) 986-4383.
Mexican-American Cultural Association , Box 614, Concord 94522, (415) 687-6222.
Mission Cultural Center, (Hispanic Culture) 2451 Harrison, San Francisco, (415) 821-1155.
Polish Club, 3040 22nd St., San Francisco, (415) 550-9252.
Puerto Rican Club, 3249A Mission St., San Francisco, (415) 550-9323.
Russian Center of San Francisco, 55 New Montgomery, San Francisco, (415) 546-0644.
Swiss Club Tell, 551 Edgewood Ave., Mill Valley 94941, (415) 388-9993.
Tri-Valley Japanese American Citizens League, (415) 833-2561.
United Irish Culture Center, 2700 45th Ave., San Francisco, (415) 661-2700. Weekend dances, Irish bands, concerts, and lectures.
Young Scandinavians Club, 6A Cazneau Ave., Sausalito 94965, (415) 331-6463.

Non-Profit Organizations

Games

Backgammon Club, 777 Jones, San Francisco, (415) 474-7328.
East Bay Go Association, 2547 8th St. #41, Berkeley, (415) 843-1973. Chess & Go lessons.
Grass Roots Cribbage, Santa Rosa, (707) 585-1577.
Santa Rosa Mah Jong Club, (707) 579-1310.

Garden

Danville/Alamo Garden Club, (415) 837-3048 or 830-9494.
Sunnyvale Garden Club, (408) 296-3805 (Nellie Durand). Odd Wednesdays, 10am, Arboretum Work Center.

Handicapped

California Handicapables, INC., 2326 Jones St., San Francisco 94133, (415) 273-5447. Meetings second Saturday of each month at the Cathedral High School Auditorium at Ellis and Franklin Sts. Luncheons, discussion groups, lectures on new legislation affecting the handicapped. Free transportation is provided for anyone who calls a few days before a scheduled meeting. All ages.

History

History Club of Los Gatos, 123 Los Gatos Blvd., Los Gatos, (408) 354-9825.
San Ramon Valley Historical Society, (415) 837-4849.

Hydroponics

Hydroponic Society of America, Box 6067, Concord, (415) 682-4193.

Men's Organizations

The Male Journey Group, Stephen Kessler, M.F.C.C., (415) 834-5399.
Men's Circle, Grand Lake area, Oakland, (415) 769-3777. Bruce Ecker, M.F.C.C.
Men's Support Group, Berkeley, (415) 548-8721 (Gary Hoeber).

Mensa

Mensa sponsors parties and other activities throughout the Bay Area. The group is limited to people with high I.Q.s. Not exclusively for singles, but a great place for meeting singles nevertheless.

Non-Profit Organizations

Mensa (continued)

San Mateo: 1732-A Marina Ct., S.M. 94403.
San Pablo: 2346 Rumrill Rd., S.P. 94806
Sonoma County: (707) 525-8494.

Minerals

East Bay Mineral Society, 2506 High, Oakland, (415) 261-4311.
San Francisco Gem & Mineral Society, 4134 Judah, San Francisco 94122, (415) 564-4230.

Model Railroads

Black Diamond Lines Model Railroad Club, 425 Fulton Shipyard Rd., Antioch, (415) 779-1964.
California Central Model Railroad Club, 4185 Bassett, Agnew, (408) 988-4449.
Golden Gate Model Railroaders, Inc., Josephine D. Randall Jr. Museum, Museum Dr., near Roosevelt St., San Francisco 94114, (415) 863-1399.
Napa Valley Model Railroaders, Inc., Napa Fairgrounds, Napa, (707) 255-9615.
Walnut Creek Model Railroad Society, 2751 Buena Vista Ave., Walnut Creek, (415) 937-1888.
West Bay Model Railroad Assn., 1090 Merrill, Menlo Park, (415) 322-0685.

Model Yachts

San Francisco Model Yacht Club, 36 Kennedy Dr., Golden Gate Park, San Francisco 94118, (415) 386-9762.

Music

Bach Dancing & Dynamite Society, Box 302, El Granada 94018, (415) 726-4143. Concerts, dinners, socials. Jazz concerts with buffet, Sunday afternoons. Classical Candlelight Dinner Concerts, Friday nights.
Band Foundation, (415) 552-3656.
Berkeley Piano Club, 2724 Haste, Berkeley, (415) 845-8488.
Etude Music Club, Santa Rosa, (707) 576-1942.
New Orleans Jazz Club of Northern California, Box 27232, San Francisco 94127, (415) 398-6652 (taped message).
Nova Vista Symphony, Sunnyvale, (408) 736-4338. Tuesdays, 7:30-10pm, Cumberland School.
Orfeo Opera Club, 13 Columbus St., San Francisco.

Non-Profit Organizations

Music (continued)

San Ramon Valley Community Concerts Association, (415) 837-3780.
Serenaders (Big Band), Sunnyvale, (408) 739-4547 (John Nebozuk).
   Wednesdays, Braly Park.
Wagner Society of Northern California, Box 590990, San Francisco
   94159.

Mysteries

Dashiell Hammett Society, John's Grill, Maltese Falcon Room, 63 Ellis,
   San Francisco 94102, (415) 986-0069.
Maltese Falcon Society, (415) 665-7644.

Neighborhood Associations

   "Today it's rare to find a sense of neighborhood in the big
cities. A study of Chicago's South Shore neighborhood revealed
that residents visit friends outside the neighborhood more often
than within the area and that almost half never visit with the
neighborhood at all!
   "In 'the good old days' it was easier to meet people, even in
big cities, "because everyone felt part of the neighborhood.
People knew and greeted each other on the street. They tended to
fall in love, marry, and raise children in the same area.
(Excerpted from **How to Find a Lasting Relationship**, Gosse, Marin
Publications, San Rafael: 1988.)
   There's no reason why you can't borrow a lesson from the past
and look to your neighbors for new friends or a romantic partner.
The first step is to be sociable anytime you see someone in the
neighborhood. Smile at them and say hello at every opportunity.
Introduce yourself and try to remember their names.
   The next step is join your neighborhood association. These
groups are most active when the neighborhood is threatened by
unwelcome development, traffic, or natural catastrophes. To find
out about your neighborhood association contact city hall. Another
option is join your Neighborhood Crime Watch Organization. To find
out about these organizations contact your local police station or city
hall.

Newcomers Clubs

   Are you new to your area? One of the best ways to get acclimated to
a new town is to contact a Newcomers Clubs. They'll do everything
they can to make you feel welcome and help you meet new friends.

Non-Profit Organizations

Newcomers Clubs (continued)

Alameda County Newcomers, (415) 490-8477.
Dublin-San Ramon Newcomers, (415) 830-4755.
Marin County Newcomers, (415) 499-0903.
Santa Clara County Newcomers, (408) 998-0313.
Sonoma County Newcomers, 2211 4th St., Santa Rosa, (707) 545-1995.

Overweight People

National Association to Advance Fat Acceptance (NAAFA), (415) 886-3550. Dinners, dances.

Photography

Redwood Empire Camera Club, (707) 539-5135.
Retlaw Camera Club, 2959 Mission St., San Francisco 94110, (415) 647-8737.
Silverado Camera Club, 4149 Linda Vista Ave., Napa, (707) 252-8468. Tuesdays, 7:30pm.
Solano Camera Club meets at the Fairfield Community Center, 1000 Kentucky St., in Fairfield. Contact: (707) 422-4415.

Poetry

Live Poet's Society, (415) 673-7213. Poetry workshops, Thursdays, 6:30-8pm, State Bldg., San Francisco. Free.

Public Affairs

American Civil Liberties Union, 814 Mission St., San Francisco 94103, (415) 621-2488.
Amnesty International, 3618 Sacramento, San Francisco 94118, (415) 563-3733.
Bay Area Urban League, 344 20th St., Oakland 94612, (415) 922-5050.
California Club, 1750 Clay St., San Francisco 94108, (415) 474-3516.
California Council for Environmental & Economic Balance, 215 Market #1311, San Francisco 94105, (415) 495-5666.
Churchill Club, Palo Alto, (415) 494-6678.
Committee to Save the Cable Cars, 201 3rd St. #900, San Francisco 94103, (415) 956-3777.
Commonwealth Club of California, 681 Market, San Francisco 94105, (415) 362-4903.
Council for Civic Unity, 870 Market, San Francisco 94105, (415) 781-2033.

Non-Profit Organizations

Public Affairs (continued)

Citizens Action League, 2988 Mission, San Francisco 94110, (415) 647-8450.
Downtown Association,582 Market,San Francisco 94104,(415)362-7842.
Ecology Center,13 Columbus Ave., San Francisco 94111,(415)391-6307.
Friends of the Earth,1045 Sansome, San Francisco 94111,(415) 433-7373.
Golden Gate Audubon Society, 2718 Telegraph #206, Berkeley 94705, (415) 843-2222.
Market St. Development, 870 Market, San Francisco 94102, (415) 362-2500.
Monterey Civic Club, 540 Calle Principal, Monterey 93940, (408) 372-9489.
Nature Conservancy, 156 2nd St., San Francisco 94105, (415) 777-0487.
San Francisco Bay Conservation & Development, 30 Van Ness #2011, San Francisco 94102, (415) 557-3686.
San Francisco Beautiful, 41 Sutter #621, San Francisco 94104, (415) 986-1010.
San Francisco Forward, 690 Market #800, San Francisco 94104, (415) 434-4466.
Save the Bay Association, Box 925, Berkeley 94701, (415) 849-3053.
San Francisco Planning & Urban Research Association (SPUR), 312 Sutter, San Francisco 94108, (415) 781-8726.
Save the Redwoods League, 114 Sansome, SF 94104, (415) 362-2352.
San Francisco Coalition of Business & Labor, (415) 982-5139.
San Francisco Democratic Party, 500 Sutter, (415) 981-8333.
San Francisco Republican Party,49 Geary,San Francisco,(415) 982-1532.
San Ramon Valley Republican Women, (415) 837-6253.
Sierra Club, 530 Bush, SF 94108, (415) 981-8634.
Sonoma County Taxpayers Association, (707) 542-0442.
Trees for the City, 740 Francisco, San Francisco 94133, (415) 775-1697.

Radio

Marin Amateur Radio Club, Hamilton Air Force Base,Novato,883-9789.
Radio-Controlled Glider Club, Pleasanton, (415) 462-9141.

Service Clubs

These clubs provide service to the community. They also raise money for charitable causes. Meetings of local chapters are listed in your local newspaper calendar of events. Some examples of service clubs are Rotary, Kiwanis, Lions, and Optimists.

Non-Profit Organizations

Sewing

Santa Rosa Nile Club, (707) 823-8235.

Skeptics

Bay Area Skeptics, 4030 Moraga St., San Francisco 94122. Critically examines paranormal claims. Free public meetings; monthly newsletter. $11,000 reward for proven psychic ability.

Singing

Mayflower Community Chorus, Mayflower Inn, 1533 4th, San Rafael 94901, (415) 456-1011.
Redwood Chordsmen, Santa Rosa, (707) 528-2661.
Silver Singers Mixed Chorus, Santa Rosa, (707) 545-8608.
Sunnyvale Singers, (408) 736-1179 (Janet Sinn). Wednesdays, 7:30-9:30pm, Homestead High School.
Sweet Adelines, Santa Rosa, (707) 578-TUNE.

Social Clubs

Campidoglio Social Club, 535 Broadway, San Francisco, (415) 392-8390.
East Side Social Club, 2377 University Ave., E. Palo Alto, (415) 323-7232.
Far East Social Club, 885 4th St., San Rafael 94901, (415) 459-9022.
North Star Social Club, 45 Jackson, San Jose, (408) 293-3529.
Old-Timers Club, 1821 Steiner, San Francisco, (415) 929-9603.
Peninsula Social Club, 100 N. B, San Mateo, (415) 343-7981.
Senior Friendship Club meets every Tuesday, 1-4 pm, at the Senior Center, 1500 Jefferson St., Napa. Contact: (707) 255-1800.
We & Our Neighbors Club, 15480 Union Ave., San Jose, (408) 559-9868.

Stamp Collecting

Japanese-American Philatelic Society, Box 1049, El Cerrito 94530, (415) 529-1045.
San Francisco Philatelic Society, 986 Guerrero, S.F. 94110, (415) 647-7637.
Sunnyvale Stamp Society, (408) 732-0531 (Bob Anderson). Tuesdays, 7-10pm, Sunnyvale Community Center.

Tall Clubs

Are you hoping to meet new friends or romantic partners that are tall? Join one of the chapters of Tall Clubs International. The height requirement is: Men - 6'2"; Women - 5'10".

Non-Profit Organizations

Tall Clubs (continued)

Redwood Empire Tall Club, 1055 Montgomery Rd., Sebastopol 95865, (707) 823-9708.
Golden Gate Tip Toppers, 750 Elizabeth, San Francisco 94114, (415) 759-6411.
South Bay Tall Club, (408) 734-1720. A social club for tall people (Women, 5'-10"; Men, 6'-2" and over). Predominantly singles.

Toastmasters Clubs

Toastmasters practice their public speaking skills each week, usually after dinner. Chapters are found throughout the Bay Area. A few are listed below.

Fountaingrove, Santa Rosa, (707) 577-3979.
Healdsburg, (707) 431-1933.
Petaluma, (707) 763-6891 or 762-6608.
Premium Toastmasters, San Ramon, (415) 842-2432.
Rohnert Park Friendlies, (707) 584-7193.
Santa Rosa, (707) 544-7233.
Toast of the Town, Santa Rosa, (707) 823-5655.

Wine & Beer

Cityscape, San Francisco, (415) 776-0215. Monthly wine tastings.
Homebrew Club, Hopland, (707) 463-1551.
Vintners Club, Box 3298, San Rafael 94901, (415) 485-1166.

Women's Clubs

American Association of University Women, (415) 820-8457.
Danville Lioness, (415) 837-3361.
Diablo Valley Business & Professional Women, (415) 866-0600.
Dublin Women's Club, (415) 829-3695.
San Ramon Valley Christian Women's Club, (415) 838-1961.
San Ramon Women's Club, (415) 828-1596.
Soroptomists
   Rohnert Park-Cotati, (707) 795-5449.
   San Ramon, (415) 846-1273.
   Santa Rosa, (707) 527-2301.
   West Santa Rosa, (707) 544-2010 x236.
Women in Mid-Life Support Group, (415) 525-8556. Mona Reeva.
Women in Telecommunications, (415) 831-1100.

Non-Profit Organizations

Other Non-Profit Organizations

For a comprehensive list of non-profit organizations and public agencies in San Francisco contact the S.F. Chamber of Commerce, 465 California St., 9th Floor, San Francisco 94104, (415) 392-4511 and ask about their **Trade Association Directory**. For a similar list for Marin County contact the Volunteer Center of Marin, 70 Skyview Terrace, San Rafael 94903, (415) 479-5660 and ask about their Guide to Volunteer Opportunities. Contra Costa County nonprofits are listed in **Directory of Organizations**. Contact Community Resource Center, 1850 2nd Ave., Walnut Creek, (415) 934-0901.

Non-Profit Organizations

DANCING

Attending a singles club that specializes in dancing is one way to meet other singles who like to dance. See the chapter on **Singles Clubs**. Many nightclubs also featuring dancing. See the chapter on **Singles Bars**.

Perhaps an even better way to meet new single friends is by taking a dance lesson. The dance instruction section of the yellow pages of your phone book lists numerous schools that teach dancing. Contact them and choose one that caters primarily to single adults. Usually at these dance lessons you will automatically meet many different partners of the opposite sex, even if you're shy!

Listed below are a few dance schools. Also listed are regular dances throughout the Bay Area that are open to both singles and couples. Of course these dances are always subject to change. For up to date information on what's going on in the Bay Area dance scene, subscribe to the **Ballroom Dancer's Rag**, a monthly magazine that lists numerous dances and dance clubs throughout the Bay Area. Send $1.45 per copy or $11.65 per year to 1448 Montego Dr., San Jose 95120 or call (408) 268-6042/252-4940.

Another valuable resource is the **Dance Directory** by Marge Gabbert, with suggestions on where to go dancing in the Bay Area, including ballroom, swing, and Latin/salsa. Send $11 to Fascinating Rhythm Dance School, 28 Prague, San Francisco 94112 or call (415) 334-9914.

98

DANCE DIRECTORY

Alameda County

ALAMEDA
  The Alameda Theater, 2317 Central. Ballroom, Sundays, 6-10pm.
  Mecca Ballroom Dance Party, 2305 Alameda Ave., Alameda.
BERKELEY
  Ashkenaz, 1317 San Pablo, 525-5054. Folk dance lessons and dances.
  Ballroom Dancing in Berkeley, Charlene Van Ness, 2600 Bancroft,
    Berkeley, (415) 848-6370.
  Berkeley Ballroom Dancers, 2525 8th St. Sundays, 4-6pm; Fridays, 7-
    10pm.
  Dance Time Studios, 1015 Camelia.
  South Indian Dance, Karen Elliott, (415) 845-3431.
  University of California, Chris Williams, (415) 527-1486. Wednesday,
    Ballroom Dancing.
  University YWCA Dance & Fitness Classes, 2600 Bancroft Way,
    Berkeley 94704, (415) 848-6370. Aerobics, yoga, flamenco, salsa, jazz,
    Polynesian, ballroom classes.
DUBLIN
  Shannon Seniors Dance Club, 1600 Shannon. Tuesdays, 1-4pm,
FREMONT
  Choices, 5399 Farwell Pl., (415) 791-1660. Tea Dance, Sundays, 5-
    9:30pm.
LIVERMORE
  Country & Western Dance Classes, 1467 Wagoner Dr., Livermore
    94550, (415) 443-9254. Nora Wilt.
  Phran Turner's Dance Classes, 635 Hemlock Ct., Livermore. Ballroom
    Dance Classes, Thursdays, 7:45 pm, Veteran's Memorial Building,
    Livermore; Tuesdays, 8 pm, Veteran's Hall in Pleasanton; Country &
    Western Dance Classes, Wednesday nights, Livermore.
OAKLAND
  Ali Baba Dance Club, Veterans Memorial Bldg., 200 Grand, (415) 465-
    0669. Fridays, 8pm-12, $7.
  Grand Dance, 3501 Grand Ave. (at Mandana), Oakland, (415) 835-
    94960. West Coast Swing, Saturdays, 8-11pm.
  National Smooth Dancers, (415) 989-2473 (Carl). 4th Saturdays.
  Romantic Ballroom, John & Cynthia Bilorusky, 473 Hudson, (415) 547-
    1069.

Dancing

PLEASANTON
Pleasanton Hotel, 855 Main, (415) 846-8106. Big Band, 1st Sundays, 5-9pm.
Popis, 3059 Hopyard. Ballroom, Tuesdays, 9-1,
Veterans Memorial Bldg, 301 Main St. Ballroom, Wednesdays, 7:30-10:30pm.
SAN LEANDRO
San Leandro Library, 300 Estudillo. Sr. Swingers Dance, 1st, 4th, & 5th Wednesdays, 1-4pm.

Contra Costa County

DANVILLE
Tea Dancing, 120 S. Hartz Blvd. Thursdays, 1-3pm.
EL CERRITO
Dancing for Fun, Belinda Ricklefs, (415) 893-1519. Swing, Ballroom, Latin, Jitterbug dance lessons for beginners.
RICHMOND
Hacienda, 12020 San Pablo. Dancing/lessons, Sundays, 4-9pm.
LAFAYETTE
Scottish Country Dancing, (415) 934-6148/837-9483 (Lafayette).
WALNUT CREEK
Acalanes Adult Center, 1963 Tice Valley Blvd., Walnut Creek, CA 94595, 935-0170. Diane and Davitt Kasdan, teachers. Swing, fox trot, rhumba, waltz, and much more.
Dance World, 15 Sage Ct., W.C. 94596, (415) 938-1434. Ballroom & social dance. 2nd Saturdays, 7-10:30pm, Dance & Lesson, $8.

Marin County

FAIRFAX
Dance Spirit, Fairfax Health Club, 711 Center Blvd, (415) 453-1613.
GREENBRAE
Body & Soul, 208 Bon Air Shopping Ctr, Greenbrae 94904, 459-0832.
SAN ANSELMO
Arthur Murray Studio of Dance, 330 Sir Francis Drake Blvd., San Anselmo 94960. Contact Cy Nabarette at (415) 258-0212.
SAN RAFAEL
DanceArts Studio, Montecito Plaza, 361 3rd St., (415) 459-1020. Dance Party, Odd Fridays, 8pm-12.
Dance-It Together, Knights of Columbus Hall, 167 Tunstead Ave., (415) 459-0983. Frank & Nancy Flores.
Mandarin House, 817 Francisco Blvd., (415) 492-1638. Ballroom dance/class, Wednesdays, 6-8pm.

Dancing

100

MISCELLANEOUS MARIN COUNTY
Dance Extravaganza, 625-6240. Ballroom classes, Mill Valley/Larkspur.

Monterey County

Chatauqua Club, Pacific Grove, 394-0270 (Harry). Dancing, Saturdays.

Napa County

NAPA
Ballroom Dancers, Inc., (707) 255-7697 (John) or (707) 224-0834 (Burl).
Boots & Belles, Welcome Grange Hall, 3275 Hagen Rd., (707) 224-8207 (days) or 255-3538 (eves). Square Dancing, Wednesdays, 8 pm.
Boot Heel Ramblers, Welcome Grange Hall, 3275 Hagen Rd., (707) 224-9046 or 552-9462. Square Dancing, Fridays, 7:30-10:30pm.
5 Star Squares, Welcome Grange Hall, 3275 Hagen Rd., (707) 224-2001. Square & Round Dancing, Tuesdays, 7:30-10pm.
International Folk Dance Classes, 1025 Napa Rd., Napa, (707) 938-2226 (June Schaal). Mondays and Thursdays, 7pm.
Napa Buzzsteppers, Welcome Grange Hall, 3275 Hagen Rd., (707) 224-5883 or 255-2180. Mainstream Plus Square Dancing, Thursdays.
Napa Town & Country Fairgrounds, Arts & Crafts Bldg., (707) 255-3330 or 255-7697. Fridays, 8:30 pm, Ballroom Dancing.
Napa Valley Folk Dance Club, (707) 944-2069. Tuesdays, catch-up class, 7-8 pm; intermediate folk dancing, 8-10pm. Kennedy Park Multi-Purpose Bldg., 2296 Streblow Dr., Napa.
Senior Center, 1500 Jefferson St., (707) 255-1800. Ballroom Dancing, Tuesdays & Saturdays, 8-11 pm. 50+ age group.
ST. HELENA
Robert Louis Stevenson Gym, 1316 Hillview Park Place, (707) 963-5706 or 965-9372. Country Dancing, Saturdays, 8 pm.
YOUNTVILLE
Yountville Veterans Home, (707) 944-4534 or 944-8158. Ballroom Dancing, Grant Hall, Sundays, 1:30-3:30 pm. No charge. All welcome.

San Francisco

Avenue Ballroom, 603 Taraval, 681-2882. Ballroom lessons & dance, Sundays, 8-11pm. West Coast swing lessons & dance, Fridays, 8pm-1. Jitterbug party, Saturdays, 8pm-1. Mainly singles.
Bach Dancing & Dynamite Society, (415) 726-3839. Dinners, dancing, and concerts.
Bay Swingers Dance Club, Box 4410, S.F. 94101 (415) 994-2856/351-9296 or 957-0177 (Joe). Free dance lessons before dancing starts.

Dancing

San Francisco (continued)

The Boat House, Skyline Blvd. Swing dancing, Tuesdays, 8-12.
The Dance Art of Isadora Duncan, Maria Villazana-Ruiz, 3435 Army St #240, (415) 587-0730.
Dancers Unlimited, Arthur Calandrelli, (415) 282-3195. Ballroom & Latin lessons.
Golden Gate Swing Club, (415) 626-1004 (Jim). Sundays, Ballroom Dancing.
International Ballroom, 50 Oak St., (415) 863-7676. Ballroom.
Juke Box Saturday Night, 650 Howard St. Dirty Dancing, Thursdays, 8-11pm.
Kimball's, 300 Grove. Swing Fever, Wednesdays, 8-12.
National Smooth Dancers, (415) 989-2473 (Carl). Ballroom Dancing.
Pick School of Ballroom Dancing, 380 18th Ave., (415) 752-5658. Ballroom dance lessons Tuesdays, Wednesdays, & Thursdays, 7 pm. Dance Party, even Saturdays, 8pm-12.
Renaissance School of Dance, 285 Ellis, (415) 474-0920 (Teddy Leigh). American smooth, Latin, ballroom lessons. Dance Party, Fridays, 9-11:30pm.
Rikudom Israeli Folk Dancers, Bethany Church, corner of Clipper & Sanchez, (415) 647-2483. Sundays, 7-10pm, $2.50 (includes one-hour lesson and request dancing for the rest of the evening). After 10pm the group goes out for ice cream.
Ritz Continental Club, (415) 469-0422. Tea dancing, mainly singles.
Ruvano Dance Studio, 1290 Sutter. Ballroom, Fridays, 8-11pm.
S.F. Bay Area Dance Coalition, Ft. Mason, (415) 673-8172 or 333-5570.
S.F. Dance Hall, 827 Hyde, (415) 771-5600. Ballroom, Fridays, 8pm-1. Swing, Saturdays, 8pm-1.
S.F. Samba Club, Studio Brasil, 50 Brady St., (415) 863-8291. Josephine Morada & Chalo Eduardo.
S.F. School of Ballroom Dancing, 63 Onondaga, (415) 333-5570. 4th Sundays.
Slavonic Cultural Center, 60 Onondaga, (415) 585-6282 (Michelle). Swing, 2nd Sundays, 5pm (lesson), 6-10pm (dance).
Scottish Country Dancing, (415) 333-9372
Vintage Dance Club, 1885 Mission St., (415) 826-1914. Swing & ballroom lessons.

San Mateo County

REDWOOD CITY
Imperial Dance Club, 822 Cassia St., Redwood City 94063, (415) 366-0504 (Rex Lewis & Denise Jourdaine). Classes in ballroom & Latin dance. Ballroom dance, Saturdays.

Dancing

SAN BRUNO
DanceParty,444SanMateo,Tuesdays,8-11:30pm;Saturdays,8pm-12:30.
SAN MATEO
Beau'n Belles Dance Club, Ballroom dancing, St. Bartholomew's Gym, Alameda de las Pulgas, San Mateo.
Peninsula Social Club, Top of Beardsleys, 1010 N. B St., (415) 659-1740 (Phil) or 886-3487 (Ed). Wednesdays, 7-9pm (lessons), 9-12 (dance).
MISCELLANEOUS
Peninsula Ballroom Dance Club, (415) 490-0479 (Henry). Fridays.

Santa Clara County

LOS GATOS
Villa Felice, 15350 Winchester. Ballroom.
MORGAN HILL
Flying Lady, 15060 Foothill Rd. Ballroom.
MOUNTAIN VIEW
Reach, 1495 El Camino Real, Mt. View, (415) 965-3018. 50s & 60s mux and swing dance lessons in a smoke-free, alcohol free environment. Cappucinos, juices, hot coco, colas, and snacks are served. Childcare is available.
PALO ALTO
Bay Area Country Dance Society, (415) 321-2773.
Garfield's, 3901 El Camino Real. Big Band.
Palo Alto Masonic Temple, 461 Florence, (415) 856-8044 (Stan). Vintage Ballroom, Mondays, 8-10pm (lesson & dance).
Pavilion, 4000 Middlefield, (415) 489-9368 (Robin). Ballroom, Fridays, 8pm (lessons), 9pm-12 (dance). $4.
Viennese Waltz Seminars (held in Palo Alto), Robin Rebello, 4932 Casper St., Union City 94587, (415) 489-9368.
SAN JOSE
California Dance Club, 938 The Alameda, San Jose 95126, (408) 297-9772. Ballroom.
Cypress Senior Center, 403 S. Cypress Ave. Ballroom.
National Smooth Dancers, (408) 739-8869 (Charlene). Mondays.
South Bay Dance & Social Club, 516 El Paseo de Saratoga, 370-6961.
SANTA CLARA
Josetta School of Dance, 3280 El Camino, Santa Clara, (408) 296- 3245.
SUNNYVALE
Hai Yuan, 711 Town & Country Village. Ballroom.
Starlite Ballroom, 1160 N. Fair Oaks, (408)745-STAR. Ballroom, Fridays ($6) & Saturdays ($8), 8pm (lesson), 9-12 (dance). Ballroom (80s music), Sundays, 7pm (lesson), 8-11pm (dance), $7.
Sunnyvale Ballroom Dance Club, (408) 248-0304 (Bob).

Dancing

MISCELLANEOUS SANTA CLARA COUNTY
Coronets, (408) 736-4255 (Paul). Thursdays.
Mates & Dates- Stardancers Club, (408) 226-5493 (Dan).
Nite Outers, (408) 267-4569 (Diane).
Sea & Tree Dance Club, (408) 724-2502 (Bob).
Stardusters Club, (408) 377-9365 (Dale). 4th Saturdays.

Santa Cruz

Ballroom Classes, Thursdays, 7-8pm, German/American Hall, 230
Plymouth.
Santa Cruz Ballroom Dance Club, 1214 1/2 Pacific Ave., Santa Cruz.
West Coast Swing, Tuesdays, Santa Cruz, Becky Adams, Box 1204,
Soquel 95073, (408) 475-4427.

Solano County

VALLEJO
Pioneer Square Dances, (707) 648-4640. Vallejo Community Center, 225
Amador. Mondays, 7-10pm,
VACAVILLE
Vacaville Senior Center, 411 Kendal St., (707) 449-5192.

Sonoma County

COTATI
Folk Dancing, (707) 823-0526.
PENNGROVE
Question Marks Square Club, (707) 546-3430.
PETALUMA
International Folk Dancing, (707) 892-9405.
SANTA ROSA
Arthur Murray Studio, (707) 575-9226. Odd Sundays, 8:30pm-12.
Bill & Juanita Robinson, (707) 542-6066.
Circle & Squares Dance Club, (707) 546-1623.
Dancetime Dance Studio, 320 W. 3rd St #H, (707) 575-0606. Swing &
Ballroom, Fridays, 7pm (lesson), 8:30-12 (dance). Country/Western,
Saturdays, 7pm (lessons), 8:30-12 (dance).
Flamingo Hotel, Swing, 1st Sundays, 1:30-6pm.
Markwesterners' Square Dance Club, (707) 528-4829.
Redwood Empire Swing Dance Club, (707) 579-0339 (Tommie). 2nd
Sundays.
Santa Rosa Folk Dance Club, (707) 546-8877.
Singles & Pairs Square Dance Club, (707) 545-1513.

Dancing

SANTA ROSA (continued)
   Traditional Jazz, (707) 542-3973 (Tom). 1st Mondays.
   West Coast Swing Dance Club, (707) 575-7633.
SEBASTOPOL
   Continentalaires, (707) 528-4829.
   Sebastopol Spinners (Square Dance), (707) 829-1944.
SONOMA
   Cabaret Sauvignon, 478 1st St. E. Ballroom, Sundays, 5-8pm.
MISCELLANEOUS SONOMA COUNTY
   Vets Club, (707) 545-7340 (Porter).

Miscellaneous

Carousel Dance Club, (415) 468-4499 (Fred). 2nd Saturdays.
Debonairs, (415) 656-6660 (Ed).
Ginga Brasil Samba School, (415) 428-0698.
International Latin & Smooth & Rhythm Dance Lessons, Dan Santiago,
   (415) 752-5658 or 755-7548.
Phil Riservato, (415) 487-7802 or 487-6287. Private or group
   lessons.
Social Dance for Shy People & Klutzes, (415) 530-4019. Laurie Ann
   Lepoff, Instructor.
Top of Beardley's, (415) 886-3487 (Ed). Wednesdays.

Dancing

SPORTS

Sports are fun, healthy, and great places to meet new friends. Generally there is a surplus of single men, so they are particularly good opportunities for women to meet a romantic partner. Start reading the sports section of your local newspaper. Learn the names of the top athletes and most successful teams. Also the rules. Attend sporting events.

How do you get involved in sports? An obvious place to start is your neighborhood. First check your parks. That's where you'll find baseball, football, rugby, softball, and tennis. Next, check your gyms for basketball, gymnastics, and table tennis. Then turn to your health clubs for aerobics, exercise, weighlifting, racquetball, and swimming. Health Clubs are listed in the yellow pages of your telephone directory.

This chapter is divided into three sections:

1. Recreation Departments
2. YMCA's
3. Sports Directory

Recreation Departments

Your local recreation department is likely to sponsor competitive sports teams and activities, many of which are coed.

ALAMEDA COUNTY

Alameda Recreation Dept., Santa Clara Ave. & Oak, Alameda 94501, (415) 522-4100.
Albany Recreation Dept., 1100 San Pablo Ave., Albany, (415) 528-5740.
Berkeley Recreation Dept., 2180 Milvia, Berkeley, (415) 644-6530.
Dublin Recreation Dept., 6500 Dublin Blvd., Dublin, (415) 829-4932.
Fremont Community Services, 3375 Country Dr., (415) 791-4320.
Hayward Area Recreation District, 1099 E St., Hayward 94541, (415) 881-6735.
Livermore Recreation Dept., 71 Trevarno, Livermore 94550, 447-7300.
Oakland Recreational Services Dept., 1520 Lakeside Dr., (415) 273-3092.
Piedmont Recreation Dept., 358 Hillside Ave., Piedmont, (415) 420-3070.
Pleasanton Recreation Dept., 200 Bernal, Pleasanton 94566, 847-8160.
San Leandro Recreation Dept., 835 14th St., San Leandro, (415) 577-3462.
Union City Recreation, Holly Community Center, 31600 Alvarado Blvd., Union City, (415) 471-6877; or Charles Kennedy Community Center, 1333 Decoto Rd., Union City, (415) 489-0360.

CONTRA COSTA COUNTY

Antioch Recreation Dept., 213 F St., Antioch 94509, (415) 757-0900.
Brentwood Recreation Dept., 724 3rd St., Brentwood 94513, 634-1044.
Concord Recreation Services, 2885 Concord Blvd., Concord, 671-3270.
El Cerrito Community Services, 10890 San Pablo Ave., El Cerrito 94530, (415) 234-7445.
Hercules Community Services, 111 Civic Dr., Hercules, (415) 799-8230.
Lafayette Recreation Dept., 500 St. Mary's Rd., Lafayette 94549, (415) 284-2232.
Martinez Recreation Dept., 525 Henrietta, Martinez 94553, 372-3510.
Moraga Recreation Dept., 2100 Donald Dr., Moraga 94556, 376-2520.
Pinole Recreation Dept., 2131 Pear, Pinole 94564, (415) 724-9004.
Pittsburg Recreation Dept., 340 Black Diamond, Pittsburg 94565, (415) 439-3440.
Pleasant Hill Recreation Dept., 320 Civic Dr., (415) 676-5200.
Richmond Recreation Dept., (415) 620-6792.
San Pablo Community Services, (415) 236-7373.

Sports

CONTRA COSTA COUNTY (continued)

San Ramon, Shannon Community Center, (415) 829-4932.
Walnut Creek Recreation Dept., 1650 N. Broadway, (415) 943-5858.

MARIN COUNTY

Corte Madera Recreation Dept., 498 Tamalpais Dr., C.M. 94925, 924-2901.
Fairfax Recreation Dept., 142 Bolinas Rd., Fairfax, 94930, (415) 453-1584.
Larkspur Recreation Dept., 400 Magnolia, Larkspur 94939, (415) 924-4777.
Marin County Recreation Dept., Marin County Civic Center, S.R. 94903,
   (415) 499-6387.
Mill Valley Recreation Dept., 180 Camino Alto, M.V. 94941, 383-1370.
Novato Recreation Dept., 917 Sherman Ave., Novato 94947, 897-4323.
Ross Recreation Dept., Lagunitas Rd., Ross, (415) 453-6020.
San Anselmo Recreation Dept., 1000 Sir Francis Drake Blvd., S.A. 94960,
   (415) 453-9055.
San Rafael Recreation Dept., 1400 5th Ave., S.R. 94901, (415) 485-3333.
Sausalito Recreation Dept., 420 Litho, Sausalito 94965, (415) 332-4520.
Tiburon Recreation Dept., 1155 Tiburon Blvd., Tiburon 94920, 435-4355.

MONTEREY COUNTY

Carmel Recreation, 15th Ave. & Monte Verde, Carmel 93923, 625-2252.
Gonzalez Recreation Dept., Box 647, Gonzalez 93926, (408) 675-2321.
King City Recreation, 411 Division, King City 93930, (408) 385-3575.
Marina Recreation, 211 Hillcrest Ave., Marina 93933, (408) 384-3715.
Monterey Recreation, 546 Dutra, Monterey 93940, (408) 646-3866.
Pacific Grove Recreation, 515 Junipero Ave., P.G. 93950, (408) 372-2809.
Salinas Recreation, 200 Lincoln Ave., Salinas, (408) 758-7306.
Seaside Recreation, 986 Hilby Ave., Seaside 93955, (408) 899-6270.

NAPA COUNTY

Calistoga Recreation Dept., 1232 Washington, Calistoga 94515, (707)
   942-5188.
Napa Recreation Dept., 1100 West, Napa, (707) 252-7800.
St. Helena Recreation Dept., 1360 Oak Ave., S.H. 94574, (707) 963-5706.

SAN FRANCISCO

Adult Sports Leagues, Jewish Community Center, 3200 California, S.F.
   94118, (415) 346-6040 (Danny Schwager).
San Francisco Recreation Dept., McLaren Lodge, Golden Gate Park, S.F.
   94117.

Sports

SAN MATEO COUNTY

Belmont Recreation Dept., 1225 Ralston, Belmont 94002, (415) 573-3561.
Burlingame Recreation Dept., 850 Burlingame Ave., Burlingame 94010, (415) 344-6386.
Daly City Recreation Dept., 111 Lake Merced Blvd., (415) 991-8004.
East Palo Alto Community Services, 2415 University Ave., 853-3144.
Foster City Recreation Dept., 650 Shell Blvd., (415) 345-5731.
Half Moon Bay Recreation Dept., 501 Main, (415) 726-1617.
Menlo Park Recreation Dept., 700 Alma, M.P. 94025, (415) 858-3470.
Millbrae Recreation Dept., 477 Lincoln Circle, Millbrae 94030, 697-7426.
Pacifica Recreation Dept., 170 Santa Maria, Pacifica 94044, (415) 875-7380.
Redwood City Recreation Dept., 1400 Roosevelt Ave., (415) 364-6060.
San Bruno Recreation Dept., 567 El Camino Real, S.B. 94066, 877-8863.
San Carlos Recreation Dept., 666 Elm St., S.C. 94070, (415) 593-8011.
San Mateo Recreation Dept., 2720 Alameda de las Pulgas, (415) 377-4704.
South San Francisco Recreation Dept., 33 Arroyo, S.S.F. 94080, 877-8560.

SANTA CLARA COUNTY

Campbell Recreation Dept., 70 N. 1st St., Campbell 95008, 866-2105.
Cupertino Recreation Dept., 22221 McClellan, Cupertino 95014, 253-2060.
Gilroy Recreation Dept., 7351 Rosanna St., Gilroy 95020, (408) 842-0221.
Los Altos Recreation Dept., 97 Hillview Ave., L.A. 94022, (408) 941-0950.
Los Gatos Recreation Dept., 123 E. Main, Los Gatos, (408) 354-8700.
Milpitas Community Services, (408) 942-2470.
Morgan Hill Recreation Dept., 17666 Crest Ave., M.H. 95037, 779-7283.
Mountain View Recreation Dept., 201 S. Rengstorff, 966-6331.
Palo Alto Recreation Dept., Mitchell Park Ctr, 3800 Middlefield, (415) 329-2487; Lucie Stern Center, 1305 Middlefield Rd., (415) 329-2261.
San Jose Recreation Dept., 151 W. Mission, San Jose, (408) 277-4000.
Santa Clara Recreation Dept., 1500 Warburton Ave., (408) 984-3223.
Saratoga Community Center, 19655 Allendale, Saratoga 95070, 867-3438.
Sunnyvale Recreation Dept., 550 E. Remington Dr., (408) 730-7350.

SANTA CRUZ COUNTY

Capitola Recreation, 4400 Jade, Capitola 95010, (408) 475-5935.
Santa Cruz Recreation, 307 Church, Santa Cruz, (408) 429-3663.
Watsonville Recreation, 20 Maple, Watsonville 95076, (408) 728-6081.

Sports

SOLANO COUNTY

Benicia Recreation Dept., 250 E. L St., Benicia 94519, (707) 746-4285.
Fairfield Recreation Dept., 1000 Webster, Fairfield 94533, (707) 428-7465.
Vacaville Recreation Dept., 1100 Alamo, Vacaville 95688, (707) 449-1830.
Vallejo Recreation Dept., 395 Amador, Vallejo, (707) 648-4600.

SONOMA COUNTY

Healdsburg Recreation Dept., 126 Matheson, Healdsburg 95448.
Petaluma Recreation Dept., (707) 778-4380.
Rohnert Park Recreation Dept., 5401 Snyder Ln., Rohnert Park 94928.
Santa Rosa Recreation Dept., 415 Steele Ln., Santa Rosa, (707) 576-5116.
Sebastopol Recreation Dept., 7120 Bodega, Sebastopol 95472, 823-1511.

YMCA

Your YMCA is another place that usually features such sports as swimming and basketball, weight-lifting, and aerobics.

ALAMEDA COUNTY

Albany, 921 Kains Ave., (415) 525-1130.
East Bay Headquarters - 2001 Allston Way, (415) 848-6800
South Berkeley, 2901 California, (415) 843-4280/848-6800.
West Berkeley, 2009 10th St., (415) 848-6800.
Central Oakland Center, 2101 Telegraph, (415) 451-9622.
Eastlake Center, 1612 45th Ave., Oakland, (415) 534-7441.
Eden Center, 951 Palisade, Hayward, (415) 582-9614.
Fremont Center, 41811 Blacow Rd., (415) 657-5200.
M. Robinson Baker Center, 3265 Market, Oakland, (415) 653-7818.
Tri-Valley Center, 400 Main, Pleasanton, (415) 462-0270.

CONTRA COSTA COUNTY

Walnut Creek Center, 1855 Olympic Blvd., (415) 935-9622.
Mt. Diablo Center, 350 Civic Dr., Pleasant Hill, (415) 687-8900.

MARIN COUNTY

Marin Center, 1500 Los Gamos Dr., San Rafael 94901, (415) 492-9622.

SAN FRANCISCO

Chinatown-North Beach Center, 965 Clay, (415) 397-6883.
Downtown Center, 620 Sutter, (415) 775-6500 (includes swimming pool).
Embarcadero Center, 166 The Embarcadero, 392-2191.
Central Y, 220 Golden Gate, 885-0460
Mission Center, 1855 Folsom, (415) 552-6790.
Stonestown Center, 333 Eucalyptus, (415) 759-9622.
Western Addition Center, 1830 Sutter, (415) 921-3814.

SAN MATEO COUNTY

Peninsula Family Center, 240 N. El Camino Real, San Mateo, (415) 342-5228.

SANTA CLARA COUNTY

Central Branch, 1717 The Alameda, San Jose, (408) 298-1717
East Valley Branch, 1975 S. White Rd., San Jose, (408) 258-4419
Milpitas Branch, 540 S. Abel, Milpitas, (408) 945-0919
Northwest Branch, 20803 Alves Dr., Cupertino, (408) 257-7160
Palo Alto Branch, 3412 Ross Rd., (415) 494-1883.
South Valley Branch, 5632 Santa Teresa Blvd., (408) 226-9622.

SANTA CRUZ COUNTY

Boulder Creek YMCA, 16275 Hwy. 9, B.C. 95006, 338-2128.
Watsonville, 27 Sudden, Watsonville 95076, (408) 728-9622.

SOLANO COUNTY

Vallejo Y, 401 Amador, (707) 643-3268 or 643-5858.

SONOMA COUNTY

Santa Rosa Y, 1111 College Ave., (707) 545-9622.

Individual Sports Directory

Badminton

Sunnyvale Badminton Club, 735-8484 (George Parker). Sundays, 4:30pm.

Sports

Baseball & Softball

Many single men love baseball and softball, so single women would be wise to consider visiting the local baseball diamond evenings and weekends during the Summer. In San Francisco, Golden Gate Park, Moscone Field (Chestnut & Buchanan), Sunset Field (39th & Pacheco) are examples. If you don't know how to play, don't worry. Just ask to play the outfield—the ball will seldom come to you out there. If you're not into playing baseball or softball just sit in the stands and find out where the team goes out drinking afterwards.

If you're more interested in watching the pros rather than amateurs, the ballpark is a great place to meet single men. Contact the San Francisco Giants, Candlestick Park, (415) 467-8000. You might also consider joining the SF Baseball Club, 555 California, SF, (415) 421-2357.

There are coed softball leagues all over the Bay Area. Contact your local recreation department (see listing earlier in this chapter).

American Legion Baseball, San Ramon, (415) 837-8412.
Coed Softball, Sunnyvale, (408) 446-1864 (Sparky). Softball clinics, group activities, parties, barbecues, ball games, wine tastings, and travel.
San Ramon Valley Adult Softball, (415) 828-4848.

Bicycling

Contact your local bicycle shop for information about local bicycling clubs.

Bombay Bicycle Riding Club, 1107 Howard Ave., Burlingame, 342-8959.
Napa Bicycle Club, (707) 257-6344.
Rhody Co. Productions, 2929 California, San Francisco 94118, (415) 387-2178. Bicycling events throughout Bay Area.
Santa Cruz County Cycling Club, 414 Soquel Ave., (408) 423-0829.
Valley Spokesman Bicycle Touring Club, San Ramon, (415) 828-5299.

Boating

Lake Merced Sailing Club, Boat House, Skyline & Harding, S.F. 94132.
Marina Sailing Society, San Francisco, (415) 368-1718.
Oceanic Society, Fort Mason, San Francisco, (415) 441-5970. Activities include sailing, classes, lectures, films, and parties.
Treasure Island Sailing Club, Treasure Island Rd., S.F. 94130, 397-7827.
Yacht Racing Association, Fort Mason, S.F. 94123, (415) 771-9500.

Boating (continued)

See Yacht Clubs in the yellow pages of your phone directory for more information about boating activities.

Boxing

Not too many women hang out at the gym to watch men exercise and practice beating each others brains out, so you'll have all the men to yourself.

Newman's Gym, 312 Leavenworth, SF, (415) 775-7020.

Bowling

Bowling is ideal for meeting single men or women. There are coed bowling leagues starting up every few months at the various bowling alleys (listed in the yellow pages of your phone book). It's easy to meet people and get to know them since you run into them each week at the bowling alley. Look up the BOWLING section of the yellow pages of your telephone book or contact the San Francisco Bowling Association, Inc., 1485 Bayshore Blvd., San Francisco 94128, (415) 467-8937.

Darts

British pubs usually feature dart boards. Dart leagues often meet at these pubs on a regular basis. Check the COCKTAIL LOUNGE section of the yellow pages of your phone book.

Barnacles Saloon, 3243 Pierce, SF, (415) 346-6824.
Mayflower Inn, 1533 4th St., San Rafael 94901, (415) 456-1011. Wednesday night is Darts night.
Penny Farthing Club, 679 Sutter, San Francisco, (415) 771-5155.
San Francisco Dart Association, 1416 Bush, San Francisco, (415) 885-6918.

Fencing

Halberstadt Fencers' Club, 621 S. Van Ness, San Francisco, 863-3838.
Pacific Fencing Club, 1249 34th Ave., Oakland, (415) 436-3800.

Fishing & Flycasting

Weekends are best for meeting single men who like to fish.

Sports

Fishing & Flycasting (continued)

Anglers' Lodge, Golden Gate Park, San Francisco.
Captain Al, San Francisco, (415) 878-4644.
Captain George's Boating Centers, Pier 39, Box CAP, San Francisco 94133, (415) 956-2628.
Captain Joe, San Francisco, (415) 673-9815

Football

San Francisco 49ers, Candlestick Park, San Francisco, 468-2249.

Golf

You can meet single men at either the driving range (where you can buy a bucket of golf balls and practice teeing off) or on the golf course (this is more expensive and requires an investment in a complete set of clubs as well as the time needed to master their use. The alternative is to just wait in the clubhouse for the men to tire out on the greens and come in for a snort. You are permitted to sit in the clubhouse of the public golf courses without being a member. Private golf courses may require that you be accompanied by a member. Both public and private courses are listed in the yellow pages of your phone book. Other resources include:

California Golf Club, 844 W. Orange Ave., South San Francisco 94080, (415) 761-0210.
San Francisco Golf Club, Junipero Serra Blvd & Brotherhood Way, S.F. 94132, (415) 585-0480.

See Fairway Singles Golf Club in the chapter on Singles Clubs.

Gun Clubs

Here's another type of club that will be "loaded" with men.

Chabot Gun Club, Box 2246, Castro Valley, (415) 569-0213.
Eagle Rock Gun Club, Empire Grade Rd., Santa Cruz, (408) 426-0623.
Green Lodge Gun Club, Cygnus Station, Suisun, (707) 864-0533.
Marin Rod & Gun Club, San Quentin, (415) 459-9845.
Pacific Rod & Gun Club, 520 John Muir Dr., San Francisco, (415) 239-9750 or 239-9613. Check the bulletin board or call to find out about social events.
Pajaro Valley Rod & Gun Club, Lakeview, Watsonville 95076, 724-7311.

Sports

Gymnastics

Gymnastic Association, (SOKOL), 847 N. San Mateo Dr., San Mateo 94401, (415) 344-6718.

Hang Gliding

One popular Bay Area spot is at Fort Funston on Skyline Blvd. near the ocean in southern San Francisco.

Health Clubs

Health clubs are an excellent place to meet single men or women. But use your head! If you're a woman, don't hand around the exercycles or aerobics classes. Go into the weight room and pump iron with all the handsome hunks. If you're a man, get on the Exercycles and join the Aerobics classes. For a list of health clubs in your area consult the **Health Club** section in the yellow pages of your phone book.

Horseback Riding

Carmel Valley Trail & Saddle Club, E. Garzas Rd., Carmel Valley 93924, (408) 659-9987.

Horse Racing

Many men love to take off for a day at the races. Just make sure that the single men you meet at the track aren't addicted. That means they're liable to be penniless. Find out at which bars they socialize afterwards.

Bay Meadows, San Mateo, (415) 574-7223.
Golden Gate Fields, 1100 Eastshore Highway, Albany, (415) 526-3020.

Lawn Bowling

Sunnyvale Lawn Bowls Club, (408) 739-1293 (James Worwood).

Martial Arts

Check the yellow pages of your phone book for local studios.

Sunnyvale Judo Club, (408) 739-3389 (David White).

Sports

Motorcycles

If you get turned on by leather and the sound of loud engines revving, here's a sport that is ideal for meeting single men. For more information on motorcycle clubs and events read City Bike, 1126 Kearny St., San Francisco 94133, (415) 982-7242.

North Bay Motorcycle Club, Fulton, (707) 526-7699.
Sadistics Motorcycle Club, 2727 Milvia, Berkeley, (415) 548-4895.
San Jose Dons Motorcycle Club, 523 Columbia, San Jose, (408) 294-5434.
Soul Brothers Motorcycle Club, 1861 Bay Rd., E. Palo Alto, (415) 853-8850.
Wicked Wheels Motorcycle Club, 5816 Foothill Blvd., Oakland, 638-9659.
Zodiac Motorcycle Club, 9500 E. 14th, Oakland, (415) 638-9188.

Orienteering

Orienteering is the Scandinavian sport of hiking. The ratio is four men for every woman.

Bay Area Orienteering Society, (415) 652-7851.
Orienteering, 3151 Hollywood Dr., Oakland 94611, (415) 530-3059.

Racquetball

Look up racquetball clubs in the yellow pages of your phone book. Many health clubs also feature racquetball, so check that section of the phone book as well.

Rowing

South End Rowing Club, 500 Jefferson, San Francisco 94109, (415) 441-9523 or 885-9564.

Rugby

No. Calif. Rugby Union, Box 15157, San Francisco 94115. Socializing afterwards at local bars.

Running & Walking

Running is the great American obsession. Millions jog regularly. Many claim to experience "runner's high", which is caused by the release of endorphines (pleasure causing hormones) into the brain while exercising. Along with improving your health and feeling better emotionally, running can also improve your social life. Fortunately both men and women enjoy running, so it is a great sport for meeting either sex. The same holds true for walking and striding.

Below are listed some competitive events for runners and walkers. For a running & walking calendar read **The Northern California Schedule**, 80 Mitchell Blvd., San Rafael 94903, (415) 472-7223.

American Heart Association, 120 Montgomery #1650, San Francisco 94104, (415) 433-2273.

April Showers Fun Run & Walk, Lois Koenig, 535 Darrell Rd., Hillsborough 94010, (415) 342-9328.

Big Sur International Marathon, Box 222620, B.S. 93922, (408) 625-6226.

Blind Date Relays, San Francisco, (415) 668-2830. 1 man/1 woman teams.

Brickyard Run, Martinez, Luka Sekulich, 1485 Darlene Dr., Concord 94520, (415) 685-5185.

Center for Living Skills, Box 1145, Lafayette 94549, (415) 284-4871.

Change of Pace, 1260 Lake Blvd. #248, Davis 95616, (916) 757-2012. Events throughout Northern California.

Charlie Wedemeyer Classic 10K Run, Tom Zades, 1230 Ridge Oak Ct., San Jose 95120, (408) 268-6693.

Chinatown Run, 855 Sacramento, San Francisco 94162, (415) 982-4412.

Christmas Classic, 528 Larch Ave., South San Francisco 94080, 583-6268.

Dash for Diabetes, Sunnyvale Medical Clinic, 596 Carroll, Sunnyvale 94086, (415) 328-1110 or (408) 287-3785.

Devil Mountain Run, Pleasanton, Box 93, Pleasanton 94566.

Dipsea, Box 30, Mill Valley 94942, (415) 381-DIPC.

DSE Lake Merced Single & Double Runs, San Francisco, (415) 668-2830.

Eden Hospital, Ellen Kushner, 20103 Lake Chabot Rd, Castro Valley 94546, (415) 889-5061.

ESL Runaway 10K, Dori Wilson, 495 Java #M-503, Sunnyvale 94088, (408) 743-6399.

Fleet Feet, 2086 Chestnut St., San Francisco 94123, (415) 921-7188.

Fujitsu 5M Classic, San Jose, (408) 922-9118.

Kennedy Drive Run, Golden Gate Park, San Francisco, (415) 668-2830.

Golden Gate Vista Run, San Francisco, (415) 668-2830.

Gonzalez Recreation Dept., Box 647, Gonzalez 93926, (408) 675-2321.

Good Samaritan Hospital League, 2425 Samaritan Dr., Los Gatos 95124, (408) 559-2555.

Human Race 10K/5K, Lois Koenig, 535 Darrell Rd., Hillsborough 94010, (415) 342-9328.

Irish Sprint & Stride, Jeff Benes, 347 Keeler Ct., San Jose 95139. Events throughout the Bay Area.

Kiwi Running Club (for women), Santa Rosa, (707) 526-2940.

Lake Merritt Joggers & Striders, Elvyn Blair, 3136 California, Oakland 94602, (415) 530-9151. Fourth Sundays.

Los Altos Hills Country Climb, Box 1286, L.A. 94022, (415) 949-5415 (Olin).

Monterey Bay Academy, 783 San Andreas Rd., Monterey 95076, (408) 728-1481 x371.

Monterey Rape Crisis, Box 2630, Monterey 93942, (408) 373-3389.

Mulberry Great Escape 5K/10K, Rae Dorough, 6154 Escondido Cir., Livermore 94550.

Napa Valley Marathon, 1325 Imola. W., Napa 94559, (707) 255-2609.

Options for Women Over 40, 3543 18th St., San Francisco 94110, (415) 431-6944.

Pacific Sun 10K, TRS, 80 Mitchell Blvd., San Rafael 94903.

Palo Alto Park & Recreation Dept., 750 N. California, P.A. 94304, (415) 329-2381.

Pamakid Runners, Box 27557, San Francisco 94127, (415) 681-2323.

Pleasant Hill Recreation Dept., 147 Gregory Lane, P.H. 94523, (415) 827-2255.

Quadruple Dipsea, Mill Valley, Jim Skophammer, 666 Orange St., Daly City 94014, (415) 994-6218.

Race/Fun Walk 1.5M, Pam Lambert, Napa Valley Bank, 940 Adams St., Benicia 94510, (707) 746-7820.

Rhody Co. Productions, (415) 387-2187. Running events throughout the Bay Area.

Rio Resolution Run, Simon & Deborah Treadmill, Carmel, (408) 624-4112.

Run & Walk for Open Space 5K, J.A. Harmes, 8 Ivy Ln., San Anselmo 94960, (415) 774-2554.

Run for the Seals, CMMC, GGNRA, Marin Headlands, Sausalito 94965, (415) 331-SEAL.

Run for the Health of It, Washington Hospital, 2000 Mowry Ave., Fremont 94538, (415) 797-1111 x4730.

Run for the Roof, Joan Runyeon, Box 13434, San Rafael 94913, 453-1063.

Run for Your Life, Joel B. Doss, 358 Searidge #1, Aptos 95003.

Runners Factory, 51 University Ave., Los Gatos 95030, (408) 395-4311.

Runner's Feet, 1004 Oak Grove, Burlingame 94066, 343-4242 or 579-7881.

Run Your Axe Off, UC Development Office, CSF, 2440 Bancroft Way, Berkeley 94720, (415) 643-7001.

Ruth Anderson 100K, San Francisco, Dick Collins, 1015 Hollywood Ave., Oakland 94602, (415) 530-6634.

Sports

San Francisco Zoo Society, Sloat Blvd. at Pacific Ocean, S.F. 94132, (415) 753-7080.

Santa Cruz Recreation Dept., Lisa McGinnis, 307 Church St., S.C. 95060, (408) 429-3477.

Serra Residential Center, Jane Bell, Box 3296, 650 Washington Blvd., Fremont 94539, (415) 657-2002.

Serra's Run, Will Franke, 2992 Lausen, Carmel 93923, (408) 375-2661.

Shoreline Run 10K, 3K, Ted Swenson, 835 E. 14th, San Leandro 94577, (415) 577-3469.

Sonoma State Intramural Office, 1801 E. Cotati Ave., Rohnert Pk 94928, (707) 664-2753.

South San Francisco Parks & Recreation Dept., Box 711, S.S.F. 94080, (415) 877-8560.

Team Challenge, Box 963, El Sobrante 904803, (415) 841-1190. Running events throughout the Bay Area.

Tri-Sports, 21 Live Oak, Berkeley 94705 (415) 540-7008. Running events throughout the Bay Area.

West Coast Knights, Box 23731, San Jose 95153, (408) 281-4599. Events throughout the Bay Area.

West Valley Track Club, Marc Lund, 1433 Norman Dr., Sunnyvale 94087, (415) 387-7172 (Flory) or (415) 482-4355 (Laury).

Windsor Whale Run, Box 237, Occidental 95465, (707) 829-9493.

Sailing

Cal Sailing Club of Berkeley, (415) 527-7245.

Scuba Diving

Alacosta Divers, 50 Entrada, Oakland 94611.

Alameda Divers, 3551 Joaquin Miller Rd., Oakland 94611.

Amphibians, 759 Lundy, Pacifica 94044.

Aqua Tutus, Box 494, San Lorenzo 94580.

Bamboo Reef, 584 4th St., San Francisco, (415) 362-6694.

Barbara Coast, 2334 Fulton, San Francisco 94118.

Bay Area Divers, 1178 Euclid, Berkeley 94708. Underwater hockey team.

Blue Coral Dive Club meets the 2nd Wednesday of each month at Whistle Stop North, on Grant Ave., Novato.

Bottom Watchers, Box 1244, Fremont 94538.

Bud Davis School of Scuba Diving, 1550 Bay, San Francisco, (415) 921-3676.

California Sport Divers, Box 4008, Mt. View 94403.

Conquestadores del Mar, Box 29356, San Francisco 94129.

Diablo Sea Bears, 4955 Boxer Blvd., Concord 94521.

Sports

Scuba Diving (continued)

East Bay Barnacles, 210 N. San Tomas-Aquino Rd., Campbell 95008.
Hydro Knights, Box 75, San Carlos 94070.
Kahunas, 1130 Deanna Ct., Morgan Hill 95067.
Lera Scuba Knights, 6150 Joaquin Murieta Dr., Newark 94560, meet
    2nd Saturday of each month at LERA Auditorium in Sunnyvale.
Lera Underwater Club, 4766 Bannock Circ., San Jose 95130.
Livermore Aquatics, (415) 443-9666.
Martinez Blue Fins, 112 Cotton Wood Dr., Vallejo 94590.
Nor Cal Club, 215 Los Altos 94590.
Outrigger Dive Club, 14291 New Jersey, San Jose. 1st Mondays, Round
    Table Pizza, Hamilton & Darryl, Campbell.
Pinnacles Dive Center, 875 Grant Ave., Novato 94947, (415) 897-
    9962. Sponsors classes.
Richmond Pelicans, 1196 Arch Ct., Concord 94520. 2nd & 4th
    Tuesdays, month, Pinole Sportsmens Club, Pinole.
Salt Water Revival, Box 573, Rodeo 94572. 1st Wednesdays, Memorial
    Park Club House in Albany.
San Francisco Cormorants, 22 Lee, San Francisco 94112. Diving, trips,
    and parties.
San Francisco Flipper Dippers, 10 Woodside, San Anselmo 94960. 3rd
    Wednesdays, Round Table Pizza, 16th & Geary, San Francisco. Diving,
    trips, and parties.
San Francisco Hammerheads, Box 1387, Pacifica 94044.
San Francisco Reef Divers, 1230 Broadway #3, San Francisco 94109.
San Jose Flipper Dippers, Box 6205, San Jose 95150.
San Jose Skin Divers, 350 Quinnhill Rd., Los Altos 94022.
San Ramon Valley Aquatics, (415) 820-9362.
Sonoma State University Scuba Club, 180 Valpariso #2, Cotati 94928.
Suisun Sea Spirits, 1035 Pintail Dr., Suisun 94585.
Tritonians, 840 Coleman, Menlo Pk 94025. 3rd Wednesdays, Stanford
    Research Institute in Palo Alto.
Underwater Photo Society (UPS), 2708 Laramie Gate Cir., Pleasanton
    94566. 1st Fridays, Fort Mason Bldg C, 3rd Floor, San Francisco.
Vacqueros del Mar, Box 882, Livermore 94550. 1st Wednesdays,
    Lawrence Livermore Lab So. Cafeteria.

Please note: For an up-to-date listing of scuba diving clubs
in Northern California, contact Central California Council of
Diving Clubs (CEN-CAL), Box 779, Daly City 94017, (415) 583-8492.
Activities include diving, hockey, underwater photography,
classes, spear fishing.

Skating

The Skating Club, Ice Arena, 1557 48th Ave., San Francisco 94118, (415) 681-6430.

Snow Skiing

The ski clubs listed below are for both singles and couples. For ski clubs exclusively for singles see the Singles Clubs chapter.

All-Seasons, (415) 236-1471 (Michael).
Alpineer Ski Club, (415) 334-3732 (Len).
Bear Valley Ski Club, 3100 Mowry #401, Fremont, (408) 379-4849 (France) or (415) 797-1368.
Berkeley Ski Club, Box 758, Berkeley 94701, (415) 236-11_7 (Bob).
Bladerunners, (415) 792-3010 (Elaine).
California Adventures, UC Berkeley, 642-4000. Young singles.
California Alpine Club, 870 Market, San Francisco 94102, (415) 334-4619.
Cal State Hayward Ski Club, 848 South M St., Livermore 94550, (415) 443-5363 (Kari)
Camber Ski Club, Box 1043, Salinas 93902, (408) 663-4616 or 757-6301. 1st Thursdays, 7pm, Lord Byron's Pizza, Northridge Mall.
Castro Valley Ski Club, Box 2032, C.V. 94546, 483-7782 or 786-3026.
Chi Ski Club, Box 5596, San Francisco 94101.
Concord Ski Club, Box 27-213, Concord 94527, (415) 676-9551 (Fred) or 671-3408.
Flexy Flyers Ski Club, 25200 Carlos Bee #94, Hayward 94542, (415) 889-6146 (Val)
Gatebusters, (408) 923-0962 (David)
Marin Ski Club, Box 334, San Rafael 94915, (707) 745-3462 (Shelly)
National Ski Club, (408) 732-9104 (Josip)
Nisei Ski Club, 1233 Taylor #1, San Francisco, (408) 371-1451 (Alice)
Oakland Ski Club, Box 12541, Oakland 94604, (415) 283-1127 (Laura)
Palo Alto Ski Club, (415) 967-5841 (Peter)
Parallelers, (415) 422-9136 (Nancy)
Peninsula Ski Club, Box 305, San Mateo 94401, (415) 574-4981 (Esther) or 591-1809.
Rut Riders Ski Club, Box 32706, San Jose 95152, (408) 729-9262 or (415) 641-4541 (Hank)
Saratoga Ski Club, 13 Sorrel Ln., San Carlos 94070.
Sierra Ski Club (Division of Sierra Club), Jerry Abad, 6454 Valley View, Oakland 94611, (415) 339-2961.
Skoalers Ski Club, 99 Crestview Dr., Orinda 94563.
Sno-Ball Express Ski Club, 729 Peekskill Dr., Sunnyvale 94087, (408) 730-9623 (Cathie)

Sports

Skiing (continued)

Snowchasers Ski Club, Box 6171, Concord 94524, (415) 930-8424.
SnoFlakes Ski Club, 1684 Spruce St., Livermore 94550
South Bay Ski Club, Box 1431, San Jose 95109, (408) 267-0802 (Maire) or
   593-7692.
Sundancer Ski Club, Box 390636, Mt. View 94039, (415) 323-4941. 40+.

Soccer

California Soccer Association, Box 12066, San Francisco 94112, (415)
   586-5800.
Marina Soccer Association, 122 Belle Dr., Marina, CA, (408) 384-4330.
Sunnyvale Alliance Soccer, (415) 967-6184.

Sports Clubs

Chinese Sportsmen Club, 773 Sacramento, San Francisco 94108, (415)
   362-9786.
Concordia Sport Club, 2355 Ocean, San Francisco 94132, (415) 239-9602.
Indoor Sports Club for Physically Disabled, 391 17th Ave., San Francisco
   94121, (415) 751-4300.
Menlo Sportsmen Social Club, 2110 Dumbarton Ave., East Palo Alto,
   (415) 326-6803, 853-8923.
Outdoors Unlimited, 500 Parnassus, San Francisco 94143, (415) 666-2078,
   is a cooperative resource center for outdoor adventures for all skill &
   experience levels.   Also offers skills clinics, reasonably priced
   equipment rental, cooperative outings, and trip planning information
   in the following areas: day hikes, nature study, backpacking,
   mountaineering, cross-country skiing, bicycling, canoeing, kayaking,
   white water rafting, windsurfing, sailing, safety & first aid. You will
   receive a free quarterly newsletter if you send a stamped,
   self-addressed envelope.
Peninsula Sportsmens Clubs, 1600 Rutgers, East Palo Alto, (415)
   853-8889.

Squash

Squash Club of San Francisco, 525 Harrison, 957-0400.

Swimming

   Most cities in the Bay Area have neighborhood pools, which
are listed under the Recreation Dept. listing for each city in the
white pages of your phone book. YMCA's often have pools as well.

Sports

Swimming (continued)

(See that section of this chapter). Best time to meet single
people is early mornings, during the lunch hour, and after work.

Other resources include:
Dolphin Swim & Boat Club, Foot of Hyde, San Francisco, (415) 441-9329.
Montclair Swim Club, 1901 Woodhaven Way, Oakland, (415) 339-2500.
Oak Hill Swim Club, 7624 Olive, Pleasanton, (415) 846-8822.
Palo Alto Swim Club, 777 Embarcadero, Palo Alto, (415) 327-7459.
Sunnyvale Swim Club, (408) 730-1999 (Debra Packard).
Valley Swim Association, San Ramon, (415) 820-4182.

Tennis

You can meet single men or women at no cost by going to any
public tennis court. An alternative is to join private tennis
clubs, which are listed in the yellow pages of your phone book.

California Tennis Association, 2455 Bush, San Francisco 94118, (415)
346-3611.
East Bay Tennis Matchmakers, (415) 548-6240. Mixed doubles, dinners,
dancing at Blackhawk Tennis Villas, Danville and Amador Valley
Athletic Club, Pleasanton.
San Ramon Valley Tennis Club, (415) 837-1643.
Sunnyvale Tennis Club, (408) 733-7848 (Jim Cunningham).

Weight-Lifting

Here's a sport that is ideal for meeting single men. If you
are a woman, go down to your local gym, health club, or Y.M.C.A.
and start pumping iron.

Wrestling

Professional wrestling events are quite popular nowadays.
Many are held at the Cow Palace in Daly City.

Sports

TRAVEL

Have you ever noticed how different people are when they're on vacation? The new locale liberates many people so that they're friendlier and more open to new friends and romantic relationships. It's not unusual for people to fall madly in love on a cruise or at a vacation resort with someone they wouldn't even notice if they lived next door!

The problem with romance away from home is that frequently you have a problem sustaining the relationship over a long distance. With that warning out of the way, you may consider looking for love on your next trip. With luck your new friend might live reasonably close to you. Call up your travel agent and ask which cruises or vacations have the most single people in the age range that interests you. Some cater predominantly to middle-aged and older; some to couples; some to singles in their 20s and 30s.

Club Med is probably the most popular vacation package for singles (although couples also attend). Your travel agent can give you the details. Incidentally, in case you've never called a travel agent, they usually work on a commission basis, which means their services are free to you, the customer. Listed below are services that specialize in meeting the needs of the single traveler.

Nationwide Travel Services for Singles

New Horizon Adventures Singles Travel Club, Box 1228, Yreka, CA 96097, (916) 842-4181 or 842-2112. Myra Benson.

Partners-in-Travel, Box 491145, Los Angeles, CA 90049, (213) 476-4869.

Singles International Travel, 668 Main St., Hyannis, MA 02601, (508) 790-0050.

Singleworld Tours, (800) 223-6490 or (212) 758-2433.

Travel Companion Exchange, Box 833, Amityville, NY 11701, (516) 454-0880.

Travel Match, Box 6991, Orange 92613, (714) 997-5273. Computerized matching service for single travelers. Members are matched on the basis of a 4 part questionnaire & as geographically convenient as possible. Same sex or opposite sex matches as the members prefer. $60 per year includes up to 12 matches per year and a monthly newsletter. The newsletter includes articles about travel. Joy Nyquist.

Travelmate, (619) 258-0220. Computer dating service that matches singles nationwide who like to travel.

Travel Partners Club, Box 2368, Crystal River, FL 32629, (904) 796-1117.

Umbrella Singles, Box 157, Woodbourne, NY 12788, (914) 434-6871. Giant singles weekends at fine hotels in the U.S. & abroad. Tennis, volleyball, swimming, ice skating, calisthenics, dance lessons, parties, rap sessions, lectures, educational programs. Leonard Moss, President.

World Travel Club, Colpitt's Travel Center, Westgate Mall, Brockton, MA 02401, (800) GO-TOURS or (617) 588-5660.

Local Travel Services

Club Voyage Marin, Greenbrae Travel, 332 Bon Air Center, Greenbrae 94904, (415) 461-4815. Singles Travel Club.

Gateway Travel, 1762 Technology Dr., San Jose, (408) 295-5600 or (800) 2483273.

Just for Singles Travelers Club, 1601 El Camino, Belmont, (415) 591-8747.

Shields World Travel, 5321-J Hopyard Rd., Pleasanton 94566, (415) 460-0555.

Travel Fun with Gloria, Gloria Dodson, 325 Rock Creek, Pleasant Hill 94523, (415) 685-4811.

Travel Time, 2307 Van Ness, San Francisco 94109, (415) 775-8725.

Vagabond Travel, 2290 W. El Camino Real, Mt. View 94040, (415) 962-0990.

Travel

SINGLES BARS

Everybody hates singles bars. Or so they say. That's despite the fact that singles bars are loaded with single people who want to meet someone nice for a romantic relationship. So why don't we all love singles bars?

Go to a singles bar on a Friday or Saturday night and you'll find out the answer. Have you heard of the 80-20 Rule? It means that 20% of baseball players hit 80% of the home runs and 20% of fishermen catch 80% of the fish. At singles bars, 20% of the people get 80% of the action. The rest go home without having met anybody nice. No wonder they hate singles bars.

You can be one of the 20% who meet nice people in bars. You just have to follow the rules. For men there are three suggestions.

1. Don't drink. Women are paranoid about meeting an alcoholic in a bar. The more you drink the less attractive you'll be. Furthermore, the more time you spend drinking the less time you'll have to meet women, which is the purpose of going to the bar in the first place. After all, you can drink at home for a fraction of the cost and not have to worry about being picked up for drunk driving. So drink at home and meet women at bars.

2. Skip the bar area and go straight out to the tables in the dark corners of the bar. That's where all the women are hiding. Most of the men will be too shy to approach them. That means that no matter how crowded the bar may be, there really isn't all that much competition. Ask a woman to dance (or if you're in a quiet bar, introduce yourself and ask if you can join her for some conversation.)
3. Don't give up until you meet someone attractive. The 80% of men who don't get their needs met in singles bars give up after one or two rejections. They rush back to the bar and order a double. If you get turned down by a woman go on to another table on the other side of the bar. Keep asking until you meet someone who finds you attractive.

Just remember that most of the women who go to singles bars aren't there to talk to their friends, get drunk, or listen to the music. They are there to meet men. Do them and yourself a favor. Make contact.

Likewise, if you are a woman, you can meet many fine men if you follow these suggestions:

1. Go alone. If you go with your friends you'll spend all night talking to them instead of meeting men. If you need a ride then enter the bar separately once you arrive. There's no reason why you can't leave together with your friends later in the evening, but don't sit with them while you're supposed to be meeting men.
2. Sit or stand at the bar, not the tables in the dark corners of the bar. The bar is where all the men are. You'll be approachable. You'll meet more men than any other woman in the singles bar.
3. Stand up for your rights and your needs. If a man is obnoxious, tell him. If he won't take a hint, then move away from him. Also, don't allow yourself to be cornered for the rest of the evening by some nice guy who is inappropriate for you. Tell him you enjoyed meeting him and would like to meet other men as well. Or, if you don't have the guts to be honest, tell him you have to

powder your nose and then return to a different part of the room.

If you don't feel comfortable in bars, that's fine. There are plenty of better places to meet people. But if you do decide to go to a singles bar, do it right. Follow the rules so that your experience will be a happy, satisfying one.

Which bars should you frequent? That depends on personal taste. There are two main types of singles bars: conversation bars and dance bars. **Conversation Bars** are places where you can easily carry on a conversation. The music is for background, not dancing. This is ideal for getting to know someone. There's only one catch. At a conversation bar it's difficult for people to meet. There's no easy, socially acceptable way to introduce yourself by asking someone to dance. So if you're a man and know you won't have the nerve to engage anyone in conversation, skip the conversation bars. If you're a woman, sitting at a table is the kiss of death. Very few men will have the guts to initiate contact.

The second type of singles bars, **Dance Bars**, are the most popular. The reason is that it's much easier to approach someone. You're just asking for three minutes of their time. The disadvantage, of course, is that it's next to impossible to carry on a conversation with the music blaring in your ears. What's the solution? Go to a place with live music, rather than a disk jockey. Every 45 minutes the band will sit down and you'll be able to converse with new friends.

What do you do if you don't like to dance and have a hard time making contact at a conversation bar? I've heard of one single woman who goes to a different bar every Monday night during the football season. She couldn't tell you the difference between a touchdown and a home run. All she does is sit in a corner and balance her checkbook. The men come over to meet her during breaks in the action because she's more interesting to them than the beer commercials.

Another option is to go to bars that feature free hors

Singles Bars

d'oeuvres (usually 5-6pm). When you see someone attractive of the opposite sex in the food line, stand behind them and ask that them what's good to eat. Even if you don't meet anybody special at least you're getting a free meal!

Singles bars throughout America are not listed in this Guide because you shouldn't have any trouble locating them. The **Cocktail Lounges** section of the yellow pages of your phone book will list many of the more popular bars. Local newspapers also list bars and the kinds of music they feature.

ALAMEDA COUNTY

ALAMEDA
  Beltline Station, 1700 Clement, 523-4668. Hors d'oeuvres, M-F, 4-7pm.
  Croll's Bar & Grill, 1400 Webster, 522-8439. Dancing, Sat.
  Top 4 Club, Bldg 585, Naval Air Station, 869-4441.
BERKELEY
  Berkeley Square, 1333 University, 849-3374. Live music & DJ. Cover.
  Blake Street Garage, 2029 Blake.
  California Dream Cafe, 2041 Center, 843-9343. Rap & funk, Fri-Sat.
  Freight & Salvage, 1827 San Pablo, 548-1761, Live music.
  Gilman Street, 924 Gilman, 525-9926. Rock music.
  H's Lordship's, 199 Seawall Dr., 843-2733.
  Kesha's Inn, 2618 San Pablo, 486-9157.
  La Pena, 3105 Shattuck, 849-2568. Live dance music.
  Larry Blake's, 2367 Telegraph, 848-0888.
  La Val's Subterranean, 1834 Euclid, 540-7743. Folk & country music.
  Roaring Rock, 1920 Shattuck, 843-2739. Good place to meet
      shuffleboard players.
  Starry Plough, 3101 Shattuck, 841-2082. Live music. Cover charge.
  Windsurf Bar & Grill, 235 University, 845-7656.
  Your Place Too, 5319 Martin Luther King Jr. Way. Live blues music.
CASTRO VALLEY
  Krayon's Gallery, 3477 Castro Valley Blvd, 581-4186. TGIF.
  Muggy's, 20920 Redwood, 582-8200.
DUBLIN
  Jimmy O'Gills, 11873 Dublin Bl, 833-2613. Music every night.
EMERYVILLE
  Carlos Murphy's, 5901 Frontage Rd., 547-6766.
  Kimball's East, 5800 Shellmound, 658-2555.
  Townhouse, 5862 Doyle, 652-5336. Live music. Cover charge.

Singles Bars

FREMONT
  Black Angus, 3101 Walnut, 794-8222. DJ every night. Young crowd.
  Choices, 5399 Farwell, 791-1660. DJ every night. Huge, elegant singles
    bar. Mainly 20s & 30s age group. Cover charge varies.
  Fremont Inn, 46845 Warm Springs Blvd.
  King's Inn, 41025 N. Trimboli, 657-2324.
  Niles Station, 37501 Niles Blvd., 794-7797. Live rock music.
  Sergio's Supper Club, 3890 Mowry, 797-7970. Live dance music every
    night.
  Sheila's Cage, 4500 Peralta, 796-8072.
  South 40 Club, 46850 Warm Springs, 657-8935. Live country music
    Wed.-Sat. and free country dance lessons Wed.-Thu., 7:30-9pm.
HAYWARD
  Amador West, 253 W. Jackson 785-5677. Dancing.
  The Beat, 24744 Mission, 881-4789.
  Calhoun's, 18974 Meekland, 276-5121. Live dance music Thu.-Sun.
  Catrina's Lounge, 225 W. Winton, 782-4030.
  Detton's, 939 B St, 537-6770.
  Garden Inn, 22821 Mission, 538-2717.
  Green Lantern, 22580 Grand, 886-6565.
  Images, 29097 Mission, 581-5393.
  La Plaza Nightclub, 22164 Mission, 889-0997.
  Le Club Moderne, 22626 Main, 581-0264.
  West 40, 871 W. A St., 783-1882. Live country music.
LIVERMORE
  The Hideaway, 2293 1st St., 455-4141. Live music every night.
  Rock House Saloon, 1840 Portola, 455-5878.
NEWARK
  Bobby McGee's, 5995 Mowry, 794-7481, DJ every night. Mainly
    singles in their 20s & 30s.
  Ike's Cocktail Lounge, 81 Lewis Ctr., 792-5455. Top 40 (DJ), Thur &
    Sun. Live music Fri-Sat.
OAKLAND
  The Cantina, 4239 park, 482-3663. Folk & country music.
  Caribe Dance Center, 2424 Webster, 835-4006, Live Brazilian, Congo,
    and Trinidad music Fri.-Sat.
  Claremont Hotel Terrace Lounge, Ashby & Domingo, 843-3000. Live
    light rock music every night of the week.
  Club Bella Napoli, 2330 Telegraph, 893-5552. Top 40 & rap music,
    Wed-Sun.
  Coffee Mill, 3363 Grand Ave., Live dance music Fri.-Sun.
  The Complex, 10 Hegenberger. Live dance music Fri.-Sat.
  Court Lounge, 132 14th, 452-1496. Live music.
  Cozy Den, 1524 Peralta, 836-9842. DJ every night. Oldies, Sunday
    afternoons.

Singles Bars

130

OAKLAND (continued)
Eli's Mile High Club, 3629 Martin Luther King Jr. Way, 655-6661. Live
West Coast Blues. Cover charge.
Escovedo's, 3285 Lakeshore, 893-7670. Live music.
5th Amendment, 3255 Lakeshore. Live dance music Tue.-Sun.
The Hill, 4100 Redwood Rd., 530-7260. Live rock music.
Larry Blake's, Oakland City Center, 12th & Broadway, 839-4163. Live
comedy and rock music. Cover charge.
Manyatta, 10-B Hegenberger, 568-9282.
The Old Warehouse Cabaret, 577 18th St., 268-0591. Live music. Cover
charge.
Omni, 4799 Shattuck. Live rock music Thu.-Sun. Cover charge.
Uptown Nite Klub, 1803 Webster, 832-8282. African music Thur-Sun.
Yoshi's, 6030 Claremont, 652-9200. Live music. Cover charge.
Your Place Keesee's Lounge, 6528 Telegraph, 652-4040. Live music.
Cover charge.
PLEASANTON
Pleasanton Hotel, 855 Main, 846-8106. Live dance music. No cover.
Sunshine Saloon, 1807 Santa Rita, 846-6108.
SAN LEANDRO
Bogie's, 101 Parrott, 357-7333. Live top 40 dance music Wed-Sun.
SAN LORENZO
Black Angus, 15800 Hesperian, 276-1400. DJ every night. Young
crowd.

CONTRA COSTA COUNTY

ANTIOCH
Delta Holiday Restaurant & Lounge, 1500 W. 10th, 778-6141.
Ugly Duck Bar & Grill, 992 Fitzuren Rd., 778-5267.
BETHEL ISLAND
Billeci's Ristorante, 6200 Bethel Island Rd, 684-3223. Live music, Fri-
Sat.
CONCORD
Fatt's, 1731 Monument, 687-6101.
Hobie's Roadhouse, 2045 Mt Diablo, 676-4417.
The Old Hangout, 1970 Concord, 682-4760.
The Ranch, 2765 Clayton, 689-1235.
Sheraton Hotel, 45 John Glenn Dr., 825-7700. Dancing to live music.
No cover charge.
DANVILLE
Bottom Line, 103 Town Country Dr, 837-5463. Live music Fri-Sat. DJ,
Thursdays.
The Club, 519 San Ramon Valley Bl, 831-0963.

Singles Bars

EL CERRITO
  Ayers Chapter 11, 10753 San Pablo. Live dance music.
  The Downtown, 10582 San Pablo. Live music Fri.-Sat. Tea dancing, Sundays.
EL SOBRANTE
  Capri Club, 4156 Appian, 223-9938.
LAFAYETTE
  Cape Cod House, 3666 Mount Diablo, Lafayette, 283-8288. Piano bar.
PLEASANT HILL
  Knights Inn, 1250 Contra Costa Bl, 682-4868.
PT. RICHMOND
  The Point, 2 W. Richmond. Live jazz.
RICHMOND
  Sho Gun Restaurant, 3044 Hilltop Mall, 222-8282. Dancing.
SAN PABLO
  El Gallero, 1472 Rumrill, 234-2645.
  Esquire Club, 2022 23rd, 237-0133. Live music Thu-Sat.
  Star Club, 14273 San Pablo, 620-9546. Live Western music Thu-Sun.
SAN RAMON
  Bobby McGee's, 3110 Crow Canyon Place, 831-1101. DJ every night. Mainly singles in their 20s & 30s.
  Canyon Lakes Sports Bar & Grill, 500 Bollinger Canyon, 735-1806.
  Charms, Marriott Hotel, 2600 Bishop Dr, 867-9200. DJ every night. No cover.
  Rusty Pelican, 2323 San Ramon Valley Blvd., 820-6160. Live rock music. No cover charge. Mainly 20s & 30s age group.
WALNUT CREEK
  After Dark, 1251 Arroyo, 933-2312.
  Crogan's Bar & Grill, 1387 Locust, 933-7800. Singles often meet here Fridays (after work) & Saturday nights.
  El Papagayo, 2995 Ygnacio Valley, 939-6211. Live light rock. No cover charge.
  HMS Endeavor, 2153 Oak Grove, 944-1844. Singles night, every Wednesday and Thursday. Live dance music.
  Margaritaville, 1829 Mt Diablo Bl, 944-6595.
  Max's Opera Cafe, 1676 N. California, 923-3434. Conversation bar. The waiters and waitresses sing opera.
  Michael's, 1536 Newell. Dancing. 40+.
  Musician's Coffeehouse, 55 Eckley, 229-2710.
  Panache, 2355 N. Main, 935-8866. DJ, Mon-Sat.
  WPLJ'S, 2112 N. Main, Walnut Creek, (415) 938-4140.

Singles Bars

MARIN COUNTY

FAIRFAX
> 19 Broadway. Live music every night.
> Perry's, 625 Redwood Highway, 383-9300. Conversation bar.

LARKSPUR
> Baxter's, 601 Larkspur Landing Cir, 461-7022. DJ every night. Always crowded. No cover charge. Mainly 20s and early 30s.

MILL VALLEY
> Eb's Muddy Water Saloon, Howard Johnson's Motor Lodge, 160 Shoreline Hwy, (415) 332-5700.
> La Bamba, 200 Shoreline Hwy. Live jazz.
> Sweetwater, 153 Throckmorton, 388-2820. Live rock & blues music every night. Cover charge on weekends.

NOVATO
> Alvarado Inn, 6045 Redwood Highway, 883-5952. Live country music. No cover charge.
> T.J. On the Boulevard, 7110 Redwood, 892-3474. Live music Wed-Sat.

SAN ANSELMO
> Cafe Nuvo, 556 San Anselmo Ave., 454-4530.
> Heartbeat, 100 Shaw, 258-0402. Smoke free.
> Ted's, 218 Sir Francis Drake Blvd., 453-8600. Conversation bar.

SAN RAFAEL
> Andaron's, Holiday Inn, 1010 Northgate Dr., 479-8800. DJ every night. Cover charge, Fri.-Sat.
> Fourth St. Tavern, 711 4th, 454-4044. Blues music.
> Mandarin House, 817 Francisco Blvd. W., 492-1638. Live dance music Thu-Sat. Mainly 40+ age group. Cover charge.
> Mayflower British Pub, 1533 4th, 456-1011. Live piano music with open mike, Fri.-Sat. Dart playing. No cover.
> New George's, 842 4th, 457-8424. Live rock music Wed-Sat.
> Royal Mandarin, 234 Northgate One Shopping Ctr, 472-5676. Dancing, live music, Fri-Sat. No cover charge. 40+ age group.
> San Rafael Joe's, 917 4th, 456-2425. Live piano bar Thur-Sat. 40+.
> Three Klicks Out, 555 E. Francisco, 454-3941. Dancing every night. Mainly 20s age group.
> Trevor's, 927 Tamalpais, 456-7044. Live rock every night. No cover.

SAUSALITO
> Bar With No Name, 757 Bridgeway. Live music Fri.-Sat. Jazz Sunday afternoons.
> Zack's by the Bay, Bridgeway & Turney, 332-9779. Live rock music. No cover charge.

Singles Bars

TIBURON

Amadeus Cafe, 20 Main, 435-3966. Live music every night.
Mr. Q's, 25 Main, 435-4550. Live music Fri-Sat nights & Sunday afternoons.
Christopher's, 9 Main, 435-4600. Live rock Fri-Sat. Cover charge.

MONTEREY COUNTY

MONTEREY

The Club, 321 D Alvarado, 646-9244. Dancing every night. Mainly singles in their 20s.
Carrera's, 414 Alvarado, 646-1415. Dancing.
Doc Rickett's, 95 Prescott, 649-4241. Live music every night.
Doubletree Hotel Lounge, 2 Portola Plaza, 649-4511. Live music. All ages.
Kalisa's, 851 Cannery Row, 372-8512.
Outrigger, 700 Cannery Row, 372-8543.

SALINAS

The Catalyst, 1011 Pacific. Live music.
The Paragon, 307 S. Main, 758-9800. Live piano music Wed.-Fri.

SEASIDE

Corral Club, 1153 Fremont, 899-2966. Live Western music every night.

NAPA

Collections, Clarion Inn, 3425 Solano, 253-7433. Live rock music Thu.-Sat. Cover charge.
Embassy Suites Lounge, 1075 California, 253-9540. Dancing to live music. No cover charge.
Junk Rock Cafe, 1017 Coombs, 224-5435.
O'Sullivan's Pub, 359 1st St., 224-5612. Live music, country swing dancing Fri.-Sat.
Tom Foolery Saloon, 600 Trampas, Napa, (707) 255-1688.

SAN FRANCISCO

Abbey Tavern, 4100 Geary, 221-7767. Folk & Country music.
A Classy Room, 32 9th, 861-2820. Dancing until 4am.
Albion, 3139 16th St., 552-8558. Folk & country music.
Amelia's, 647 Valencia, 552-7788. Disco Thur-Sat.
Balboa Cafe, 3199 Fillmore, 922-4595. Fern bar for conversation.
Bajone's, 1062 Valencia St., 282-2522. Live music. Cover charge Fri-Sat.
Bentley's, Sutter & Kearny, 989-6895. Live music Tue-Sun.

Singles Bars

SAN FRANCISCO (continued)

Bo Grumpus, 561 Geary, 885-1464. Rock music.
Bopper's, 650 Howard, (415) 896-1950. 50s & 60s music (DJ). Cover charge.
Bouncer's, 64 Townsend, 397-2480. Live music Tue-Sun.
California Cafe, 50 Broadway. Live music Mon-Fri.
Cal's, 2001 Union, (415) 567-3121. Live music Wednesdays.
Camelot, 3231 Fillmore, 567-4004. Top 40, Fri-Sat.
Capurro's Pier 47, 300 Jefferson, 771-0377 Live music every night.
Caribbean Rose, 1039 Ocean. Live Caribbean & Jamaican music.
Cats, 48 Peter Yorke Way, 771-3309. DJ, Top 40 music. Cover charge.
Cesar's Latin Palace, 3140 Mission, 648-6611. Live Latin music, Fri.-Sat., 9pm-2. Cover charge.
Chatterbox, 853 Valencia, 821-1891. Live music Fri-Sat.
Chi Chi Club, 440 Broadway, 392-6213. Live music & DJ. Cover charge.
Club DV8, 55 Natoma, 777-1419. Live music Wed-Sat.
Club 412, 412 Broadway, 391-8282. Live music Sat.
Club Metropolis, Market at 11th, 621-5001. Dancing Wed-Sat. Cover charge Fri-Sat.
Club Mirage, 2 Kansas, 431-9046. Top 40, Fri-Sat.
Coeur Samba, 1015 Folsom, 626-2899. Afro-Caribbean music, Fri.
Covered Wagon Saloon, 917 Folsom, 974-1585. Dancing every night.
Creativity Explored, 3245 16th St., 821-6210. Rock music.
Crystal Pistol, 842 Valencia, 695-7887. Dancing Thur-Sun.
Das Klub, 1015 Folsom. Live music Wed.-Sun.
DNA, 375 11th St., (415) 626-1409. Live music Sat.-Sun.
El Rio, 3158 Mission, 282-3325. Dancing Fri.
Fairmont Hotel, California & Mason, 772-5000. Live music every night in the New Orleans Room and Tonga Room.
The Farm, 1499 Potrero, 826-4290. Live music. Cover charge.
The Fillmore, 1805 Geary, 922-3455. Rock, new music, reggae, jazz, comedy.
Firehouse 7, 3160 16th St., 621-1617. Live music and happy hour daily. All ages.
Full Moon Saloon, 1725 Haight, 668-6190. Live rock. Cover charge.
Galleon, 718 14th St., (415) 431-0253. Live music.
Goat Hill Pizza, 300 Connecticut, 641-1440. Live music.
Gold Dust Lounge, 247 Powell, 397-1695. Live music every night.
Golden Grommet, 834 Irving, 564-6627. Blues music. Cover charge.
Great American Music Hall, 859 O'Farrell, 885-0750. Live music. Cover charge.
Greek Taverna, 256 Columbus, 362-7260. Greek dancing.
The Hall, 827 Hyde, 771-5600. Ballroom dancing.

Singles Bars

SAN FRANCISCO (continued)

Hard Rock Cafe, 1699 Van Ness, 885-1699. Loud rock music (taped), but no dancing. Plenty of singles in their 20s and 30s.

Harry's, 2020 Fillmore, 864-2779.

Holiday Inn, Van Ness & Pine, 441-4000. Dancing, DJ, every night.

Hyatt Regency Hotel, 5 Embarcadero Ctr, 788-1234. Live big band dance music Fridays, 5:30-8:30 pm. Mainly 40+ age group.

I-Beam, 1748 Haight, 668-6006. Rock music every night. Cover charge.

Ireland's 32, 3920 Geary, 386-6173.

John Barleycorn, 1415 Larkin, 564-1233.

Kimball's, 300 Grove, 861-5555.

La Terraza, 3472 Mission, 285-1236. North Mexican music every night.

Le Montmarte, 2125 Lombard, 921-9921. Live Latin & salsa music every night. Cover charge.

Last Day Saloon, 406 Clement, (415) 387-6343. Live music.

Lipps, 201 9th St., 552-3466. DJ. Cover charge.

The Little Shamrock, 807 Lincoln, 661-0060. Good place to meet softball players and bicyclists on Sunday afternoons.

Lost & Found Saloon, 1353 Grant, 397-3751. Rock music.

Lou's Pier 47, 300 Jefferson, 771-0377. rock music.

Mabuhay Gardens, 443 Broadway, 956-3315. Live music.

Mangia, Mangia, 1 Embarcadero Center, 397-8799. DJ (rock & disco) and light show. No cover charge.

The Mart, 32 9th St. DJ Fri.-Sat.

Maxwell's Restaurant, 900 North Point, 441-4140. Rock music.

Morty's, 1024 Kearny, 986-MORT. 50s & 60s music.

Mulhern's, 3653 Buchanan St., (415) 346-5549.

Mumms, 2215 Powell, 433-3414. Private dinner-dance club. Non-members with reservations may stay for dancing. On weekends only members are allowed.

New Eagle Bar & Grill, 4 Embarcadero Center, 397-2056. Rock music, DJ.

New Tar & Feather's, 2140 Union, 563-2612. Rock music.

Nightbreak, 1821 Haight, 221-9008. Live music Wed.-Sun.

Nine, 399 9th St., 863-9990. Live rock music. Cover charge.

Oasis, 11th & Folsom, 621-8119. Rock music (live or DJ). Cover charge.

Onna No Shiro, 359 Grant, 398-6464. Piano bar.

Off Union Saloon, 2513 Van Ness, 928-1661. Live music.

Palladium, 1031 Kearny, 434-1308. Afterhours bar, 9pm-6am. Cover charge.

Park Bowl, 1855 Haight, 752-2366. Rock & oldies (DJ).

Passand, 1875 Union, 922-4498. Live music. No cover charge.

Pat O'Shea's Mad Hatter, 3rd & Geary, 752-3148. Rock music.

Paul's Saloon, 3251 Scott, 922-2456. Live country music every night.

Singles Bars

136

SAN FRANCISCO (continued)

Perry's, 1944 Union, 922-9022. Most famous singles bar in San Francisco. Conversation bar.

Pierce Street Annex, 3138 Fillmore, 567-1400. Top 40 music (DJ) every night.

Pier 23 Cafe, The Embarcadero, 362-5125.

P.J. Montgomery's, Montgomery & Broadway. DJ on two dance floors every night.

Plough & Stars Irish Pub, 116 Clement, 751-1122. Live Irish folk music. Cover charge Fri.-Sat.

Rasselas, California & Divisadero, 567-5010. Rock music.

Regent Cafe, 952 Clement, 752-0354. Live Top 40 music Wed.-Sat. DJ, Sundays. Cover charge Fri.-Sat.

Remy, 2001 Union, 567-3121. Rock music (DJ).

Rockin' Robbins, 1840 Haight, 221-1960. Dancing every night. Cover charge Fri-Sat.

Rockin' Robbins Downtown, 133 Beale, 543-1961. 50's & 60's music every night. No cover charge.

Rocky Sullivan's Bar & Grill, 4737 Geary, 386-0909.

Roland's, 3309 Fillmore, 921-7774. Live jazz. Cover charge.

Sacred Grounds, Hayes & Cole, 387-3859. Rock music.

The Saloon, 1232 Grant, 989-7666. Blues music. Cover charge Fri.-Sat.

Silhouettes, 524 Union, 398-1952. 50's & 60's music.

Silhouettes at the Wharf, 155 Jefferson, 673-1954. 50's & 60's music.

16th Note, 3160 16th St., 621-1617. Dancing. Cover charge.

Sound of Music, 162 Turk, 885-9616. Live music.

The South Side, 1190 Folsom, (415) 431-3332. Top 40 music, DJ. Cover charge Fri-Sat. 25-45.

Stan's Bar, 1401 Valencia, 826-3600. Talent Showcase, Thur-Sat. Music, poetry, films, comedy, etc.

Starlite Roof, Sir Francis Drake Hotel, Powell & Sutter, 392-7755. Live ballroom and top 40 music. Mainly 40+ age group. Expensive but classy.

St. Francis Hotel, Powell & Geary Streets, 397-7000. Top 40, pop, & disco music (live & DJ) in the Compass Rose and Oz Club every night.

The Stone, 412 Broadway, 391-8282. After hours bar, Midnight-6 am Fri.-Sat. Live rock music. Cover charge.

Studebaker's, 22 4th St., 777-0880. 50s-80s music Mon-Sat.

The Underground Club, 201 9th St., 552-3466. Live modern music.

VIS Club, 628 Divisadero, 567-0660. Live rock music. Cover charge.

Washington Square Bar & Grill, 1707 Powell, 982-8123. Conversation bar.

Wolfgang's, 901 Columbus, 441-4333. DJ. Cover charge.

Singles Bars

SAN MATEO COUNTY

BELMONT
Iron Gate, 1360 El Camino, 592-7893. Live music Wed.-Thu.
BRISBANE
De Marco's 23 Club, 23 Visitation. Live swing and modern country music.
BURLINGAME
Bobby McGee's, 150 Anza, 579-7807. DJ every night. No cover.
Fisherman Restaurant, 1492 Bayshore Hwy, 697-1490.
Hyatt Burlingame, 13333 Old Bayshore, 342-7741. Live music.
Mr. K's Cabaret, 1819 El Camino, 697-4042. Live music.
Route 66, 261 California, 347-3669. Live music Wed-Sat.
Safari Run, 1306 Bayshore Hwy, 347-8406.
Saluto's, 1600 Bayshore Hwy, 697-6565.
DALY CITY
R.V.'s Super Club & Bar, 6287 Mission, 991-4006.
FOSTER CITY
Black Angus, 1299 Chess, 345-9971. DJ every night. Mainly 20s & 30s age group.
Le Paradis, 1221 Chess, 570-5700. DJ.
HALF MOON BAY
Miramar Beach Inn, Highway 1. Live music Fri.-Sun.
MENLO PARK
British Bankers Club, 1090 El Camino, 327-8769.
MILLBRAE
Bit of Rhythm, 1741 El Camino, 588-6151. Live music, Fri-Sun.
PACIFICA
Miramar Beach Inn, Magellan & Mirada, 726-9053.
Nick's Rockaway, 100 Rockaway Beach Ave., Pacifica. Live music.
REDWOOD CITY
Barney Steel's, 590 Veterans Blvd., 366-1238. Live music Fri.-Sat.
La Terrasse, Hotel Sofitel, 223 Twin Dolphin, 598-9000. Piano & Dance Trio, Thu-Sat.
Tommy's Club, 1794 Broadway, 368-8514.
SAN MATEO
Borel's, 2951 Campus, 341-7464.
Charlie Brown's, 3025 Clear View Way, 574-8330.
Club Ante, 223 S. B St., 348-2683.
Occa, 217-A Baldwin, 579-7282. Live music every night.
The Planet at Tingle's, Dunfey Hotel, 1770 S. Amphlett, 572-8400. DJ every night.

Singles Bars

SOUTH SAN FRANCISCO
  Railroad Station, 206 Grand, 588-0206.
  Silver Dollar, 320 Grand, 589-0596. Live music Fri.-Sun.
  3 Amigos Nightclub, 206 Grand, 588-7081.
  Tony's Hofbrau Lounge, 151 S. Spruce, 583-8200.

SANTA CLARA COUNTY

CAMPBELL
  Baja Cafe & Cantina, 499 E. Hamilton, 374-4290. DJ every night. Cover charge.
  Boswell's, 1875 S. Bascom, 371-4404. Live rock every night. Usually no cover charge.
  Fricn Frac's Cabaret, 1545 W. Campbell, 378-1121. Live rock, Thu.-Sat.
  Kixx, 300 Orchard City, 374-4500.
  L.A. Rocks, 300 Orchard City Dr., 866-5666. Live music Tue-Sun, 9:30pm. Cover charge varies.
  Perrone's, 1777 S. Bascom, 377-6060. Live top 40 music.
  Puma's Rock & Roll Club, 33 S. Central, 993-2697. Live music Wed-Sat, 9:30 pm. Cover charge.
  Remington's, 1730 W. Campbell, 370-3280. Live music. Cover charge. Sundays, Singles night. Tuesdays, Parents Without Partners night.
  Sebastian's, 1901 S. Bascom, 377-8600, Dance music (DJ), Wed-Sat., 9pm-1am. No cover charge.
  Smokey Mountain, 33 S. Central, 866-8288. Live rock every night.
  Southern Comfort, behind Hamilton House, 371-1861. Live music, Thu-Sat.
  The Terrace, 750 The Pruneyard, 371-3801. Live music Thu.-Sat.
COYOTE
  Coyote Inn, 102 Monterey Rd., 463-0452. Live country music, Fri-Sat., 9:15 pm. No cover charge.
CUPERTINO
  Allstars, 10905 N. Wolfe, 725-8488. DJ every night, 9pm-1:30am. No cover charge.
  Blue Pheasant, 22100 Stevens Creek Blvd., 255-3300. 50s & 60s music (DJ). Mainly 35+ age group.
  Night Kap, 20020 Steven's Creek Blvd., 252-1100. Live music Mon-Sat. $2 cover charge Fri-Sat.
  Peacock Bar & Grill, 19980 Homestead, 253-2141. Live music Fri-Sun. No cover charge.
  P.J. Mulligan's, 19979 Stevens Creek, 255-0588.
  Rusty Pelican, 10741 N. Wolfe, 255-6240. Live music, Thu.-Sat.

Singles Bars

EAST PALO ALTO
Club Afrique, 583 O'Connor, (415) 322-3912. Live Caribbean and recorded music every night. Cover charge varies.
Collins Club, 1983 University, 329-1710.
Pena Moai, 1944 University, East Palo Alto, (415) 321-1944.

GILROY
Sandrino's, 420 1st St., 848-3811. Live rock music, Fri-Sat. Mainly 20s & 30s age group.

LOS ALTOS
Main Street Bar & Grill, 169 Main St., (415) 948-4332. Live music.

LOS GATOS
At the Hop, Old Town Center, 50 University, 354-4677. 50s & 60s & Top 40 dance music (DJ), Wed-Sun., 8pm-2am.
The Cats, 17533 Santa Cruz Hwy, 354-4020. Live rock music.No cover.
Il Nido, 170 W. Main, 354-8108. Live music Fri.-Sat., 9pm-2am. No cover charge.
Johnny's, 14675 Winchester, 395-6888. Live top 40 music Tue-Sat, 9pm-1:30pm. Cover charge.
La Hacienda, 18840 Los Gatos/Saratoga Rd., 354-6669. Piano bar every night.
Los Gatos Lodge, 50 Saratoga, 354-3300. Live rock Tue-Sat.
Mountain Charley's, 15 N. Santa Cruz, 354-2510. Live music Tue-Sun, 9:30pm-1:30am. Cover charge varies.
#1 Broadway, 102 S. Santa Cruz, 354-4303. Live piano or quartet music Thu-Sat., 8pm-1am. No cover charge.
Scarlett La Rue's, 15940 Los Gatos, 356-2404. Live ragtime & dixieland jazz music, Fri & Sat., 9:30pm-1:45am. No cover charge.
University Club, 50 University, 354-5959. Live music Fri.-Sat., 8:30pm-12:30am. No cover charge.

MILPITAS
Brandon's, 1800 Barber, 432-6311. DJ Mon.-Sat., 4pm-2am. Cover charge.
Holiday Inn, 777 Bellew, 945-0800. Live music every night. No cover charge.
Nino's, 1181 E. Calaveras, 946-4667. DJ, Fri.-Sat., 10pm-2am. No cover charge.
Riffs, 1801 Barber, 943-0600.

MOUNTAIN VIEW
Doug's Cocktails, 1313 W. El Camino, (415) 940-9707. Live music, Fri-Sat.
J.J.'s Blues Cafe, 165 E. El Camino Real, (415) 968-2277. Live blues music every night. Cover charge.
No Jacket Required, 2540 California, (415) 949-1800.

Singles Bars

MOUNTAIN VIEW (continued)

Sports Page, 1431 Stierlin, (415) 961-1992. Live music Fri-Sat, 9:30-1:30am. No cover charge.

Wagon Wheel, 282 E. Middlefield, (415) 967-1244. 50s-70s music (DJ), Wed-Sat., 8:30 pm-1:30am. No cover charge.

PALO ALTO

British Bankers Club.

City Lights, 575 High, 322-8731.

Dinah's Shack, 4269 El Camino Real, (415) 493-9510. Live music Tue-Sat. No cover charge.

Fanny & Alexander's, 271 University, (415) 328-7700. Live piano & vocals, Tue.-Sat.

Gatehouse, 265 Lytton, Palo Alto, (415) 326-1330. Live music Thu-Sat., 9pm-1:30am. No cover charge.

The New Varsity, 456 University, (415) 321-1246. Live rock music Fri.-Sat.

Vortex, 260 California, (415) 324-1402. DJ, Thu.-Sat. After hours dancing until 4am, Fri.-Sat. Cover charge varies.

SAN JOSE

Almaden Feed & Fuel, 18950 Almaden Rd., 268-8950. Live music every Fri-Sat, 9:30 pm. No cover charge.

Barrington's Lounge, Ste. Claire Hilton, 302 S. Market, 295-2000. Live music Fri-Sat, 9pm-1am. No cover charge.

Beau's Annex, 35 N. San Pedro, 292-9277. Live music Mondays and Fri-Sat. Cover charge varies.

The Cabaret, 370 Saratoga Ave., 248-0641. Live rock music. Cover charge varies.

Calico Paints, 2250 Stevens Creek, 247-6050. Live rock music.

Cowtown, 3840 Monterey, 225-4277. Live country music, Tue-Sun. No cover charge.

D.B. Cooper's, 163 W. Santa Clara, 279-5867. DJ, Mon.-Sat., 9pm-2am. Cover charge.

El Rancho Grande, 301 S. Capitol, 259-7281. Live music.

El Tanampa, 1151 S. King, 258-8440. Disco dancing.

Essex Club, 510 El Paseo Shopping Ctr, 378-4433.

The Fairmont, 170 S. Market, (408) 998-3960. Live orchestra Tues-Sun. Cover charge.

Garden Alameda, 1520 The Alameda, 998-1415. Live piano music, 6-10:30pm, Tue.-Sat.

Garden City, 360 Saratoga Ave., 244-3333. Live piano, flute, vocals, bass, guitar, and jam sessions every night. No cover charge.

Ida's Fireside Inn, 2152 S. 1st, 297-4831. Live music Thu-Sat. No cover.

JJ's Lounge, 3934 Stevens Creek, 243-6441. Live blues music every night, 9:30 pm.

Singles Bars

SAN JOSE (continued)

Joey's Lounge, 2058 N. Capitol, 263-3200. Country music Fri.-Sat., 9 pm. No cover charge.

Le Baron Hotel, 1350 N. 1st, 288-9200. Live light rock music every night, 6:30-10:30 pm. No cover charge.

The Loft, 951 Town & Country Village, 246-6672. Live music.

Lou's Village, 1465 W. San Carlos, 293-4570. Live piano music, Fri-Sat., 7-11 pm. No cover charge.

Marsugi's, 399 S. 1st, 286-8345. Live music Wed-Sat, 9:30 pm. Cover charge.

Miguelito's, 406 Blossom Hill, 226-0330. Live music Fri-Sat, 9:30pm-1:30am. No cover charge.

Mr. P's, 285 S. First, 295-8511. Live music Wed.-Sat.

Oasis, 200 N. 1st, 292-2212. Rock music (DJ) every night. Cover charge.

Pacific Fish Co., 177 W. Santa Clara, 298-7222. Live music. Usually no cover charge.

Paradise Beach, 175 N. San Pedro, 298-9283. Recorded music. 20s age group.

Ritz Pub & Pizzeria, 5180 Moorpark, 996-8870. Live music Wed-Sat, 8-11:30pm. No cover charge.

Saddle Rack, 1310 Auzerais, 286-3393. Live country music Tue.-Wed., 9pm. Also dance lessons. Usually no cover charge.

The Sanctuary, Calico Kate's, 4400 Stevens Creek, 296-2332. Live music every night, 9:30 pm. Cover charge.

Spartan Pub, San Jose State University, 7th & San Carlos, 924-1855. Live music Tue-Thu. No cover charge.

Studio 47, 47 Notre Dame Ave., 279-3387. DJ. 20s age group.

3 Flames Restaurant, 1547 Meridian, 296-3133. Live music Tue-Sat, 9 pm. No cover charge.

3 Plus One, 675 E. Gish, 293-6289. DJ.

Time Out Sports Bar & Cafe, 111 N. San Pedro, 279-4330. Live music Thu-Sat.

Tony Roma's, 4233 Moorpark, 253-4900. Live music.

Tropicana Twin Ballroom, King & Story, 926-4321.

Village Retreat, 7028 Santa Teresa, 226-5424. Live music Fri. & Sat. DJ, Sun.-Thu.

Willows Lounge, Hyatt Hotel, 1740 1st, 993-1234. Live music, Thu-Sat. No cover charge.

Zorba's, 1850 S. Bascom, 293-7170. Live music & belly dancers, Tue-Sun, 9:15pm-1am. No cover charge.

SANTA CLARA

A.J.'s Cypress Lounge, 1031 Monroe, 243-0589. Live rock and top 40 music Fri-Sat., 9:30 p.m.

Arthur's, 2875 Lakeside, 980-1666.

Singles Bars

142

SANTA CLARA (continued)
Chips, Doubletree Hotel, 5101 Great America Pkwy., 986-0700. Top 40 music Tue-Sat., 8pm-2am, cover charge. Live jazz in the lobby, Fridays, 5pm, no cover.
Horseshoe Club, 2655 El Camino, 248-4100.
Lord John's Inn, 3190 The Alameda, 984-0475. Live music Tue-Sat., 9:30pm-1:30 am. Cover charge.
McNeil's, 800 Kiely, 244-4038. Live music Mon-Sat. Usually no cover charge.
One Step Beyond, 1400 Martin, 727-0901. Modern music, Thur-Sun. Cover charge.
SARATOGA
Crazy Horse Lounge, 14455 Big Basin, 867-4711. Live music. No cover.
Duke of Wellington, 14572 Big Basin, 867-7070. Live music Thu-Sat. No cover charge.
SUNNYVALE
Beefy's Cabin, 1028 W. Washington, 736-7141. Live music every Fri-Sat, 9 pm-1am. No cover charge.
Bold Night, 769 Mathilda, 782-4357.
Caribbean Cajun Restaurant, 172 Murphy, 737-7056. Live music Fri-Sat. No cover charge.
Donna's Dukes, 919 El Camino Real, 733-5575. Live country music, Wed-Sun. No cover charge.
Faces Cafe, 685 E. El Camino, 479-1288.
Hard Disk Cafe, Lawrence/Central Expwys., 733-2001. Live music Fri-Sat, 9 pm. No cover charge.
Jay Bird Lounge, 1102 W. Evelyn, 739-7939. Live country music, Fri-Sun. No cover charge.
Michael's, 830 E. El Camino Real, 245-2925. Live piano music, Tue-Sat., 8:30pm-12:30am. No cover charge.
Odyssey Room, 799 El Camino Real, 245-4448. Live top 40 music every night, 8 pm. Cover charge.
Spot Cafe, 1010 Sunnyvale-Saratoga, 733-6000.
Stardust Lounge, 1183 W. El Camino Real, 732-5570, Oldies music (DJ) & dance lessons. Cover charge.
Starlite Ballroom, 1160 N. Fairoaks, 745-7827. Country dance music, Thursdays; top 40 music, Fri-Sat.

SANTA CRUZ COUNTY

APTOS
Aptos Club, 5 Post Office Dr, 688-9888.
Seascape, 610 Clubhouse Dr., 688-3254. Dancing.
Severino's, 7500 Old Dominion, 688-8987. Live rock music. No cover.

Singles Bars

SANTA CRUZ
Bonny Doon Vineyard, 10 Pine Flat, 425-3625. Live music.
The Catalyst, 1011 Pacific, 423-1336. Live rock music, Thu-Sat. Cover charge.
Coconut Grove, 400 Beach, 423-5590. Live music.
Edgewater Club, 215 Esplanade, 475-6215. Dancing every night & Sunday afternoons.
Kuumbwa Jazz Center, 320-2 Cedar, 427-2227. Live music almost every night. Cover charge.
SOQUEL
O.T.'s, 3660 Soquel, 476-3939.
WATSONVILLE
Pasa Tiempo Club, 126 Main, 722-0605.

SOLANO COUNTY

BENICIA
Sundowner, 1401 E. 5th, 745-2600.
CORDELIA
Pure Energy, 364 Pittman, 864-0185. DJ. Young crowd.
FAIRFIELD
Duffy's, 150 Acacia, 425-7141.
Fairfield Landing, 2470 Martin, 429-2370. Live rock music. Mainly singles in their 20s and 30s.
Geronimo Room, 2030 N. Texas, 425-6413. Dancing Wed.-Sun.
Hickey's Brass Rail, 837 Texas, 425-4975.
Moon Room Lounge, Muffin Treat Restaurant, Hwy. 80 at N. Texas, 429-1519. Live music every night. Mainly 40+ age group.
SUISUN
Vista Club, E. Cordelia & Kellogg, 422-0584. Live music Wed.-Sun.
Zowie's Cafe Cabaret, 701 Main, 422-1613.
TRAVIS
Cecil's, 666 Parker, 437-3610. DJ every night.
VACAVILLE
Brigadoon's, 1591 E. Monte Vista, 448-8446. Live rock or country music.
Monte Vista Pub, 1072 E. Monte Vista, 448-8173. Live country music.
VALLEJO
Harbor House, 23 Harbor, 642-8984. DJ. 35+ age group.
Jenicas Lounge, 1711 Solano, 554-1073.
Maritime Station, 117 Maritime Academy Dr, 643-2012.
Nitty Gritty Lounge, 2065 Solano, 642-4413. Dancing.
Outlaw Josie Wales, 1504 Sears Pt., 554-0107. Live country music.

VALLEJO (continued)

Talk of the Town, 326 Virginia, 555-2600. Live music. Open after hours.

The Village, 732 Tuolumne, 648-9497. Live county music every night.

Vallejo Country Club, 1801 Solano, 552-8157. Live music.

SONOMA COUNTY

COTATI

Cotati Cabaret, 85 La Plaza, 795-7622. Dancing Thu.-Sun.

EL VERANO

Little Switzerland, Grove & Riverside, 938-9990. Waltz & polka dancing, Saturday evenings & and Sunday afternoons & evenings. 50s & 60s music, Fridays.

HEALDSBURG

Skylark, 245 Healdsburg, 433-6789. Live music Fri-Sat.

PETALUMA

Aquarium Lounge, 1030 Petaluma Blvd., 762-9814. Live rock or country music.

McNears, 23 Petaluma Blvd., 765-2121. Dixieland jazz Thu.-Fri. Live country Fri.-Sat.

Steamer Gold, 1 Water St., 763-6876. Live music every night.

ROHNERT PARK

Maxi's Lounge, Red Lion Inn, 1 Red Lion Dr., 584-5466. Live rock music. No cover charge. All ages.

Smitty's Bar & Grill, 5000 Commerce, 584-0235. Live music.

SANTA ROSA

Daily Planet, 578-0952. Dancing Wed-Sun. Mainly 20s and 30s age group.

El Rancho Tropicana, 2200 Santa Rosa Ave., 542-3699. Live top 40 music Tues-Sat. No cover charge.

Magnolia's 107 4th, 526-1006. Live top 40 music Wed-Sat.

New Joe Frogger's, 527 4th, 526-0539. Live music every night.

Santa Rosa Inn, 4302 Santa Rosa Ave., 584-0345. DJ.

Studio Kaffe, 418 Mendocino, 523-1971. Live music or comedy, Mon-Sat. Cover charge.

SEBASTOPOL

Marty's Top O' the Hill, 8050 Bodega, 823-5987. Live country music Thu-Sun. No cover charge.

Paradise Alley, 6930 Burnett, 823-3778. Live music.

SONOMA

Cabernet Sauvignon, 478 1st St. East, 996-3600. Live music Wed.-Sat.

Singles Bars

LONG DISTANCE ROMANCE

Back in the days of the Old West there was a tremendous shortage of single women. Pioneer single men who wanted to settle down and raise a family were forced to import women from the more populated areas of the country. These women became known as "mail-order" brides. Today there is no such shortage. Nevertheless, many singles prefer to correspond with other singles around the country and also overseas, rather than limit themselves to singles in their own geographical areas. There are three types of singles who choose to correspond with people far away:

1. Singles in small towns and rural areas who complain that "all the best ones are already married". If you have already dated all of the suitable partners in your area your only alternative is to date people from other areas.
2. Singles who hope to move to a new locale where "the grass is greener". If you are tired of your current area and hope to move to a new one where there is more excitement, better weather, or greater financial opportunity, one way is to find a romantic partner in that area.

Long Distance Romance

3. Singles who enjoy writing. Millions of people around the world of all ages write to "pen-pals". There's no rule that says your "pen-pal" relationship has to be platonic.

Correspondence Services

Millions of people around the world hope to immigrate into the United States. Due to American immigration quotas, only a small percentage are admitted to the U.S. each year. One way to hasten the process is to marry an American citizen. As a result, there are many companies that help American men meet foreign women. Usually they publish a directory of foreign women, including photo and brief descriptive profile. American men are encouraged to correspond with these foreign women through the mail.

There is nothing illegal about these correspondence dating services. What is illegal, however, are sham marriages that are often arranged by unscrupulous companies that charge foreign women thousands of dollars to come to the U.S. to marry American men whom they have never met. Usually these marriages are never consummated sexually and a divorce follows shortly. The U.S. Immigration Service is quite aware of this scam and has tightened procedures to prevent the success of such unscrupulous companies.

The basic problem with these services is that eventually either you or your "pen pal" have to travel a long distance in order to meet each other. In the case of American men seeking foreign women, almost inevitably it is the American who winds up paying for the plane fare.

A second problem with international dating services is the potential for being exploited. As soon as your mate becomes naturalized, you may be expendable. Also, it is common for foreign brides to want to bring their entire families over to the United States eventually. Guess whose home they'll be staying at while they are getting established?

Not all correspondence dating services involve American singles meeting foreign singles. There are many such

Long Distance Romance

services that entail a "pen pal" relationship between American singles.

Correspondence Services Directory

American Asian Worldwide Services, Box 2777, Orcutt, CA 93455, (805) 937-5230. Louis & Tessie Florence, Directors.
American Colored Club, Box 18331, Philadelphia, PA 19120.
American Friendship Club, Box 761, Rouses Pt., NY 12979.
American Social Club, Box 18353, Philadelphia, PA 19120.
Anachron, Box 326, New York, NY 11367. Specializes in older woman/younger man and older man/younger woman relationships.
Anticipations, Box 2307-D, Makati, Philippines.
Arts World, Box 833, Amityville, NY 11701.
Asian-American Matchmakers, Box 10187, Glendale 91209.
The Asian Experience, Box 1214, Novato, CA 94948, (415) 897-ASIA.
Asian Sweethearts, Box 929, Carmichael, CA 95609.
Asiatic Manor, Box 2044, Madison Square Station, New York, NY 10159.
Be Happy Ltd, Box 2175, Ramona, CA 92065. European women.
Bibliobuffs, Box 995, Ingram, TX 78025.
Black Dating Service, 103-24 Northern Blvd., Flushing, NY 11368. West Indies and Africa.
Blue Horizons, 862 Farmington Ave., Bristol, CT 06010, (213) 584-5712.
Central American Bureau, Box 650, Concord, CA 94522. Latin women.
Cherry Blossoms, Box 1021, Honokaa, Hawaii 96727, (808) 961-2114. Directed by John Broussard & Kelly Pomeroy. Asian women.
Christian Singles, Box 203, Union City, CA 94587. Pen Pal Club for Bible believing Christians, U.S. and Canada.
Christian Singles Exchange, Box 83211, San Diego, CA 92138, (619) 266-8602. International.
Christian Singles Outreach, Box 9020, Van Nuys, CA 91409. Meet by phone or mail. Profile dating.
Christian Friendship Fellowship, The Ridings, Holberrow Green, Redditch, Worcester, England B96 6SE.
Christian Introductions, 4118 10th Ave. N., Lake Worth, FL 33461. Computer dating service. Dennis Lombard, Director.
Classical Music Lovers Exchange, Box 31, Pelham, NY 10803. (914) 738-3684. T. Montique Conroy, Director.
Club Devotion, Box 549, Dublin, VA 24084, (703) 674-GIRL. Woman from islands.
Club MLF, Box 2152, Loves Pk, IL 61130. Nationwide.
Club Revelation, 16 S. White Rd., San Jose, CA 95127. International.
Col International, Hillsdale, IL 61257. Profile & photo dating.

148

Correspondence Services (continued)

Colortech Image, 7341 Clairemont Mesa Blvd. #106-192, San Diego, CA 92111. Video tapes of South American single women.

Concordia-International Penpals Club, Box 185, Snowdon, Montreal, Canada H3X 3T4.

Dateline, Box 118, Brooklyn, NY 11218, (800) 727-3300. Nationwide matchmaking service. Arthur Goldberg, Director.

Di's Meet People, 6812 Hill Pl, Crystal, MN 55427. Asians & Europeans.

East Meets West, 910 N. Bushnell Ave., Alhambra, CA, (714) 641-7333 or Box 92, Cooper Station, New York, NY 10276. Women from Far East.

Ebony/Ivory Society, Box 4245, West Chicago, IL 60815, (312) 231-2455. Interracial dating service.

FA Worldwide Friendship Society, Box 8851, Karachi-3, Pakistan.

Fantasy, 1812 Grant Ave #713, Novato 94947. Filipinas.

Field's Exclusive Service, 41 E. 42nd St. #1600, NYC 10017, (212) 391-2233. Worldwide, for religious singles, all ages.

Filipinas Video Enterprises, 456 Brook Ave #B, Tooele, UT 84074.

Friends Around the World, Box 3582, Seattle, WA 98328.

Friends By Mail, (800) USA-MATE.

Friends Exchange, Box 297, Tillamook, OR 97141.

Friendship International, 4959 Hollywood, Hollywood, CA 90027, (213) 662-3184.

The Friendship Office, Box 5248, Stn. A, Calgary, AB Canada T2H 1X6. Asian women.

Friends Unlimited
East, Box 1457, Groton, CT 06340.
West, Box 27185, Ft. Worth, TX 76127.

Friends With Pens, Box 6410-C10, Denver, CO 80206. Computer matching according to interests and hobbies.

Global Introductions, Box 2123, San Francisco, CA 94126. Asian women.

The Graduate Single, Box 3602, Lawrence, KS 66044. International. You must have a Bachelor's Degree.

Guiding Light Club, Box 11434, Fort Worth, TX 76109. Nationwide.

Handicap Introductions, Box 48, Coopersburg, PA 18036, (215) 282-1577. For both handicapped and non-handicapped, U.S. & Canada.

Harmony International, Box 1920, Evanston, IL 60204.

Heart Match Intnl, L. Valencia, 2015 Bedle, Linden, NJ 07036.

Home Services, Box 477, Chetwynd, B.C., Canada V0C 1J0. International.

Ideal Companion, Box 7697-H, Albuquerque, NM 87194. South American women.

Identity, Box 315, Royal Oak, MI 48068. Nationwide.

Interamerican Club, 55 Sutter #513, San Francisco, CA 94104. Latin women. Hector Secchi, Director.

Long Distance Romance

Correspondence Services (continued)

Intercontact, Box 12, Toronto, Ontario, Canada M4A 2M8.
International Correspondence, Box 1027, Orangevale, CA 95662.
International Friendship, 7439 La Palma Ave. #555, Buena Pk, CA 90620.
International Introduction Dynasty, 334 N. Central Ave., Glendale, (818) 243-0330. International Introductory Service, (213) 469-3481.
International Love Network, Box 720438, Houston, TX 77272.
International Neighbors, Box 443, Lingsborg, KS 67456.
International Pen Pal Club, Leslie Jacobs, 3024 Secretariat Dr., Atwater, CA 95301.
International Romances, 24194 Amberly, Moreno Valley, (714) 656-2538 or 656-4604.
International Singles Network, 2700 N. Main, Santa Ana, (714) 558-1402.
Intro, 2995 Woodside Rd. #400-136, Woodside, CA 94062. Asian women.
Intro International, Box 163, Lutherville, MD 21093.
Intro Services, 3518 Cahuenga, LA, CA 90068, (213) 876-6200. 5-10 abstracts (75 words each) of your matches are mailed to you at a time. Nationwide, but mainly California.
Japan International, Box 1027, Orangevale, CA 95662.
Jewels of the Orient, Box 1708, Bloomfield, NJ 07003. Asian women.
Jewish Introductions International, 1-800-442-9050. U.S. & Canada. Local & personalized.
Kenner Publications, Box 272124, Tampa, FL 33688.
Latins International, Box 1716, Chula Vista 92012. (619) 425-1867. Latin, Asian, European, American women.
Letterline, Box 30711, Lincoln, NE 68503.
Lew Dick Enterprises, Box 25038, Tamarac, FL 33320, (305) 721-8257. International.
Lifemates, Box 56953, Phoenix, AZ 85079, (602) 973-9676. Asian women.
Makati Productions, Box 203533L, San Diego, CA 92120, (619) 281-2270. Videotapes of Phillipine women.
Matchline USA, (516) 933-1320. Computer dating. Nationwide.
Matchmakers, Box 18018, Memphis, TN 38181.
Matchmakers International, 701 N.E. 67th St., Miami, FL 33138.
National Advisors Astrological Dating Service, Box 6410, Denver, CO 80206. Computer dating, matches by astrological profiles.
National Singles Paper, Box 8645, Denver, Co 80201.
Nationwide Exchange, Box 1576, Timmins, Ontario, P4N 7W7, Canada. U.S. and Canada. V.A. Ferri, Director.
Nationwide Friendship Exchange, Box 12, Wells River, VT 05081.
Nationwide Introductions, Box 5637, Reno, NV 89513.
Nationwide Singles, Box 1472, Ashland, KY 41105.
North America Matchmaker Service matches Asian women with American men, (415) 585-0919. Matchmaking.

Long Distance Romance

Correspondence Services (continued)

Oriental Beauty, Box 691693, Hollywood, CA 90069.
Oriental Introductions, (406) 526-3565. Video tapes.
Oriental Ladies, Box 875323, Los Angeles 90087.
The Oriental Listing, Box 1920, Evanston, IL 60204, (312) 731-8769.
Orient-West Singles Encounter 11343 Biona Dr., Mar Vista, (213) 391-0193 or 391-2851.
Over 40 Club Newsletter, Box 309, West Chester, PA 19380.
Pals, Box 4457, Ft. Lauderdale, FL 33338.
Pearls of the Orient, Pal Dept. 19, Blanca, CO 81123, (303) 379-3228. Filipinas. Photos & video. Directed by Kurt Kirstein.
Pen Pal Newsletter, 6318 Van Buren, Hammond, IN 46324.
Penpals, Box 443, Lindsborg, KS 67456.
Perlas International, Box 906, Los Banos, CA 93635. Filipinas.
Philippine Nexus, Box 1751, Alameda, CA 94501.
PIC-AIM, Box 652, Easley, SC 29641.
Playtime International, Box 3355, York, PA 17402.
Private Search, Box Intro, Studio City, CA 91604.
Romance International, Box 727, Eatonville, WA 98328.
Rural Network, Rt.2, Gays Mills, WI 54631.
Sampaugita, Box 742, Jasper, IN 47546, (812) 482-3064. Filipinas.
Sandy Sandmire, 584-M Fry St., St. Paul MN 55104. Philippine & American women.
Scanna International, Box 4, Pittsford, NY 14534. Americans, Scandinavians, English, Australians.
September Singles Club, Box 84, St. Ann 63074. Matchmaking. 50+.
Show Business, Chefredaktion, Jos Kempa-019, Route de Luxembourg, 9125 Schieren, Luxemborg.
Signal International, 522, P.O. Box 150, Fl-15111, Lahti, Finland. Scandinavian & foreign singles. Photos, addresses, pen pals.
Single Adults Intro Club, Box 17994, Atlanta, GA 30316.
Single Booklovers, Box 117, Gradyville, PA 19039, (215) 358-5049. Bob & Ruth Leach, Directors. US, Canada, foreign countries.
Single Christian Correspondence, Box 45, Sanders, AZ 86512.
Singles Connection & Network (SCAN), Box 4561, Parkersburg, WV 26104. Profile Dating Service. Louise Chambers, Editor.
The Singles Directory, Box 667, Azusa 91702, (818) 334-4077. Free profiles, all ages.
Singles Exchange, Box 43217, Louisville, KY 40243, (502) 245-6585. Michelle Lee, Editor. Profile Dating Service.
Singles International, Metropolitan Plaza, 2480 S. Main St., Salt Lake City, UT 84114. European singles.

Long Distance Romance

Correspondence Services (continued)

Singles International, Box 1132, NYC 10023.
   Asian women, (212) 787-3111
   Hispanic Women, (212) 787-3155
   Black & White Network, (212) 787-3177.
   Super Achievers Club for MDs, JDs, MA's, etc., (212) 787-2899.
Singles International, Box 74758, Los Angeles, CA 90004.
Singles International, Rt. 2, Box 234, Owatonna, MN 55060.
Single Profile Nexus, Box 748A, Orlando, FL 32854.
South American Service, Ces, Apartado Aereo 1814, Cali, Colombia.
State to State Date, Box 17861-14, Columbus, OH 43207.
Sunshine International Correspondence, Box 260, N.Hollywood, CA
   91603 or Box 5500, Kailua-Kona, HI 96745, (808) 325-7707. Asian
   women.
Sweet & Sexy Seniors, Box 8691, La Jolla 92038, (619) 584-5902.45+.
Talk of the World, Box 1442, Des Plaines, IL 60018.
T.E. Thacker's Pen Pal Club, 2018 Red Oak Dr., Irving, TX 75060.
T.K. Publications, Box 1411, Canton, OH 44708.
Today's Single, Box 11394, Kansas City, MO 64112.
Transcor, Box 2321, Manila, Philippines. Filipinas.
Trans-Pacific Dream Makers, Inc., (714) 838-5683.
TravelMate, (619) 258-0220. Computer Dating Service that matches
   singles nationwide who like to travel.
TrueMatch, Box 18000-5, Las Vegas, NV 89114. Monthly personal ads
   and photos. Nationwide.
Unique Singles, Box 15861, Stn F, Ottawa, Ontario, Canada K2C 397.
United Singles Access, Box 62, Attica, IN 47918. Nationwide.
USA Christian Dating Service, Box 193, Camby, IN 46113.
US-Asian Agency, Box 915, Temple City, (818) 447-9000.
US-Asian Connection, 3342 S. Sand Hill #9-227, Las Vegas, NV 89121.
USA/Worldwide Pen Pals, AIM, Box 116, Goldsboro, NC 27533.
Videorient, Box 22-32, Bangkok 10220, Thailand.
World Friends, Box 15010-C1, Sacramento, CA 95851.
World International, Box 68013, Virginia Beach, VA 23455.
World Wide Club, Box 2001, Chicago 60690.
Worldwide Correspondence Magazine, Lawanda's, Box A 81331, Mobile,
   AL 36608.
World Wide Singles, Box 1472, Ashland, KY 41105.
Yellowphone, (900) USA LINK. Telephone personal ads. Nationwide.
Zodiac Singles Cklub, 72 N. Clinton, Poughkeepsie, NY 12601.

Long Distance Romance

Personal Ads

Another method for meeting singles from other areas is by placing a personal ad in a publication in that locale. See the Advertising for Love Chapter. Below are publications that specialize in personal ads from across the nation.

American Jewish Singles Magazine, Box 728, Bloomfield, CT 06002, (203) 243-1514. U.S. (mainly New England) & Canada.

Carol's Singles Org., Box 998, Rootstown, OH 44272, (216) 296-8051.

Chocolate Singles, Box 333, Jamaica, NY 11413, (718) 978-4800. Barbara Miles, Editor. Monthly personals for middle class black singles.

Concerned Singles Newsletter, Box 555, Stockbridge, MA 01262. Monthly personals for peace-oriented singles.

The Connector, Box 24331, Omaha, NE 68124, (402) 551-7257. Jewish.

Cupid's Destiny, Box 5637, Reno, NV 89513. K. Williams, Publisher. National personal ads & photos.

Homestead Hotline, 720 Morrow Ave., Clayton, NJ 08312.

Jewish Singles Magazine, Box 247, Newton, MA 02159, (617) 244-5677.

Mailbox Swapshop, Box 652, Easley, SC 29641. Worldwide.

National Singles Register, 13821 San Antonio, Norwalk 90650, (213) 868-8259. Largest collection of personal ads in the U.S. (1500 ads).

Singles Choice, Box 118, Brooklyn, NY 11218, (718) 941-7550. Monthly.

Singles Monthly, Box 121999, Ft. Worth 76121, (817) 831-1895.

ADVERTISING FOR LOVE

Are you the adventurous type? If so you might try placing or responding to a personal ad. According to US Magazine, June 1, 1987, "each year at least 10,000 people who meet through personals get married" in the United States each year.

It is now socially acceptable to both place and respond to personal ads. According to the US article, "2 million men and women run personal ads each year, and over 10 million answer them."

Most newspapers accept personal ads, as well as many magazines. A number of singles publications are listed below which are also ideal for personal ads.

Should you place an ad or respond to one? Assuming you can afford it, the ideal way to use the personal ad columns is to place an ad yourself. The reason for this is that if you only respond to ads, you may be one of dozens of people responding to a particular ad. The odds are against your being selected by the person placing the ad. If you place the ad however, you're in the driver's seat. You can choose from the many different types of people who will hopefully be responding to your ad.

What should you say in your ad? Honesty is the best

154

policy. Tell who you are and who you are looking for. Be aware, however, that a price has to be paid for honesty. Dishonest people who exaggerate their attractiveness are going to get many more responses than you. The advantage of being honest, however, is that people won't be disappointed when they meet you.

Try to be original, clever, and funny if possible. You'll get many more times the responses than if your ad is serious and similar to others. Make your ad stand out.

Avoid being too specific about who you are looking for. Remember, each characteristic or quality that you require diminishes the number of responses. The less people you have to choose from the less likely you will find a person who is right for you.

On the other hand, if you're too vague (e.g., "I want to meet someone nice"—who's going to admit they're not nice?) you'll get a lot of responses that are totally unsuitable for you. So try to strike a happy medium.

If physical appearance is important to you, request that responding letters include a recent photograph. Ask them to describe themselves physically, emotionally, educationally, etc. as thoroughly as possible. Be sure to send them a photo of yourself also.

How do you select who to meet from those who respond to your ad? Some people keep an open mind and meet everyone who responds to their ad. They enjoy meeting people and are willing to take a chance. Others are very selective. They correspond through the mail and converse over the phone to the point that they feel fairly confident that they're going to like the person before they schedule a face-to-face meeting. Either method works.

Where should you meet? That depends on how cautious you are. If you're afraid of meeting a weirdo you might want to meet at a public place during the day. This is obviously a lot safer than giving someone your home address and telephone number. Do what feels comfortable to you.

What kind of singles are you liable to meet through

Advertising for Love

personal ads? The same kind of people you'll meet anywhere else. Some will be winners and some will be losers. Your job is to choose wisely so you wind up with someone appropriate for you.

Hopefully you will approach personal ads in a spirit of fun. Here's your opportunity to meet a lot of nice people like yourself who are looking to meet someone special for a romantic relationship. So don't be too serious. And don't be disappointed if you don't meet Mr. or Ms. Right. Just have a good time and keep trying.

If you are placing an ad yourself get a sample copy of some of the publications listed in this chapter and compare them with your local newspaper. Determine which publication has the most ads of people you'd like to meet at the most reasonable cost. That's the publication that's right for your personal ad.

Personal Ad Directory

Call of the Wild Radio Reporter, KORK Radio, 127 E. Napa St., Sonoma 95476, (707) 996-9125. Free personal ads.

The Dating Magazine, Box 1357, Marina 93933, (408) 646-0717 publishes low cost personal ads for Monterey & Santa Cruz Counties.

Dollar Saver, 37365 Centralmont, Fremont 94536, (415) 792-4052, publishes a low cost "Companions Column" each week.

Fairfield Daily Republic, Box 47, Fairfield 94533, (707) 425-4646. Singles Connection section daily.

Goodtimes, Box 1139, Santa Cruz 95061, (408) 426-8430, publishes personal ads weekly.

Lifestyle, 421 W. MacArthur Blvd., Oakland 94609, (415) 420-1381. David Sawle, Publisher.

Metro, 410 S. 1st St., San Jose 95113, (408) 298-8000. Weekly.

97-Match, (415) 976-2824. Voice personal ads only. $2 plus toll, if any.

976-Date, Voice personal ads only. $2 + toll charge if any.

Open Mind, 5271 Dry Creek Rd., Napa 94558, (707) 255-5022. Single File section. Quarterly. Free ads.

Pacific Sun, 21 Corte Madera Ave., Mill Valley 94941, (415) 383-4500.

Photointroductions, 928 Snowberry Ct., Hayward 94544. Publishes personal ads with passport photo.

San Francisco Bay Guardian, 2700 19th St., San Francisco 94110, (415) 824-7660.

Personal Ad Directory (continued)

San Francisco Weekly, 230 Ritch St., San Francisco 94107, (415) 541-0700.

San Francisco Focus, 680 8th St., San Francisco 94103, (415) 553-2821.

San Francisco Magazine, 45 Belden Pl., San Francisco 94104, (415) 982-2700.

Selections, (415) 391-0757. Voice personal ads only. Dial 1-900-999-3700. 89 cents per minute.

Single Again, Box 384, Union City 94587, (415) 656-0322.

Singles Network, 1-900-844-6600. Voice personal ads only. 95 cents per minute.

Trellis Singles Magazine, 1260 Persian Dr. #6, Sunnyvale 94089, (408) 747-1455 or (415) 941-2900. Bimonthly. Publishes more personal ads per issue than any other periodical in Northern California. Paul Reese, Publisher. Voice personal ads, (900) 844-4445. 89 cents per minute.

Whole Valley Catalogue, 2801 Ygnacio Valey Rd., Walnut Creek, (415) 939-3777.

Advertising for Love

DATING SERVICES

Suppose you hate going to lectures, classes, dances, and parties, and you don't like outdoor sports? What do you do? Why not join a dating service? They're usually more expensive than the non-profit singles clubs, but you get a professional organization working for you to increase your chances of meeting someone special.

There are many dating services to choose from ranging from the very inexpensive (often as little as $30 for a three month membership) to the ones requiring thousands of dollars. You can find out about them by reading the Introductions or Business Personals sections of your daily newspaper. Or you can contact the dating services listed below.

There are two basic categories of dating services: Matchmaking and Self-Service.

Matchmaking Dating Services

Matchmaking Dating Services do not allow you to directly choose from membership files. Instead, the service goes through the files looking for a match for you. These services may be divided into two categories: Computer Dating Services and Personal Introduction Services.

Computer Dating Services

With computer dating you fill out a questionnaire describing yourself and the person you want to meet. The computer matches you with several people whom you can telephone. If you prefer, you can wait for your "match" to telephone you.

The main advantage of computer dating is that it is usually quite cheap (often only $30 for three months). Ideally, this enables the service to enroll a vast membership. The computer then can go through the membership files efficiently to find the one person who has all the qualities you seek. Of course, in real life this doesn't always happen. Some computer dating services have so few members that the computer is only a joke. You could personally thumb through the files in minutes without a computer.

"Garbage in, garbage out" is an old computer adage. In the case of computer dating, it means that frequently people lie when they fill out the questionnaires. Don't blame the computer if it matches you up with someone 5 foot 3 when you wanted someone over 6 feet tall. The computer doesn't administer a lie detector test.

What kinds of lies do singles tell the computer? The most common lies from men pertain to their height and occupation. Men know that women like to date tall men who have a status job and a high income. Women tend to lie about their age and their weight, since most single men prefer young, slim women.

Personal Introduction Services

Many matchmaking services scoff at their competitors who use computers. They claim that you can't program a computer to find a person for you to spend the rest of your life. That takes the "human touch". Personal Introduction Services claim to have an intimate knowledge of their members and suggest they can do a better job of matching

Dating Services

than a computer. Unfortunately, these Personal Introduction Services charge a great deal more than Computer Dating Services for using a "personal touch" (from $200 to thousands of dollars).

Think of dating someone through this kind of service as being similar to a blind date, except instead of a friend matching you up for free you are paying a professional to do that for you. Here you are relying on the intuition of the matchmaker who interviews you personally and then makes recommendations on who you should meet.

Self-Service Dating Services

Self-Service Dating Services are often critical of matchmaking services. They argue that it is ridiculous to expect someone else to find the right person for you for a romantic relationship. How can the matchmaker or computer know what turns you on? Self-service dating services allow you to go through their membership files to find the right person. There are several types of Self-Service Dating Services:
Profile Dating Services
Photo Dating Services
Video Dating Services

Profile Dating Services

Profile dating services are usually the least expensive of the self-service dating services. As a member you will receive a collection of profiles of other members. You decide which members you wish to contact and other members have the same opportunity to contact you. One word of caution: some of the information in profiles may be fictitious. As with computer dating, members sometimes lie about age, height, weight, looks, and occupation.

Photo Dating Services

Wouldn't it be nice if you could see a photo of each person next to their profile before deciding to meet them? That's the logic behind the photo dating services. They allow you to go through photo albums of the members. Alongside the photo is a full page of information about the person. When you see someone you'd like to meet, the club contacts them on your behalf so they can come down and view your photo and profile sheet. If there is mutual attraction the telephone numbers are released so the two of you can arrange to meet one another.

As with profile dating and computer dating, be prepared for members of photo dating to occasionally lie about themselves. The added dimension of deception in photo dating pertains to the photo. Often it is not current. The slim young woman or handsome distinguished man you think you're going to meet may be only a memory.

Video Dating Services

With Video dating you have all the advantages of photo dating plus the opportunity to see and hear your prospective date on television before you go out. There are many advantages. For one thing, you have more than a snapshot to base your decision. Even the Hunchback of Notre Dame would look good if you photographed him properly! With video dating you get the opportunity to watch the person for five minutes from many different camera angles. You also get to view their body language, hear their voice, and get a feel for their personality. You are more likely to choose the right person through video dating than through photo dating. The catch is that you have to pay more for this added video dimension.

Dating Services

How to Choose a Dating Service

There are many things to consider when choosing a dating service:

1. How long have they been in business? Over 90% of small businesses in the United States fail in their first year. This is also true for dating services. Joining a brand new dating service can be risky. **Warning**: you may find that many of the dating services listed in this guide have gone under since publication.
2. How many active members do they have? Some dating services claim to have hundreds or thousands of members, but many of these may be unavailable due to marriage, committed relationships, heavy work schedule, moving out of the area.
3. How many active members do they have in the geographical area you prefer? It does you no good to join a service with thousands of members if none of them live close enough to you to facilitate meeting them. Local dating services usually have a preponderance of members in the immediate vicinity of their offices. The further away you live from their offices the less likely they are to have many potential partners for you. With the matchmaking services you will frequently find that if you limit them to a small geographical radius they will not be able to find even one person who has the qualities you seek in a romantic partner. They will pressure you to "expand your horizons" and date people outside of your immediate area.
4. What percentage of the members are men and what percentage are women? Usually the vast majority of almost any dating service will be male. Single women tend to be reluctant to join dating services either because they feel more vulnerable than men or because they tend to earn lower incomes than men.
5. What percentage of the members are in the age range you prefer? Most dating services have a surplus of young men in their 20s and women over 40. Dating services are

usually good investments for women in their 20s and early 30s and for men over 40, because those are the age categories in shortest supply. Many dating services offer free or reduced price memberships for women in their 20s and early 30s.

6. What is the cost of the service? There is often a wide difference in prices from one service to the next.

7. How long is the membership? Are there alternative membership plans?

8. What are the privileges and limitations of each membership plan?

9. If it is a photo or video dating service, are you committed enough to go down to their office each time someone selects you in order to view their photo or video?

10. Do you feel comfortable with the process employed and the people working at the dating service office?

11. Does the dating service have a good reputation? If you don't know any of the members and therefore don't have any testimonials, what does the Better Business Bureau or local Chamber of Commerce have to say about the dating service?

An additional question is, "Do I want to have the opportunity to see what the other person looks like before I go out with them?" If so, you would best join a photo dating or video dating service. Usually computer dating and profile dating services do not provide a photo of the person you are to meet. Often matchmakers do not provide a photo either.

Of course the flip side of the coin is, "Do I want the other person to see what I look like before we meet?" If you are not photogenic, you may not get your money's worth joining a service where a photo or videotape of yourself is seen **before** the other person decides whether or not to meet you. If you have a "heart of gold" and communicate well through the mail or over the phone, you might be better off joining a service where external beauty is not a factor before the initial meeting.

Dating Services

Many singles fail to properly investigate and analyze the dating services they join. They end up feeling "ripped off". If you take the precautions listed above you can make a wise choice and get your money's worth. Shopping for a dating service is no different than shopping for a used car. Caveat emptor!

The dating services listed below enable you to meet someone close to your home. Other services help you to correspond with singles of the opposite sex throughout the U.S. and across the seas. See the chapter on Long Distance Romance.

DATING SERVICE DIRECTORY

Nationwide Dating Services

Please note: even though the services in this section are nationwide, they will introduce you to singles in your geographical area.

Datique, 1347 Divisadero, San Francisco 94115. Low cost profile dating.
Dateline, 1-800-727-3300. Low cost matchmaking. Many offices:
  Northeast, 132 W. 24th, NY, NY 10011
  Southeast, 4801 E. Independence Bl #1000, Charlotte, NC 28212
  East Central, 18055 James Couzens Hwy, Detroit, MI 48235
  North Central, 39 S. LaSalle St., Chicago, IL 60603
  South Central, 3540 Summer Ave #307, Memphis, TN 38122
  Midwest, 7001 N. Locust #102, Kansas City, MO 64118
  Northwest, Seattle 1st Natl Bank Bldg #3618, Seattle, WA 98154
  Southwest, 8609 NW Plaza #300, Dallas, TX 75225
  West Coast, 256 S. Robertson Bl, Beverly Hills 90211
Fields Dating Service, 41 E. 42nd St. #1600, NYC 10017. (212) 391-2233. For religious singles, 18-30.
International Society of Introduction Services, 1028 E. Juneau Ave #5, Milwaukee 53202, (414) 272-5595. Bob Aldrich. Non-profit.
Jewish Introductions International, 264 H ST #8110, Dept 113, Blaine, WA 98230, (800) 442-9050. Barry Turner. Jewish only.
Matchline USA, (516) 933-1320. Computer dating.
Someone for Everyone, Tod House, Box 4769, Chicago 60680. Profile dating.
Zipcode Date Club, Box 84, St. Ann, MO 63074. Matchmaking.

Dating Services

Local Services

ANTIOCH
  Connections, Box 3241, Antioch 94531, (415) 778-6883. Matchmaking after psychological testing.
CAPITOLA
  Compatibility Plus, Box 1235, Capitola, CA 95010, (408) 462-1457. Computer dating. Allan Gleicher.
  New Friends, Box 1235, Capitola, CA 95010, (408) 462-5662. Computer dating for singles with herpes.
CONCORD
  Matters of the Heart, 3015 Grant St., Concord 94520, (415) 676-7542. Matchmaking. Maria Isola.
  Video Introductions, 1950-D Market, Concord 94520, (415) 676-2399. Video dating. Norm Mickey.
CUPERTINO
  Dinner Introduction & Networking Group, Box 1510, Cupertino 95015, (408) 257-1450. Matchmaking and dinner club.
HAYWARD
  Photointroductions, 928 Snowberry Ct., Hayward 94544.
  Select Introduction Service, 24032 Hesperian #161, Hayward 94545. Matchmaking.
MILL VALLEY
  The Right One, 591 Redwood Hwy, Mill Valley 94941, (415) 381-3283. Video & computer dating. Also social events and travel discounts.
MONTEREY
  Foto Date, (408) 372-2280. Photos of your matches are mailed to you.
MOUNTAIN VIEW
  Great Expectations, 2065 Landing, M.V. 94043, (415) 964-2985. Video.
NAPA
  Confidential Dating Service, Napa, (707) 255-0414. Matchmaking.
  Patricia Moore Group, (707) 579-3037. Matchmaking.
  Reliable Singles, Box 3706, Napa, (707) 252-2002.
OAKLAND
  Opposites, Box 3845, Oakland 94609, (415) 654-6565. Matchmaking (interracial) and parties. 9 months/$150. Chandler Fairchild.
  Something in Common, 484 Lake Park Ave. #272, Oakland 94610, (415) 530-6903. Partners and pals for every interest: theater, single parent outings, hiking, movies, symphony, skiing, musicians. All ages.
  Unique Dating Service, 484 Lake Park Ave. #226, Oakland 94610, (415) 420-5880. Matchmaking. $45 for three matches.

Dating Services

PLEASANT HILL
  Big Alternatives, 363 Gladys Dr., Pleasant Hill 94523, (415) 676-3635.
  Matchmaking for overweight singles.
PLEASANTON
  Upscale Choices, 4625 1st St #230, Pleas. 94566, (415) 462-6913. Self-
  service photo dating. Aletha Dier.
REDWOOD CITY
  Sunrise Dating Service, 368-2446. Self service photo dating.
SAN FRANCISCO
  Amicus, 1347 Divisadero, S.F. 94115, (415) 359-6900. Photo dating.
  Datique, 1347 Divisadero, San Francisco 94115, (415) 359-6900 or (408)
  295-8600. Profile dating. Marty Siders, Linda Simmons.
  Foto Date, (415) 937-3285. Photos of your matches are mailed to you.
  The Jewish Connection, 3569 Sacramento, S.F. 94118, 221-5683.
  Matchmaking.
  John Wingo & Associates, 44 Montgomery St., San Francisco 94104,
  (415) 955-2722. Matchmaking.
  May-December Introduction Svc, 2940 16th St.#308, SF 94103, Matches
  younger men with older women. Women pay no fee. Constance Polk.
  New Partners, SF Jewish Community Center, 3200 California, S.F.
  94118, (415) 346-6040. Matchmaking. $125 fee. Barrett Moore.
  The Original Matchmaker, 887-1010.
  The Patricia Moore Group, Box 31130, San Francisco 94131, (415)
  337-1551 or 321-9655. Matchmaking.
  Perfect Strings, Box 22291, San Francisco 94122, (415) 566-7774.
  Matching by similar musical interests for attending symphony,
  concerts, opera, ballet or for playing and singing your favorite music.
  SelectraDate of Northern California, Box 11149, S.F. 94101, (800) 232-
  3283. Computer dating. $55. Minimum of 5 matches.
  Singles & Sidekicks, 285-0843. Introductions for single parents.
  Yellow Phone, 870 Market #428, S.F. 94102, (415) 765-4321 (S.F.) (408)
  737-7770 (Sunnyvale), (415) 944-0744 (Walnut Creek), (800) 538-7289.
  Zachary Pavlides. Computer dating & personalized matchmaking.
  Telephone personal ads with personalized attention, (900) USA LINK.
SAN JOSE
  Ananda Astrological Matching Service, 99 Wilson, S.J. 95126, (408) 947-
  5958.
  Brown Sugar Soul Singles, Box 32595, San Jose 95152. $35. Black dating
  service. 21-45.
  The Dating Center, (408) 479-9635. Photo matchmaking.
  Foto Date, 913 Willow #101, S.J. 95125, 286-7000 (24 hrs).
  Matchmaking. Photos of your matches are mailed to you.
  More to Love, 395-7417. Big men & women and those who love them.
  2010 Singles Club, (408) 253-6200. Self-service photo dating.

Dating Services

166

SAN MATEO
  Venus Computer Matchmaking Service, 2228 S. El Camino #80, S.M. 94403.
SAN RAFAEL
  California Singles, 4 Highland Ave., San Rafael 94901, (415) 456-5683. Non-profit, free profile dating.
SANTA CLARA
  Futures, 4675 Stevens Creek #110, S.C. 95051, 243-3848. Video dating.
SANTA ROSA
  Enjoy Life, Box 2593, S.R. 95405, 575-1006. Matchmaking, seminars.
SAUSALITO
  Barbara Tackett, 3030 Bridgeway, Sausalito 94965, (415) 927-1562. Personal Relationship Counseling & Matchmaking.
  Great Expectations, 2330 Marinship Way #105, Sausalito 94965, (415) 332-2353. Video dating.
SONOMA
  Select Singles, Box 350, Sonoma 95476. Profile dating.
SUNNYVALE
  John Wingo & Associates, 1250 Oakmead Parkway, Sunnyvale 94086, (408) 730-6806. Matchmaking.
UNION CITY
  Christian Singles, Box 203, Union City, CA 94587.
  Kings & Queens, 4719 Loretta, U.C. 94587, (415) 489-4395. Jo Ann Larez.
WALNUT CREEK
  Foto Date, 1615 Bonanza #207, W.C. 94596, (415) 937-3283. Photos of your matches are mailed to you.
  Great Expectations, 1280 Civic Dr., 1656 Oakland Bl #200, Walnut Creek 94596, (415) 944-4900. Video dating.
  John Wingo & Associates, 1990 N. California Blvd., Walnut Creek 94596, (415) 932-7057. Matchmaking.
  Marriage Minded, Box 4313, Walnut Creek 94596. Matchmaking.
  Successful Singles International, 2175 N. California #150, W.C. 94596. Matchmaking.
  The Professional Connection, 778-6883. Martin Schaaf. Matchmaking with psychological screening.
MISCELLANEOUS
  The Activity Connection, American Meeting Svc, 976-3283. Computer matching by 130 activities, via telephone. $2 + toll, if any.
  Ethnic Connections, (415) 778-6883. Matchmaking for Black, Asian, Hispanic singles.
  Introphoto, 796-1706. Photos mailed to your home.
  New Age Connections, 861-3554, x26. Matchmaking.

Dating Services

SINGLES CLUBS

There are hundreds of clubs in the Bay Area created specifically to meet the need of singles. Most people who attend these clubs are hoping to meet someone special for a romantic relationship. A smaller number aren't ready for romance (they're bouncing back from an unpleasant experience with the opposite sex), but they're still looking for new friends.

What is the typical age of people who attend singles clubs? That varies from club to club. Most singles who attend are 40+. Usually there is a shortage of men at these clubs, since there is a surplus of women in America in the 40+ age bracket. There are some clubs, however, that cater specifically to singles in their 20s or 30s. The **Singles Club Directory** that follows specifies which clubs attract younger singles.

Many people refuse to go to singles clubs. You may be one of them. You probably have one or more reasons for this:

1. **"Only losers go to singles clubs"**. The fact of the matter is that you get a cross-section of people at singles clubs. Some are winners and some are losers, as in any other social situation. You are just as likely to run into losers at work, at church, on the beach, or at private dinner parties. If you want to avoid meeting losers, stay home. Otherwise, take your chances at singles clubs.

2. **"I went to a singles club once and didn't meet anybody."**
That's usually the case for everyone. You can't expect to
fall in love the first time you attend a singles club. Keep on
going anyway. If you visit singles clubs often enough
eventually you'll meet the kind of people you want.
3. **"I don't want to broadcast to the world that I'm single and
looking."** Here's pride rearing its ugly head. Are you
going to let it get in the way of meeting new friends or a
romantic partner?

There are many different types of singles clubs and
organizations:

1. Church clubs
2. Dance clubs
3. Outdoor & sports clubs
4. Parents clubs
5. Exclusive clubs
6. Miscellaneous singles clubs
   A description of each category follows.

1. Church Clubs

Most singles clubs meet at churches. There are several
reasons for this. First, the church usually provides the
meeting site at low cost. Secondly, a church is a very safe
environment for meeting people. Single women in particular
feel more comfortable meeting someone at a church than at
a bar or hotel. Third, many churches are committed to the
Singles Ministry, that is, reaching out to single people in the
area to help them meet their spiritual, social, and emotional
needs.

Church-sponsored singles clubs fall into two categories:
religiously oriented and secular. A religiously oriented club
usually features worship services and/or Bible study.
Obviously, if you are a non-religious single, you might feel
uncomfortable attending. Most church-sponsored singles
clubs, however, are more secular in their orientation.

Typically they sponsor lectures, discussions, potlucks, picnics, parties, dances, trips, and sports. You will rarely hear any mention of religion at their activities. It is also important to realize that you do not have to be affiliated with a particular faith in order to attend these church singles clubs.

Catholic Singles Clubs

There was a time when churches were negative towards divorced people, particularly the Catholic Church. This is no longer true. Separated & Divorced Catholic Support Groups meet at churches throughout America. Typically they have a free weekly support group. In addition they often sponsor parties, potlucks, and dances. The Catholic Church also sponsors **Beginning Experience**, which is a weekend retreat for newly separated, divorced, and widowed. Catholic Alumni Clubs, for college graduates eligible to marry within the Catholic Church, are located in most major cities in the U.S.

Protestant Singles Clubs

Most Protestant denominations sponsor singles activities, particularly Presbyterians, Methodists, Lutherans, Baptists, Assembly of God, and Mormons. Often their groups are called FOCAS (Fellowship of Christian Adult Singles) or FOCUS (Fellowship of Christian United Singles).

Jewish Singles Clubs

Jewish Community Centers (JCC) almost always have singles clubs. Jewish synagogues and temples also frequently sponsor singles clubs. In addition, the JCC is similar to a YMCA or YWCA in terms of a whole host of activities such as lectures, discussions, dancing, swimming, and volleyball. These are great ways to meet people. JCCs in large cities also operate JASSline, a 24 hour recording of Jewish singles activities.

170

Unitarian Singles Clubs

What do you do if you're comfortable going to Catholic, Protestant, or Jewish places of worship? Go to the Unitarian Church. Unitarians don't have any dogmas, so we're all theoretically Unitarian. Most Unitarian churches have singles clubs.

2. Dance Clubs

Dancing is a great way to meet other singles. The perfect opening line is "Wanna dance?" It's a socially acceptable way to approach a complete stranger and ask for three minutes of their time. While you can dance at ballrooms, night clubs, bars, and discos, you might prefer to join a singles club that specializes in dancing.

Square dancing is a good example. Bachelors 'n Bachelorettes is a national square dancing associations with chapters throughout America. Numerous other singles clubs specialize in square dancing. Folk dancing is usually featured at Jewish Community Centers. While not limited to singles, folk dancing is a great way to meet people.

Many singles clubs specialize in ballroom dancing. Singles Club Association of California (SCAC), for example, has chapters throughout the state that feature ballroom. Most singles clubs also sponsor dances to contemporary music.

"But I've got two left feet", you object. No sweat. There are dance classes in most areas that will teach you everything from ballroom to disco. Men in particular would be wise to sign up for these classes, because most women love dancing and complain that it is difficult to find a good dance partner. Make sure you go to a class that caters to single people rather than couples. You will effortlessly meet new people each time that instructor advises you to change partners.

3. Outdoor & Sports Clubs

Outdoor & Sports Clubs feature hiking, bicycling, river rafting, etc. An example is the Sierra Club, which is not a singles club but has singles clubs under its banner. Loners on Wheels has chapters nationwide. Members are predominantly 50+ and own Recreational Vehicles.

There is a league of singles ski clubs in the Bay Area. What if you don't ski? Join anyway. The rumor is that 30% of the members don't ski! They're just looking for an excuse to meet new friends.

4. Single Parents Clubs

Do you have kids? Sometimes they can cramp your social life when you can't find a babysitter. But for every cloud there's a silver lining. Parents Without Partners (PWP), has over 700 chapters throughout the U.S. In order to join you have to be the single parent of a living child. Your child could be 50 years old. You're still eligible to join PWP, and you don't even have to have custody of your 50 year old!

PWP sponsors dozens of activities for singles each month. Some are family-oriented and others are for adults only. To learn more about PWP call the local chapter listed in the white pages of your phone book. The first step is to attend an orientation meeting (free). If you aren't a single parent you are still invited to attend their monthly open dances.

5. "Exclusive" Clubs

What do you do if you're a snob and want to meet "quality singles"? There are many clubs throughout the nation that cater specifically to single "professionals." They often require men to wear a coat & tie. Usually they meet at country clubs, luxurious private homes, or elegant hotels. They also tend to be more expensive than other singles clubs.

These groups seldom turn anyone away for reasons of

income or occupation. The aura of exclusivity, however, tends to attract large numbers of singles to their events.

One group that limits its parties to invited guests is Who's Who International, with chapters in most major U.S. cities.

6. Miscellaneous Clubs

There are also singles clubs specifically for Minorities, Non-Smokers, Overweight Singles, Widows & Widowers.

Starting Your Own Singles Club

Are you unhappy with the choices for singles activities in your area? Why not start your own singles club! Here's the easy way to do it.

1. Enlist the help of your single friends. Call a meeting at your home for anyone who might be interested in helping to start a singles club. "Many hands make light work."
2. Choose a free or inexpensive meeting place or places for your group. Private homes are an obvious option. Your local church is another. Most churches are conscious of the need for a "singles ministry" and are receptive to singles clubs meeting at the church for little or no cost.
3. Publicize your group free through the news media. Most newspapers have an events calendar for non-profit organizations. Local radio and television stations may be willing to run a free public service announcement about your meetings.
4. Make newcomers feel welcome at your meetings. First-timers usually feel uncomfortable and need to be greeted warmly, introduced to other members, and then encouraged to participate in club activities.
5. Be sure to notify me about your singles club for a free listing in the next edition of Singles Guide to the San Francisco Bay Area. Send information to American Singles, 4 Highland Avenue, San Rafael, CA 94901, (415) 459-3817.

The **Singles Club Directory** lists as many singles organizations as I could locate. Unfortunately there are many more that are so obscure that I've never heard of them. Singles Clubs usually don't have an advertising budget, so it's difficult to find out about them other than through word of mouth.

One method for locating other singles clubs in your area is to call your local churches. They usually sponsor a singles club or can tell you of a church nearby that does.

Another method is to check the listings in the calendar or events sections of your local newspapers. Many of the singles clubs receive free listings due to the fact that they are non-profit organizations.

A third method is to attend meetings of different singles clubs and ask people where other clubs meet.

Listed below are singles clubs throughout the San Francisco Bay Area. If you know of any others that were omitted or if you are aware of any inaccuracies please contact us so we can include the information in the next edition of Singles Guide to the San Francisco Bay Area. Our address is: American Singles, 4 Highland Ave., San Rafael 94901, (415) 459-3817.

Please don't be offended if some of the listings below are outdated. When your new telephone directory arrives on your doorstep each year, many of the listings are already obsolete. The same holds true with listings of singles clubs.

One way to keep current about new singles clubs and also find out what the old ones are doing is to check the calendar section of your local newspapers and magazines. Listed below are some publications that feature special sections for singles clubs and their activities.

Publications Featuring Singles Club Activities

Enjoy Life Singles Magazine, Box 2593, Santa Rosa 95405, (707) 575-1006. Violet Young, Editor. North Bay singles calendar each month.

In the Know, 634 Broderick, San Francisco 94117, (415) 346-7783. Juliette Smith, Editor. Monthly. Singles parties and other activities throughout Bay Area.

Lifestyle, 421 W. MacArthur Blvd., Oakland 94609, (415) 420-1381. David Sawle, Publisher. Bi-monthly. Singles parties and other activities throughout Bay Area.

Trellis Singles Magazine, 1260 Persian Dr., Sunnyvale 94089, (415) 941-2900 or (408) 747-1455. Bi-monthly singles calendar throughout Bay Area. Singles events listings over the phone, (900) 844-4445. 89 cents per minute.

SINGLES CLUB DIRECTORY

BAY AREA WIDE

Advanced Degrees, Box 455, Woodland Hills 91365, (800) 333-4937. For singles with master's, doctoral, or professional degrees.

Bay Area Jewish Singles Hiking Club, 30 N. San Pedro Rd., San Rafael 94903, (415) 479-2000 (Jeanette Carr). Hikes throughout the Bay Area. Also activities include trips to Yosemite and skiing. 21+.

BAYJASS (Bay Area Jewish Association of Singles Services), 3200 California, San Francisco 94118, (415) 931-JASS or (408) 356-0058. 24 hour hotline of weekly events for Jewish singles.

California Singles, 4 Highland, San Rafael 94901, (415) 456-5683. Socials, dances, & classes.

Catholic Alumni Club, (415) 344-7952, 441-8470, 447-3312 (Jean) or (408) 479-1846. For singles eligible for marriage within Catholic Church.

Divorced Catholics, Archdiocese of San Francisco, Sister Jane McKinlay, 445 Church, San Francisco 94114, 565-3624. Divorce adjustment program, support groups, socials.

Fairway Singles Golf Club, 830 Rigel, Foster City 94404, 349-8191, 349-5822. Meets at golf courses throughout the Bay Area Saturdays & Sundays. Ron Gabel, Director.

Graduate Degrees, (415) 420-1381. Socials.

International Club Elite (ICE), Box 241512, Los Angeles 90024, (415) 330-8166. Elegant parties throughout California.

March of Dimes Bid for Bachelors, (415) 468-7400. Charity auction of eligible bachelors with a prearranged date package going to the highest female bidder.

Singles Clubs

BAY AREA WIDE (continued)
Near Escapes, Box 3005, San Francisco 94119, 921-1392 (Kay Grant). Visits to museums, aquariums, baseball games, amusement parks. Mainly singles.
Pacific Heights Club, Ed Woods, 808 Post St. #709, San Francisco 94109, 641-4909. Parties. Coat and tie/cocktail dress. Mainly 30s & 40s.
Sierra Singles, Sierra Club, 6014 College, Oakland 94618, 548-0591 (Phil Gale). Hiking, bicycling, camping, parties. 21-40.
Single Travelers, (415) 420-1381 (Dave). Networking, socials.
Solo Sierrans, Sierra Club, 568 Fairmount Ave., Oakland 94624, 658-9977, or 654-4163 (Joe Dorst). 40+. Hiking, backpacking, sailing, potlucks, slide shows throughout Bay Area.
Treasure, 5461 Lawton, Oakland 94618, 655-9990. Lectures, parties, and dances. Mainly 30s and 40s.
Trellis, 1260 Persian #6, Sunnyvale 94089, (415) 941-2900 or (408) 747-1455. Lectures, discussions, dance parties, live big band dances, comedy. Mainly 30s and 40s. Paul Reese.
Who's Who Intl. Natl organ. of singles that sponsors elegant parties by invitation only. Mainly 40+. In Alameda, Contra Costa, Marin, San Francisco, & N. San Mateo counties contact Alyce Dunn, 111 E. Court, Foster City, (415) 570-6847. In Monterey, Santa Clara, S. San Mateo, and Santa Cruz counties contact Joy Smith at 6412 Camden, San Jose 95120, (408) 997-3141.
Young Jewish Singles, Jewish Comm. Fed., Young Adult Division, 121 Steuart, San Francisco 94105, 777-0411. Blue Monday dances. Cultural, social, & fund-raising. 21-39.

ALAMEDA
Island City Singles, 1148 Fleet St., Oakland 94610, (415) 865-5024 or 530-4326. Public speaking, Mondays, 7pm, Citicorp Bldg Conference Rm, Haight at Webster, Alameda.
St. Joseph's Parish Ctr Separated & Divorced Catholic Support Group, 1119 Lafayette, Alameda, (415) 865-0653. Potlucks, odd Thursdays, 7pm. Discussion & support group, even Fridays, 7:30pm.

ALBANY
Single Adoptive Parents, Sandy McQuillin, 1309-B Solano Ave., Albany 94706, (415) 236-4064. Workshops for single people who want to be parents.

ANTIOCH
1st Assembly of God Church Singles, 640 E. Tregallas, Antioch 94509, (415) 757-1837. Sundays, 9:30am. Tuesdays, 7pm.
Parents Without Partners, Box 1317, Antioch 94509, (415) 757-3591.
Separated & Divorced Catholic Support Group, Antioch, Bob Arieta, 197 Oakview, Pleasant Hill 94523, (415) 939-1356.

Singles Clubs

176

APTOS
Assembly of God Singles, 7200 Freedom Blvd., Aptos 95003, (408) 688-3312 (June Barber).
Twin Lakes Baptist Church, 2701 Cabrillo College Dr., Aptos 95003. 3 singles clubs: 1. New Life (mainly 45-65), (408) 475-5284. Sunday school, 9:45am. Bible study, Wednesdays, 7pm. Also socials. 2. Open Door, (mainly 21-40), (408) 475-5284. Sunday school, 9:45am. Bible study for women, Tuesdays, 7pm, 160 Loma Place, Aptos. Dinner & Bible study for men, Thursdays, 6:45pm, 310 Monte, Santa Cruz. Bible study for both men and women Wednesdays, 7pm, at the Church. Also game nights, dinners, sports, beach. 3. Single Parents Support Group (mainly 21-35), (408) 475-5284. Potlucks, 4th Fridays, 6:30pm, at church.
BELMONT
Just for Single Travelers Club, 1601 El Camino, Belmont, (415) 591-8747.
Mid-Peninsula Jewish Singles 2440 Carlmont Dr., Belmont 94002, (415) 591-4438 or 334-0749 (Jack). Dances, house parties, lectures/discussions, camping. 35+.
Singles Adjustment Meetings, 592-1573. Free weekly discussions dealing with being single.
BENICIA
Benicia Fellowship Church Divorce Recovery Workshops, 963 Jefferson, (707) 746-5673 Bill Price, Pastor. One evening per week for 8 weeks.
BERKELEY
Berkeley/Richmond Jewish Community Ctr, 1414 Walnut St., Berkeley 94709, (415) 840-0222 or 848-0237. Parties, trips, films, and theatre for singles. 3 singles clubs: 1. Interest Network (33+). 2. Shabbat dinners for single parents and their kids. 3. Young Adults (20-33).
Berkeley Singles, Box 456, Berkeley 94710, (415) 236-8840. Ballroom dancing to live music, even Fridays, 8:30pm-12:30am, Cerrito City Club, Potrero & Kearney, El Cerrito. Mainly 40+.
Berkeley Singles, 848-7041 (J. Haney). Square dancing.
Berkeley Singles Ward (Mormon), 2368 Le Conte Ave., Berkeley, (415) 848-1918. Sunday church services, camping, hiking, white water rafting, and socials.
Cal Singles, Alumni Assoc. of UC Berkeley. Bill Reichle, 642-1945. Dances, speakers, trips. Mainly late 30s+. You do not have to have attended Cal in order to join.
East Bay Jewish Singles, Diane Scott, Box 9792, Berkeley 94709, (415) 540-5403. Cocktails, Wednesdays, 5:30-7:30pm, H's Lordships Rest., 199 Seawall Dr., Berkeley. 35+.
1st Presbyterian Church 20-20 Singles, 2407 Dana St., Berkeley 94704, (415) 848-6242. Worship and fellowship Sundays, 5:45pm, at 22-35. Also Divorce Recovery Workshop.

Singles Clubs

BERKELEY (continued)

Single Adults Counseling Group, 3048 Deakin St., Berkeley 94705, (415) 548-3434 (Joe Cristofalo, MFCC) or 653-5665 (Alice Large, LCSW).

Single Gourmet, social dining, 25-60s. Karen Nordeen, Dakota Grill & Bar, Shattuck Hotel, Berkeley 94707, 841-2848.

Star Sport & Social Club, (415) 956-1110 or (800) 242-3648.

Temple Beth El Singles (Jewish), Arch & Vine, Berkeley, 848-3988 or 464-5063 (Mary Moore, days).

Tennis Matchmakers, (415) 548-6240. 30+.

UC Squares, 535-0812 (B. Ferretti). Square dancing.

Unitarian Singles, 1 Lawson Rd., Kensington 94706, 891-9672 (Margaret). Discussions, Sundays, 7:30pm. Also socials. Mainly 35+.

BURLINGAME

Burlingame Recreation Department Singles Dances, 850 Burlingame Ave, Burlingame 94010, 344-6386. 250+ singles, live band. 35+.

1st Presbyterian Church, 1500 Easton, Burlingame 94010, 342-0875. Rev. Dan Meyer. 3 singles groups: 1. New Beginnings Transition Support Group, Joy Carroll. 2. Single Friends of Burlingame (30+). Bible study, volleyball, bicycling, Thursday socials. 3. YAMS (Young Adult Singles, 22-30), 347-7265 (Cheryl Toliver). Wednesdays, 7:30pm. Bible Study, volleyball, socials.

Guys & Dolls, Box 5, Burlingame 94010, (415) 342-8471 (Laverne Parker). Ballroom dancing, live music, Fridays, Burlingame Women's Club, 241 Park Rd., Burlingame. Mainly 40+.

Single Parents Drop-in Discussion Group, 696-5400. Tuesdays, 7-9pm, Peninsula Hospital, 3rd Floor Solarium, 1783 El Camino Real, Burlingame 94010. $2.

CAMPBELL

Home Church Singles, 1711 S. Winchester, Campbell 95008, (408) 370-1500. 1st Fridays, 7pm. Non-sectarian. All ages. William Ray. Spirit Group, 264 E. Everett St., Campbell 95008.

CASTRO VALLEY

Cathedral at the Crossroads 3 Crosses Singles, 20600 John Dr., C.V. 94546, 537-4690. M. Cash.

1st Baptist Church Singles, 18550 Redwood Rd, C.V. 94546, 582-0515.

1st Presbyterian Church Alive for Christ, 2490 Grove Way, C.V. 94546, 581-6203. Bible Study, Sunday nights. Also movies, potlucks, brunches. 26+.

Friends First, Box 20189 #200, C.V. 94546. Socials. Mainly 20s.

Redwood Chapel Community Church (nonsectarian), 19300 Redwood Bl, C.V. 94546, 886-6300. Socials. 3 clubs: 1. Chai Alpha (18-early 20s), Sunday school, 11am. 2. 20-20 Singles (24-30), Sunday school, 8:10am, Little Chapel. 3. Single Career (working full-time, mainly 30s), Sunday school, 11am. Bible study, Wednesdays, 7pm.

Singles Clubs

COLMA
The Love of Your Life, 205 Village Lane, Colma 94015, 991-0288. Workshops, classes, and support groups on creating ideal relationships. Susan Scott, Dir., also does counseling for singles.

CONCORD
Bethel Baptist Church Singles, 3578 Clayton Rd., Concord 94521, 798-7470. Bible study, Sundays, 9 & 10am. Also potlucks & parties. All ages.

Calvary Baptist Church Singles, Hwy. 24 at Olivera Ct., Box 846, Concord 94522, (415) 685-1424. Craig Hadingor.

Concord Christian Ctr Singles, 4255 Clayton Rd, Concord 94521, 687-2020. Potlucks, singing at convalescent homes, socials. 25+.

Fairoaks Baptist Church Singles 1925 Risdon Rd., Concord, 687-4810. Sundays, 9am. Potlucks, barbecues, swimming.

1st Presbyterian Church Contra Costa Christian Singles, Colfax & Salvio, Concord 94520, 458-5470, 682-4241. 1st Fridays. Volleyball, potlucks, parties, fellowship. Nonsectarian.

Full Gospel Church Singles, 2120 Olivera Ct., Concord 94520.

Gateway Singles Ministries, 3018 Willow Pass Rd #204, Concord 94519, (415) 686-5851. Bill Rose, Director. Mondays, 7:30-9, Fubar's Comedy Club, 1150-C Arnold Dr., Martinez. Lectures, discussions, concerts, sports.

Merry Mixers, Box 993, Concord 94522. Ballroom dancing or dinners, Fridays & Sundays. Mainly 40+.

Parents Without Partners, Box 6347, Concord 94520, (415) 689-1826.

Single Doglovers Association, Box 272245, Concord 94527. Showing, hunting, breeding of dogs. Also socials.

Singles Drop-in Support Group, 1810C Willow Pass Rd., Concord, (415) 676-2399. Thursdays, 7:30-9pm. $10 per session. Led by Mae Bragen, M.F.C.C.

Singles Scene, Box 4242, Concord.

Tabernacle Baptist Church Singles, 4380 Concord Blvd., Concord 94521.

Trinity Baptist Church Singles, 3525 Chestnut, Concord 94514, 686-1400 or 945-8147. 2 groups: 1. People's Group, mainly singles under 30, most of whom have never been married. Bible study and socializing Sundays, 6:30pm. 2. Divorced & Widowed (mainly 30+, 686-5130). Potlucks & discussions 4th Sundays, 7-9pm, in private homes. Also lunches, attending plays, and socializing.

Yellow Rock Singles, 1844 Clayton, Concord 94520, 671-0730 (Mervin Burnworth). Square dancing.

DALY CITY
Grace Presbyterian Church Singles, 515 Winchester, D.C. 94014, 586-5681.

DANVILLE
Community Presbyterian Church Christian Singles, 222 El Pintado, Danville 94526, 837-5525 or 947-1842 (Liz Edwards). 30+. Religious service, speaker, social, Wednesdays, 7:30pm. Bible study, Fridays, 7pm.

Singles Clubs

DUBLIN
  Shannon Community Ctr Seniors Dance Club, Shannon & San Ramon
    Rd., Dublin, (415) 828-9394. Tuesdays, 1-4pm. Free.
  Valley Christian Ctr Singles, 10800 Dublin Blvd., Dublin 94568, 828-4549.
    2 groups: 1. FOCAS (30+). Bible study and socializing every Wednesday,
    7:30pm, Fireside Room. 2. LOGOS, 25-35. Bible study and socializing
    in a private home in Dublin.
EL CERRITO
  St. John the Baptist Church Separated & Divorced Catholic Support Group,
    11150 San Pablo Ave., E.C. ;94530, (415) 525-6577 (Denise Cree).
EL SOBRANTE
  Church of the Nazarene Singles, 4600 Appian Way, (415) 223-1576.
  El Sobrante Church Singles, 670 Appian Way, Richmond 94803.
FAIRFIELD
  Bereavement Recovery Club, Fairfield Senior Ctr, 1200 Civic Ctr Dr.,
    642-7148 (Stanley Cornills). 2 Thursdays each month, 10:30am.
  Community United Methodist Church Singles Circuit, 1875 Fairfield,
    428-3558 (Sherwood) or 422-3752 (Ruth Anne Harris). Sundays, 7-9pm.
    Lectures, dancing, and parties.
  Creative Living Ctr Singles, Solano County Health Dept. and Fairfield
    and Suisun City Adult School. 429-6931 (Ruth Washington) or 864-1334
    (Emily Valenzuela). Wednesdays & Thursdays, 10am-2pm, Moose
    Lodge, 623 Taylor St. Trips, crafts, arts, games. All ages.
  Mormon Singles Hotline, Fairfield, (707) 426-4950.
  Our Lady of Mt. Carmel Catholic Church DAWN. (Divorced And
    Widowed Neighbors), 2700 Dover or Box 3283, Fairfield 94533, (707)
    426-0920 (Phil Correia) or 425-8623 (Mary). Support group, Wednesdays,
    7pm.
  Parents Without Partners, Box 277, Fairfield 94533, (707) 429-1526.
  Singles Outdoor Activities & Recreation (SOAR), Box 209, FF 94533.
    422-4694. Sailing, hiking, backpacking, camping, rafting, horseback
    riding, canoe trips, picnics, barbecues, diving, windsurfing.
FOSTER CITY
  Central Peninsula Church Singles Community Groups, 1005 Shell Blvd.,
    F.C. 94404, 349-1132. Bible study and socials every other Wednesday,
    7:30pm. Also socials. All ages, mainly 20s.
  Foster City Singles. Even Thursdays, Recreation Ctr, 650 Shell. Also dances
    with live music, 2nd Fridays. 35+.
FREMONT
  Centerville Presbyterian Church Genesis (22-35), John Knox House, 4360
    Central Ave, Fremont 94536, 793-3575. Bible Study, Wednesdays,
    7pm. Also brunches & socials. Garrett Starmer, Minister.
  1st Assembly of God Singles Alive, 4760 Thornton, Fremont 94536,
    793-8687. Worship, Wednesdays, 7:30pm. Also picnics, barbecues,
    & potlucks. All ages & all faiths. Roger McCarthy, Singles Pastor.

Singles Clubs

FREMONT (continued)
  Fremont Community Church, 39700 Mission Bl, Fremont 94539, 657-0123.
    Bible study, socials. 2 nonsectarian groups: 1. College/Career Singles
    (never-married, 18-24), Sunday school, 9am. 2. 25+ group, Sunday
    school, 10:45am.
  New Horizons, 34469 Shenandoah, Fremont 94536, 794-8596. House
    parties, activities, volleyball, rafting. Mainly 35-45.
  Parents Without Partners, Box 1814, Fremont 94538, 796-4327. Dancing
    with DJ, Thursdays, 8:30pm, Fremont Inn, 46845 Warm Springs Bl,
    free. 40+.
  St. Leonard's Catholic Church Reaching Out Support Group, 3600 St.
    Leonards Way, Fremont 94538, 651-8009 (Jerry) or 489-1355 (Betty).
    Wednesdays, 7:30pm. Lectures, games, picnics, dining, movies, socials.
  Tri-City Church of Religious Science Serendipity Group, 40155 Blacow,
    Fremont 94538, 656-9955. Dinners, beach parties, and discussions.
    Betty O-Brien.
GILROY
  Gilroy Presbyterian Church Singles, 842-3000. Dinners & trips.
  Parents Without Partners, Gilroy Chapter, Box 969, Morgan Hill 95037.
GREENBRAE
  Club Voyage Marin, Greenbrae Travel, 332 Bon Air Ctr, Greenbrae 94904,
    (415) 461-4815. Singles Travel Club.
HAYWARD
  Black Catholics, 21062 Gary #113, Hayward 94546, 582-7632 (Marlene
    Jones-Lovett). Free support group, 3rd Sundays, 2pm. Socials, 3rd
    Fridays, 7:30pm. Wine tastings, potlucks, fundraisers, workshops.
  Eden Singles, 21455 Birch St., Hayward 94541. Ballroom dancing, 3rd
    Saturdays, 377 Paseo Grande, San Lorenzo. Mainly 40+.
  Elmhurst Baptist Church, 380 Elhurst, Hayward 94544, 783-8062. Bible
    study & fellowship, Sundays, 9am. Nonsectarian. Divorce Recovery
    Workshop, Tuesdays, 7-9pm. Also parties, dances, movies, trips, and
    sports. Mainly 25-50. Ralph Starling, Single Adult Minister.
  Hayward Bible Chapel Singles, 22416 Meekland Ave., Hayward 94541.
  Parents Without Partners, Box 3341, Hayward 94540, (415) 357-1768
    or 782-3008 (Anita).
  Successful Christian Singles, 354 B St., Hayward 94541. Carl Serfass.
KENTFIELD
  Single Soles, Box 726, Kentfield 94904.
LAFAYETTE
  Lafayette Orinda Presbyterian Church, 49 Knox, Lafayette 94549, 283-8722.
    Giant meetings, Sundays, 7:30pm, $3, featuring your choice of a
    Transition Support Group, a Newcomers group, or any of three
    speakers. Socializing afterwards at Black Angus Cocktail Lounge in
    Pleasant Hill and other cocktail lounges. Numerous discussions, parties,
    volleyball, and other activities throughout the week. 6 groups:

Singles Clubs

LAFAYETTE (continued)
  1.Bereavement Outreach, 938-3292, support group & info for widowed persons, odd Thursdays. 2. Castaways (20s), (415) 284-1425. 3. Shipmates (30s & early 40s). 4. Single Ship (40+). 5. Singles Toastmasters, public speaking, Mondays, 7:30-9:30pm. 6. Transition Support Group, Sundays, 7:30pm. For singles less than 6 months out of a relationship. Members share experiences and provide support and acceptance.
  Our Savior Luth. Church Singles, 1035 Carol, Lafayette 94549, 283-3722. Brunches, fellowship, retreats, dinners, lectures. Mainly 30+.
  Single Scene America, Mary Berkowitz, 3361 McGraw Lane, Lafayette 94549. Soup, sandwiches, & discussion of world-wide topics.
  Touchstone, Box 494, Lafayette 94549, (415) 686-5851. Mondays, 7:30-9pm. Bible study, concerts, theatre, speakers, parties. Nonsectarian.
  Widows Network, 3483 Golden Gateway #2, Lafayette 94549, 283-7174 (1-5pm). Financial discussion groups, workshops, potlucks, Travel Club. Young Widow/Widowers Support Group (under 40), Saturdays, 10am.
LIVERMORE
  Parents Without Partners, Box 303, Livermore 94550, 443-0458 or 443-0802.
  Tri-Valley Community Singles, Box 3015, Livermore 94551, 447-2573. Sundays, 7:15-9:30pm, Livermore Presbyterian Church, 5th & L, Rm. 10. Lectures, potlucks, dinners, plays, and hiking. 35+.
LOS ALTOS
  Divorced Catholics, Diocese of San Jose, 7600 St. Joseph Ave., Los Altos, 94022, (408) 294-8953. Fr. William O'Keeffe, Coordinator.
  1st Baptist Church Singles, 625 Magdalena Ave., Los Altos 94022, (415) 948-5698. Single Parents Club, (408) 948-5698, and College/Career Singles (20s). Rev. Roger Draves.
  St. Nicholas Catholic Church New Dawn Support Group, Lincoln & Sherman, (415) 948-2158. 3rd Tuesdays. Monthly potlucks. Molly Keezer, 150 Flynn Ave., Mt. View 94043, 961-6102 or Marion Kirk, 948-5208, or Kay Boynton, 961-3286.
LOS ALTOS HILLS
  Temple Beth Am, 26790 Arastradero, Los Altos Hills, (408) 493-4661 or (415) 965-3913. San Mateo and Santa Clara counties. Weekly support group, hiking, wine tastings, picnics, dances, pool parties, discussions. 2 groups: 35+ Singles & Chai Society (21-35).
LOS GATOS
  Calvary Baptist Church Singles, 2522 S. Bascom Ave. #8, Campbell 95128.
  Congregation Shir Hadash Singles, 16555 Shannon Rd., L.G. 95032, (408) 358-1751. 21-40.
  Los Gatos Christian Church Singles 16845 Hicks Rd., Los Gatos, 268-1411. Parties, games, socials. Nonsectarian. Bob Anderson, Singles Pastor.

182

LOS GATOS (continued)
Selective Singles, Fridays, 7:30pm, Los Gatos Neighborhood Ctr. Discussions, lectures, game night, potlucks, and hiking.
South Bay Jewish Community Ctr Singles, 14855 Oka Rd., Los Gatos 95030, (408) 358-3636. Parties, dances, biking, sports, cultural, barbecues, discussions. Mindy Goodman. 3 groups: 1. 20-50. 2. Single Parents. 3. Young Energetic Single Seniors (YES), 60+.
St. Mary's Catholic Church New Vistas Support Group, N Ave. Socials. (408) 246-2153 (Loretta McNicholas).
Your Winning Edge, 15466 Los Gatos Blvd. #109-317, L.G. 95032, 354-7060. Offers Side by Side, a relationships seminar.
MARIN
In Interest Of, (415) 383-1146. Socials, 2nd Tuesdays.
Single Cyclists, Bx 684, Kentfield 94904, (415)258-8067. Bike trips. 25+.
Widowed Persons of California, Marin Chapter, (415) 453-6562. Dinners, 3rd Saturdays.
MENLO PARK
Menlo Park Presbyterian Church, 950 Santa Cruz Ave., Menlo Park 94025. 4 groups: 1. Singles Together, 40+. Sundays, 11am, free. Parties, dances, dinners, rafting, attending performing arts, retreats. 2. Middle Singles (30s-early 40s), Dinner & lecture, every other Friday, 6:45-10pm. 3. Young Adult Fellowship (20s & 30s), (415) 323-8631. Sundays, 6pm. Also rafting, dinners, parties. 4. Divorce Recovery group, Mondays, 7:30-10pm.
New Life Church Singles, 71 Bay Rd., Menlo Park, (415) 322-3696. Charismatic church. Mondays, 7:30pm.
Singles Supper Club, (415) 321-0388.
MILL VALLEY
MAC Singles, Miller Avenue Church, 285 Miller Ave., Mill Valley 94941, (415) 388-5993 (church) or 927-1895 (Nancy). Bowling, sports, parties, dinners, movies. Divorce Recovery Workshop, Wednesday evenings.
United Methodist Church Jugglers, Camino Alto & Sycamore, Mill Valley 94941, (415) 383-2368. Single parent support group. Potlucks, 2nd Tuesdays, 6pm.
MILPITAS
Calvary Assembly of God College/Career Singles, (Pentecostal), 1115 Ayer, Milpitas 95035, 262-6551 (The Tolberts). Bible study & fellowship, Thursdays, 7pm, private home. Also socials. All faiths.
Parents Without Partners, Box 360277, Milpitas 95035, (408) 251-7982.
MONTEREY
Church of Religious Science Singles, 400 W. Franklin, Monterey 93940, (408) 372-7326.
Emmanuel Fellowship Singles, 761 Lighthouse, (408) 646-0121.
1st Presbyterian Church Singles, 501 E. Dorado, Monterey 93940, (408) 373-3031. 30s & 40s.

Singles Clubs

MONTEREY (continued)
  Monterey Outdoor Singles (M.O.S.) Box 51416, Pacific Grove 93950, (408) 624-0202. Volleyball, Tuesday nights. Also biking, hiking, skating, sailing, monthly potluck. Mainly 30-60.
  Parents Without Partners, Monterey County, Box 4382, Salinas 93912.
MORAGA
  Lamorinda Connection, St. Monica's Catholic Church, Box 128, Moraga 94556, 376-6900. Also St. Perpetua's Church (Lafayette) & St. Maria's Church (Orinda). Trips, retreats, lectures, support group.
MORGAN HILL
  1st Assembly of God Church Singles, Box 755, Morgan Hill 95037.
  Hillside Nondenominational Church Singles, Morgan Hill.
  Mormon Singles Hotline, (408) 779-0670
  Parents Without Partners, Box 969, M.H. 95037.
  South County Singles, Box 204, M.H. 95037, 637-9138. Wednesdays, 7-10pm. Speakers, game nights, Western dancing. 30s to 60s.
MOUNTAIN VIEW
  Bay Area Winners, 801 W. El Camino #189, Mountain View 94040. Discussions, seminars, socials.
  Bows & Beaus, 3631 Evergreen, Palo Alto, 494-8236 (M. West). Square dancing, Mondays, Monta Loma Sch.
  Judean Society Catholic Support Group, 1075 Space Park Way #336, Mt. View 94043, (415) 964-8936 (Frances Miller).
  Sierra Singles, Loma Prieta Chapter, Box 391775, Mountain View 94039. 21+. Hiking, cross country skiing, sailing, social activities, bicycling, white water rafting, backpacking, volleyball, conservation.
  Single Squares, 720 Laguna Seca Ct, San Jose, 227-2162 (G. Carnes). Square dancing, Thursdays, Mt. View H.S.
  South Bay Christian Ctr Singles 1134 Miramonte Ave., Mt. View 94040, (415) 961-5781. Tuesdays, 7pm.
NAPA
  Catholic Social Svcs Support Group for Separated & Divorced, 2510 Old Sonoma, Napa 94558, 224-4403. Wednesdays, 7-9pm. All faiths & ages. Also therapy.
  Dinners for Singles, 224-6631 or 255-1327. Socials & dinners.
  1st Christian Church Singles, 2659 1st St., Napa 94558, 253-7222. Bible study & fellowship, Mondays, 7pm. Also movies, bowling, camping. 20s & 30s. Open to all faiths.
  Hillside Christian Ctr Singles (Assembly of God), 100 Anderson, Napa 94559, (707) 255-3036. Bible reading & fellowship, Tuesdays, 7pm. Also potlucks, water/snow skiing, trips to the city, game nights, and camping. 20-45. All faiths. Mark Hawkins.
  Napa Valley Singles, (707) 255-1327, 255-0268. Hiking, potlucks, overnights, brunches, dining out.
  Parents Without Partners, 224-0118, 557-4308, 224-2512, 643-5470.

Singles Clubs

NAPA (continued)

Singles Network, (707) 257-8525 (Jane). Discussions/speakers, Thursdays, 7:30pm, 1st United Methodist Church, 625 Randolph. TGIF, Fridays, 6pm, Embassy Suites Hotel. Gourmet dinner, last Sundays.

Singles Outdoor Activities & Rec. (SOAR), 255-8610 (Rosemarie).

Support Group for Separated, Divorced, or Widowed, Napa County Mental Health, 253-7715. Thursdays, 7-9pm, Adult Services Bldg, 2344 Old Sonoma Rd., Napa 94558. Free.

NOVATO

Church of the Open Door Singles, 897-5556 or 897-8206 (Phil & Vickie Holmes). Bible study, socials.

Marin Solos, Box 335, Novato 94948, 479-3827. Ballroom dancing to live music, 1st Saturdays, 9pm, $6, Isabel Cook Recreation Ctr, 1000 Sir Francis Drake Bl, San Anselmo. Dress code. Mainly 40+.

Our Lady of Loretto Church Separated & Div. Catholic Support Group, 1806 Novato Bl, Novato 94947, 897-9116 (Jef Stansfield). 2nd Fridays.

OAKLAND

Allen Temple Baptist Young Adult Singles, 8500 A St, Oakland 94621, 569-9418 or 430-9298/445-5150 (Ted Carter). 1st Saturdays. Workshops, potlucks, theater. Mainly singles, 23-38.

Alliance for Displaced Homemakers, 3800 Harrison, Oakland 94611.

Beginning Experience, 185 Wildwood Ave., Piedmont 94610, 654-9588. Weekend workshops for newly single Catholics.

Committee for Jewish Involvement Singles, Jewish Federation of the Greater East Bay, 401 Grand, Oakland 94610, 839-2900 (David Cohen). Social, educational, & cultural activities.

Entertainment Connection, Bill Ferrier, 7266 Homewood, Oakland 94611, 339-8460. Dance parties, Veteran's Hall, Piedmont.

Graduate Degrees, 420-1381. For singles with masters degrees or higher.

Greek Orthodox Church of the Ascension, 4700 Lincoln Ave., Oakland 94602, (415) 531-3400. Spiritual and social activities. Limited to Greek, Russian, and Antioch Orthodox. Attracts members from all over N. Calif. 2 clubs: Orthodox Singles (25-40) & 39ers (39+).

Happy-Go Lucky Singles, 3059 Georgia #3, Oakland 94602, 530-4483. Dining, dancing, barbecues, min. golf, bowling, picnics, parties.

High IQ Singles (Mensa Society spin-off), 547-4815. Fridays, 6pm, Via Veneto Restaurant, Oakland. Led by Dr. Marilyn Ducati.

Lifestyle Dining Club, 419 W. MacArthur Blvd., Oakland 94609, (415) 420-1381. Meets at restaurants in San Francisco & Alameda County.

Mormon Singles Hotline, (415) 531-6686.

Northern California Christian Singles, Shiloh Christian Fellowship, 3295 School, Oakland 94602, 261-2052 or 843-9117 (Annabel Wann). Annual retreat for Christian singles, with 30 churches attending. Nonsectarian. Sunday school, 9am.

Oakland Bible Church Singles, 2640 108th, Oakland 94605. Barbara Reese.

Singles Clubs

OAKLAND (continued)

Oakland/Piedmont Jewish Community Ctr Single Persuasion, 3245 Sheffield, Oakland 94602, 653-9790 (Lisa Wadsworth). Volleyball, films, tours, dinners, discussions, Shabbat dinners. 30-55.

Parents Without Partners, Box 1497, Oakland 94604, (415) 893-5995.

Powder Hounds Singles Ski Club, Box 12763, Oakland 94604, (415) 769-7669. Tuesdays, 8pm, Sheanigans, Jack London Square. Volleyball, Thursdays. Also baseball & camping.

Solos & Pairs, 1799 Euclid, 848-7041 (J. Haney). Square dancing, Wednesdays, Rockridge Arts.

PACIFICA

Beginning Experience, Dorothy Stanek, Box 1074, Pacifica 94044, (415) 355-7236. Weekend workshops for newly single Catholics.

Parents Without Partners, Box 745, Pacifica 94044, (415) 359-3779.

PACIFIC GROVE

1st United Methodist Church Singles, Box 60, P.G. 93950, 372-5875.

PALO ALTO

Albert C. Schultz Jewish Community Ctr Singles, 655 Arastradero, Palo Alto, (415) 493-9400 (Hephzivah Kolban). Volleyball, Tuesdays, 8-10pm, $1, (415) 424-9045. Also canoeing, sailing, tennis, hiking, potlucks, dining, wine tasting, workshops, games, bridge, discussions. 35-50.

Congregation Kol Emeth Singles, 4175 Manuela Ave, (415) 948-7498.

1st Methodist Church Singles, 625 Hamilton, P.A. 94301. Mary Kelly.

Grace Lutheran Church Singles, 3149 Waverly St., Palo Alto 94306.

Inner Growth Seminars, Box 1107, Palo Alto 94302, (415) 328-8552. Gloria Wilcox leads "Breaking Through Barriers to Intimacy".

Los Amigos, YMCA, 3412 Ross, (408) 494-1883. Ballroom dancing, Thurs., 8pm, Sundays, 8pm, & even Saturdays, 8:30pm. Also bridge.

Mormon Singles Hotline, Stanford, (408) 494-9136.

Palo Alto Singles Ward (Mormon), 3865 Middlefield, Palo Alto, (415) 494-8899. Sunday worship, camping, hiking, rafting, volleyball.

Parents Without Partners, Box 60834, Palo Alto 94306, (415) 326-0426.

Peninsula Bible Church Singles, 3505 Middlefield Rd., Palo Alto 94306, (415) 494-3840. Worship service & small group discussion & socializing, Sundays, 9-10:45, at Menu Tree, Showers Dr., Mt. View. Also parties & dances. Mainly 20-49.

Stanford Bachelors, Box 2345, Stanford 94305. Large singles dances at hotels & country clubs from to San Jose. Coat & tie.

Stanford Quads, 3280 Ross Rd., 494-0603 (P. Curtis). Square dancing, Sundays, Old Union Clubhouse.

Stanford Singles, (415) 859-5341, 322-7280. Lectures, seminars, parties. Mainly 40+.

TGA Singles, YWCA, 4161 Alma St., Palo Alto, 494-0972 or 969-9772 (Antonio Fernandes). Ballroom Dancing, odd Saturdays & dance classes, Tuesdays, 7-8pm, followed by dancing.

Singles Clubs

PALO ALTO (continued)

Unity Palo Alto Community Church Singles, 3391 Middlefield, Palo Alto 94303, (415) 969-1167. Even Thursdays, 7:30pm. Metaphysically oriented. Discussions, lectures, parties, potlucks, weekend hikes.

UU South Bay Singles, Unitarian Church, 505 E. Charleston Rd., Palo Alto 94306, (415) 494-0541, (415) 967-8764 (Sandy), or (408)554-6360 (Lisa). Socials co-sponsored by Unitarian Churches in Redwood City, Palo Alto, San Jose, and Los Gatos.

PENINSULA

Mid-Peninsula Jewish Singles, 155 Upland, San Francisco 94127, 334-0749 (Jack Ploscowe). Co-sponsored by Peninsula JCC, Temple Sholom, & Temple Beth El. Parties, discussions.

PETALUMA

Petaluma Singles, 726-0749 (Charlene).

PINOLE

How to be Single & Happy Growth Group, (415) 787-1360. Thursdays, 7:30-9:30pm, at the Pinole YM.

PLEASANT HILL

Hope Ctr (Evangelical Church), 2275 Morello Ave., Pleasant Hill 94523, 685-4673. Carpenters (18-25), discussion group, Sundays, 6pm, free. Also parties, dinners, and skiing.

Christian Fellowship Church Contacts, 40 Cleveland, 676-1584. Sundays, 8:30-10am, Oaks Restaurant in Walnut Creek. Also socials.

Diablo Singles, 26 Lagunitas Ct., Martinez 94553, 228-3654 or 798-5797. Square dancing, Thursdays, 7:30pm, Fair Oaks Sch.

Hope Ctr (Evangelical Church) Lighthouse 2275 Morello, Pleasant Hill 94523, 685-4673. Discussion group, Thursdays, 7:30pm, free. Also parties, dinners, skiing. 25+.

Separated & Divorced Catholic Support Group, Family Life Ctr, 2446 Estand Way, P.H. 94523, 671-9339 (Diocese of Oakland), 939-1356 (Bob Arieta) or 228-3389 (Kit Wilkinson). Tuesdays, 7:30pm, discussion group for newly single. Thursdays, 7:30pm, discussion on being happily single. 1st Wednesdays, 8pm, $1. Beginning Experience, weekend workshops for newly single Catholics.

Singles Outdoor Activities & Recreation (SOAR), Box 23928, P.H. 94523, 934-9080 (Shirley). Sailing, hiking, backpacking, camping, rafting, horseback riding, canoe trips, picnics, barbecues, diving, and windsurfing.

Tons of Fun Social Club, 334 Strand, P.H. 94523, 676-3635, 841-7946, 676-4875. For overweight, all ages. Speakers, socials games.

PLEASANTON

Bota Baggers Singles Ski Club, Box 772, Pleasanton 94566, 443-4451 (tape) or 275-0317. Tuesdays, 8pm, Velvet Turtle, Sheraton Hotel.

Pleasanton Singles, (415) 484-3513 or 449-7015. Square dancing at Camp Parks, RFTA, Bldg. 790, Dublin 94568.

Singles Clubs

PLEASANTON (continued)

Single Women's Group, 4725 1st St. #205, Pleasanton 94566, 846-2085.

St. Augustine's Catholic Church Genesis Support Group, 900 E. Angela, 846-3531. Serves the Tri-Valley area. Every other Monday, 7:30pm.

Widowed Men & Women of N. Calif., 422-1153 (Nick). 3rd Mondays, 7:30pm, Chabot Community Ctr, 4637 Chabot, Parties, dancing, dinner, trips every weekend. Members from throughout East Bay.

REDWOOD CITY

Beginning Experience, Redwood City, (415) 366-0323 (Christine Kenny). Weekend workshops for newly single Catholics.

Redeemer Lutheran Church Singles, 468 Grand St., Redwood City 94062.

St. Pius Church Separated & Div. Catholic Support Group, 1110 Woodside, R.C. 94061, 322-7694 (Margaret Moore) or 322-2220 (Claire Moran).

RICHMOND

1st Baptist Church THEOS Widows Group, 234-4395 or 724-9124.

Singles Class, 3037 Groom Dr., Richmond 94806.

SALINAS

Cypress Community Church Singles, Monterey Hwy, 484-2141. Every other Fri. Bible study, potlucks, discussions, lectures, games. 2 clubs, 21-32 and all ages.

1st Baptist Church New Life Singles, 1130 San Vicente, Salinas 93901, (408) 663-2724. Volleyball, Thursdays, 7:30pm.

1st Presbyterian Church Single & Single Again (S.A.S.A.), 830 Padre Dr., Salinas 93901, (408) 422-7811. Socials, lectures, divorce recovery. Pete Cantu, Singles Minister.

Parents Without Partners, Box 4382, Salinas 93912, (408) 449-3511, 757-8532, 424-0562, 757-1640.

Sacred Heart Catholic Church New Directions, 14 Stone, 424-1458 or 757-4568. Guest speaker & support group, Thursdays, 7:30pm.

Vineyard Christian Fellowship, The Gathering, 1000 S. Main St. #216B, Salinas 93901, (408) 422-5321.

Word of Life Christian Fellowship Singles (Evangelical), Box 4657, Salinas 93912, (408) 449-1030 or 675-3272.

SAN BRUNO

St. Robert's Church Separated & Divorced Catholic Support Group, 1380 Crystal Spgs, San Bruno 94066, 873-7399, 285-1219 (Mary Ann Camacho). 2nd Thurs.

SAN FRANCISCO

Bachelors 'n' Bachelorettes, John Kelly, 55 Garcia 94127, 566-3563 or (415) 681-4843. Square dancing, Fridays, Ebenezer Lutheran Church, 678 Portola Dr.

Beginning Experience, (415) 921-1367 (Barbara Elliott) or 469-9842 (Sue Brumer). Weekend workshops for newly single Catholics.

Bethel Temple Caring Christian Singles, 1325 Valencia, San Francisco 94110, 285-1433. Discussions, brunches, T.G.I.F., volleyball, concerts,

SAN FRANCISCO (continued)

Calvary Presbyterian Church Singles Together 2515 Fillmore, San Francisco 94115, 346-3832, 221-3821 (Ron Wong) or 692-7439 (Frank Osgood). Parties, potlucks, movies, theatre outings, hiking, barbecues. 30s and 40s.

Catholic Young Adults, Chris Fitzsimmons, 755 Ashbury, San Francisco 94117, 665-4400. 21-35.

Commonwealth Club of California, 681 Market, San Francisco 94105, (415) 362-4903. Occasionally sponsors lectures for singles.

Congregation Emanu-El Circle Singles (Jewish), 2 Lake, San Francisco 94118, 751-2535. Monthly Shabbat services & dinners. 21-40.

Congregation Sherith Israel Modern Community of Adults, 2266 California, 346-1720 (Don Plansky). Monthly Shabbat services. Speakers, dances, cultural/socials.

Creative Cooking for Singles, Carl Levinson, 1508 Taylor #4, San Francisco 94133, 441-0675. Weeknights, 6-8:30pm. Mainly 25-45.

Finance Meets Fashion sponsors a gigantic dance party and fashion show each year, co-produced by Camp Productions, 931-6591 and San Francisco Modeling Company, 626-1191.

1st Baptist Church, Market & Octavia, 863-3382. Sunday school, 9am. Bible study, picnics, fairs, charitable, socials. 3 groups: 1. 40+. 2. 25-40. 3. College/Career (mainly college age).

1st Unitarian Church Singletarians, 1187 Franklin, San Francisco 94109. 776-4580. 40+. Potluck/Dance, last Saturdays.

Going Places, San Francisco Jewish Community Center, 2200 California, (415) 346-6040. Shabbat Dinner for singles, 1st Fridays.

Guardsmen, 115 Sansome #310, San Francisco 94104, 781-6785. Businessmen who raise money for charity and sponsor one party per month.

In the Know, 634 Broderick, San Francisco 94117, 346-7783. Parties. Juliette Smith.

Jewish Singles Over 40, Box 15055, San Francisco 94155, 243-9202 (Lynne Levi). Lectures, 1st Thursdays, 5:30-7:30pm, Hyatt-Union Square Hotel Also parties, swing dances, dinners, art galleries.

L'Chaim Singles (Jewish), Ed Epstein, 31 Meadowbrook, San Francisco 94132, 731-9166. Sundays, 7:30-9pm. Games, speakers, discussions, dances, dinners. 50+.

Mormon Singles Hotline, (415) 345-0077 or 572-9273.

Mothers Without Custody, Helga McCamley, 1040 Carolina, San Francisco 94107, 824-8052. Support group.

Musical Theater Lovers United, Box 4384, San Francisco 94101, 552-5045 or 552-2222. Bonnie Weiss. Sing-alongs and parties.

Networking Breakfasts, San Francisco, Marianna Nunes, (415) 673-6775. Mainly singles.

New Age Singles Dance Parties, Daphne Laurel at (415) 863-4048.

Singles Clubs

SAN FRANCISCO (continued)

19th Ave. Baptist Church Singles 1370 19th Ave., 564-7721 (Bill Smith). Bible Study, Sundays, 10am. Socials. 24-40s.

Pacific Ski & Trail Club, 235 Montgomery #860, San Francisco 94104, 398-7372. Dances, skiing, sports, flea markets, matchmaking.

Parents Without Partners, Box 4014, San Francisco 94101, 750-3076 or 337-2546.

Positive Connections, 776-8437 (Georgina Ong) or 826-7234. Dinners, 2nd Wednesdays & last Saturdays. Networking, seminars, dances,tours.

Renaissance School of Dance, 285 Ellis, 474-0920. Buffet dinner & dance lesson & party for singles, Fridays.

San Francisco Club, Box 26347, SF 94126, 681-7525 or 346-5776. Parties. Proceeds go to charities.

San Francisco Jewish Community Ctr Singles, 3200 California, San Francisco 94118, 346-6040. Sunday brunches, lectures, workshops. Going Places (ages 20-40) sponsors Wine & Cheese/Lectures, Tuesdays. Also skiing, river rafting, brunches, dinners, concerts, dances.

San Francisco Singles Ward (Mormon), Pacific & Gough, 441-9897, 441-4983.

San Francisco Ski Club, Box 421765, San Francisco 94101. Tuesdays, 8pm, Seven Hills Restaurant, 252 California St.

Singles Dining Out Club, 1978 23rd Ave., San Francisco 94116, 731-8026. Visits restaurants, wineries, & breweries. Mainly 30s & 40s.

The Singles Organization of Calif. Renee de Segur, 815 Garfield, SF 94132, 587-1779. Parties in San Francisco & along the Peninsula. 40+.

Spinsters, Leslie Taglio, 1840 Union #102, San Francisco 94123, 346-2460. Fund-raising parties open to public. Membership is limited to college educated women, 22-35, who have never been married.

St. Peter Church Separated & Divorced Catholic Support Group, (Spanish speaking). 1st Tuesdays, St. Peter School, 1200 Florida, San Francisco 94110. 469-8765 (Esperanza Martinez) or 826-4457 (Victor Madrigal).

St. Stephen's Catholic Church New Dimensions Support Group, 475 Eucalyptus, San Francisco 94132, 586-4154 (Janet Arpin) Even Mondays.

St. Vincent de Paul Catholic Church New Tomorrow Support Grp, 2320 Green, San Francisco 94123. 346-7733 (Rita Beaulieu). Odd Wednesdays.

Temple Emanu-El, Arguello & Lake, Box 18247, SF 94118, 751-2535. Shabbat dinners/speakers. 2 grps: 1. Circle (20s & 30s); Singles Plus (40+).

Univ. of San Francisco New Wings Catholic Support Group, Turk & Parker, San Francisco 94117, 661-4198 (Cliff Pfluger). Even Wednesdays.

Urban Life Ctr Christian Singles, 1101 O'Farrell or Box 14611, San Francisco 94114, 333-6019 (John Dillman). Bible study, Sundays, 6pm. Mid 20s-mid 40s. Barbecues, socials.

Valley Baptist Church Singles 305 Raymond, San Francisco 94134, 467-6055. Jim Pittman, Minister. Potlucks and socials.

Young Republicans, 331-4053.

Singles Clubs

SAN JOSE

Agape Singles (Christian), Box 6531, San Jose 95150, (408) 236-3396. Monthly social.

Almaden Neighborhood Church Singles, Box 20696, San Jose 95160.

Bachelors 'n' Bachelorettes, Bill Gates, 965 Katherine, San Jose 95126, 249-1609, or Mike, (408) 374-6148. Square dancing, Tuesdays, 8-10:30pm, Rogers School, 4835 Doyle Rd. Mainly 40+.

Beginning Experience, 1879 Bethany, San Jose 95132, 926-3929 or Box 36003, San Jose 95158, 244-3684 (Pat Rupel). For newly single Catholics.

Bethel Assembly of God Church (Pentecostal) Singles, 1201 S. Winchester, San Jose 95128, 246-6790. Outings, barbecues, sightseeing, parties, potlucks, lectures, discussions, films. All faiths. 3 groups: 1. Agape Singles (55+). Sunday classes, 9:30am. 2.Career Singles (20s & 30s), Sundays, 11a.m. 3. Single Spirit (30s, 40s, & 50s), Classes, Sundays. Also Santa Clara Valley Christian Singles sponsors large combined events with singles clubs at 6 churches. Open to all faiths.

Calvary Community Church Singles, 1175 Hillsdale Ave., San Jose 95118.

Cathedral of Faith Chapel Singles Helping Singles (Pentecostal), 2315 Canoas Garden, San Jose 95125, 267-4691. Worship & speaker, Sundays, 9:15 am, & Wednesdays, 7:30pm. Also dinners, beach parties, and retreats. 25+. Mike Garcia, Pastor.

Christian Singles Ballroom Dancing. Judy Walter at (408) 736-7211.

Crossroads Bible Church, 1670 Moorpark. Seminars.

Exploring Singles Perspective (ESP), 737-8254. Discussions, dances. 1st Baptist Church Singles, 800 Ironwood Dr., (408) 265-9000.

1st Church of Religious Science Phoenix Singles, San Jose, (408) 294-1828.

1st Congregational Church Singles, 1980 Hamilton, San Jose 95125. 688-6611. 45+. Brunches, cards, theater, golf.

Gloria Dei Lutheran Church Singles, 121 S. White Rd., San Jose 95127.

Holy Family Catholic Church New Horizons Support Group, 4848 Pearl, 267-2574 (Maynard Ellis) or (408) 265-4040 (Fr. Pat Doherty). 1st & 3rd Sundays.

Immanuel Presbyterian Church Divorce Recovery, 3675 Payne, 244-5298.

Jubilee Christian Ctr Singles, 110 Nortech Pkwy., San Jose 95134, 262-0900.

Live Entertainment Going Singles (LEGS), C. Kelleher, 1048 Oaktree, San Jose 95129. 253-5353. Excursions to live entertainment.

Men-Gals, Box 1145, Campbell 95009, 298-6391 (Kathleen). Ballroom Dancing, odd Fridays, 9pm, American Legion Hall, 1344 Dell. 40+.

Mormon Singles Hotlines, Almaden, 268-7677; East San Jose, 259-5740; San Jose (408) 448-1113 or 298-5156

Over 40 Singles, Box 9593, San Jose 95157. Ballroom Dancing.

Parents Without Partners, Box 5096, San Jose 95150, (408) 225-4415.

Professional Guild, Ron Hanner, 1211 Utopia Place, San Jose 95127, 272-3966. Parties for single professionals in elegant settings.

Singles Clubs

SAN JOSE (continued)

Queen of Apostles Church Separated & Divorced Catholic Support Group, 4911 Moorpark, 253-7560, 253-7560 (Fr. Jim Misfud) or (408) 448-3268 (Jeannette Cherney). Odd Tuesdays.

Singles Dinner Club, (408) 257-1450. Monthly dinners at gourmet restaurants, ski, trips.

Solo Notes, 99 Almaden Blvd. #400, San Jose 95113, (408) 287-7383. Cocktail parties for singles at symphony performances.

St. Christopher's Catholic Church Four Seasons Support Group, 1576 Curtner, San Jose, (408) 269-2226.

St. Frances Cabrini Church Separated & Divorced Catholic Support Group, 15333 Woodard, 629-8160 (Clarence Tarmann).

St. Martin of Tours Church Separated & Divorced Catholic Support Group, 200 O'Connor, 294-8953 (Fr. Bill O'Keeffe). Even Sundays, 7-9pm, 2 groups: 20s & 30s & Catholic Widows or Widowers (Odd Sundays, Mary Ellen George, 354-0371).

St. Patrick's Catholic Church New Goal in Your Life Support Group, 389 E. Santa Clara, San Jose 95113, 294-8120 or 292-2782 (Cristina Molina). Spanish speaking. 2nd Wednesdays.

St. Victor's Church, Separated & Divorced Catholic Support Group, 3108 Sierra, 259-0713, 262-6506 (Bill) or 272-0295 (Chuck). 25-45. Crossroads sponsors a support group for newly divorced and separated odd Sundays. 252-7560 (Fr. Candido Lim), 251-7712 (Sue Kneer) or 272-8421 (Nancy Zecchini).

Trinity Presbyterian Church Singles, 3151 Union Ave., San Jose 95124.

Vineyard Christian Fellowship Singles, 3550 Stevens Creek Bl #345, 243-7238.

SAN LEANDRO

Beginning Experience, 1392 Advent Ave., San Leandro 94579, (415) 357-2988. Weekend workshops for newly single Catholics.

Calvary Lutheran Church Singles, 17200 Via Magdalena, S.L. 94580.

San Lorenzo Singles, 16871 President, S.L. 94578, 278-6957 (Eldon) or 490-4096. Square & round dancing Tuesdays, 7:30-10pm, Ashland Community Ctr, 167th Ave., in San Leandro. Mainly 40+.

Soiree Socials, Box 2493, C.V. 94546, (415) 886-1625 (24 hr. hotline) or 568-5086. Volleyball, Mondays. Parties, dances, lectures, T.G.I.F.s. Mainly 40+.

St. Felicitas Church Separated & Divorced Catholic Support Group, 1604 Manor, S.L. 94579, 657-6956 (Chuck Dal Pozzo). Thursdays, 7pm.

SAN MATEO

Bachelors 'n' Bachelorettes, Marvin G. Smith, 3633 Colegrove #12, San Mateo 94403, (415) 345-9853, or Ben, 278-3290. Square dancing, Mondays, Shoreview Recreation Center, 950 Ocean View Ave..

Crystal Springs Bible Church College/Career Singles, 2645 Alameda de las Pulgas, San Mateo, (415) 341-5096.

SAN MATEO (continued)

1st Baptist Church Christian Singles Fellowship, 2801 Alameda de las Pulgas, San Mateo 94403, 345-1965. Bible study, Thursdays, 7pm. Socials. 22-37.

1st Presbyterian Church Singles, 194 W. 25th, 345-1633. Lectures, 1st Sundays. Brunches, 3rd Sundays, 12:15pm. All ages.

Inskiers Ski Club, Box 5065, San Mateo 94402, 494-8243 (Bonnie Soeas) or 364-5490 (Sandy). Tuesdays, 8 pm, Sand Bar Cocktail Lounge, San Mateo Municipal Golf Course. Also potlucks, happy hours.

Jewish Singles Over 40, Box 4156, San Mateo 94404, 243-9202 (Ellen Sandler). Socials, speakers.

Parents Without Partners, Box 1954, San Mateo 94401, 344-6406. Singles Adjustment Group, Mondays, 7:30pm, Belmont Community Center, 592-1576 or 369-8551.

Peninsula Singles, Brookridge Institute, 349-9675. Potlucks, 3rd Saturdays, 7:30 -10:30pm, 1209 Palm Ave. Singles interested in consciousness, spirituality, parapsychology, and new connections with Greens, Elmwood Institute, USSR/US Initiatives, Beyond War.

Positive Thinkers Toastmasters, 341-1707 (Jim Schwandt). Public speaking, Mondays, 6:30-7:30am, Denny's Rest., 3190 Campus.

Temple Beth El Young Singles, 1700 Alameda de las Pulgas, San Mateo 94403, 341-7701 (Phyllis Shispinski). Dances, dinners, shows, parties. 18-30.

SAN PABLO

St. Paul's Catholic Church Young Adult Fellowship, 1845 Church, S.P. 94806, 232-5931. 25-35. All faiths. Outings, sports, discussions, potlucks, picnics, and Bible sharings. Brother Rufino, Director,

SAN RAFAEL

Apple Single Parent Support Group, 7 Skyview Terrace, San Rafael 94903, 492-0720. Potluck & discussion, odd Mondays, 6-8pm, Corte Madera. $2 + potluck contribution. Child care available. Must pre-register. The group also meets in Novato.

Beginning Experience, Marin, Jack France, (415) 472-2477. Weekend workshops for newly single Catholics.

Christ Presbyterian Church Singles, 620 Del Ganado, San Rafael 94903.

Fall Line Ski Club, Box 2367, San Rafael 94912, 381-8579 (Harriette West). Odd Tuesdays, Christopher's Restaurant, 9 Main, Tiburon. Skiing, volleyball, socials.

In Interest Of, 714 C St. #201, San Rafael 94901, (415) 456-7596 (De). Catered socials, private homes throughout Marin, 2nd Tuesdays, $15.

1st Presbyterian Church Sojourners, 1510 5th, San Rafael 94901, 456-6760. 40+.

1st United Methodist Church Single Parent Coalition, 9 Ross Valley Dr, San Rafael 94901, 453-8716. Betty Pagett.

Singles Clubs

SAN RAFAEL (continued)

Marin Covenant Church, 195 N. Redwood Dr., San Rafael 94903, 479-1360. All ages. No alcohol. 3 groups: 1. Career Singles (24-31, starting their careers). 2. Divorce Recovery Workshops, Tuesdays, 7:30pm. 3. Me & the Kids (single parents), Potluck & discussion, odd Thursdays, 6pm. Child care. $2. 892-3319.

North Bay Jewish Adults, Marin Jewish Community Ctr, 30 N. San Pedro, San Rafael 94903, 479-3441 or 499-1223 (Sharon). Discussions & socials. 25-45.

Single Parent Resource Ctr, 408 4th St., San Rafael 94901.

The Renaissance Club, Box 12718, San Rafael 94913, (415) 897-6067. Lectures in private homes.

Team Singles, Box 13072, San Rafael 94901, 461-2090, 456-3331 or 456-1748. Dances to live music, 4th Saturdays, 9pm, St. John's Hall, Ross, $7. Also parties, lectures, picnics, trips, biking, bridge, tennis. 45+.

SAN RAMON

Eagles Nest Fellowship Single Fire, 833-8283. Bible study & dinner. Mainly 18-35.

Life Community Church Singles, 2525 San Ramon Valley Rd., San Ramon 94583, 867-4640.

SANTA CLARA

1st Baptist Church Singles, 3111 Benton St., Santa Clara 95051, (408) 241-7635.

1st Presbyterian Church Singles, 2499 Homestead, (408) 984-0804.

Mormon Singles Hotline, (408) 446-4636

Parents Without Partners, Box 2265, Santa Clara 95054, (408) 984-1088.

Progressive Christian Singles, 2408 Karen Dr. #D, Santa Clara 95050.

Resurrection Lutheran Church Singles, 2495 Cabrillo Ave., (408) 241-2728.

Single Ballroom Dancers, (408) 268-6042 (Dick Wilson). Thursdays, 8-11pm, Senior Ctr, Fremont & Monroe, Santa Clara.

Single Clara, 1802 Amelia #2, 244-1668 (M. Wyman). Square dancing, Fridays, Kinderwood Pre-Sch.

United Methodist Church Singles, 1700 Lincoln, (408) 296-7411.

SANTA CRUZ

Attractions meet every Thursday, 7-9pm at the Barn, S. Park Way, in Santa Cruz. Activities include discussions and outings.

Green Earth Singles, Box 7933, Santa Cruz 95061, 338-2366. TGIF, 7-9pm, Peachwood's, Pasa Tiempo exit off Hwy. 17. Volleyball, Mondays, 7-9pm. Outdoor activities.

1st Church of Religious Science Uno's, 429 Pennsylvania, Santa Cruz 95062, 423-9520 or 426-5999 (Gwen Lee).

Live Oak Senior Ctr Singles, Capitola Rd. & 17th Ave, 423-8468. Sundays, 8:30-10am. For senior citizens.

Mormon Singles Hotline, (408) 423-8516.

Singles Clubs

SANTA CRUZ (continued)
   Star of the Sea Catholic Church New Expectations, 515 Frederick, 438-3190 (Pat). Lectures, 2nd & 4th Wednesdays, 7pm. Also socials, dances, raps, potlucks, breakfasts, games.
   Temple Beth El Jewish Community Ctr Singles, 920 Bay, 423-3012. Parties, hikes, beach, picnics, theater.
   Unity Temple Singles, 407 Broadway, Santa Cruz 95060, 423-8553 or 462-4152. Volleyball, potlucks, dances, parties.
SANTA ROSA
   Christian Covenant Community Church Singles, 1315 Pacific, Santa Rosa 95404. Christian Singles, 1620 Sonoma Ave., Santa Rosa 95405.
   Dinner at 8, 1330 N. Dutton, Santa Rosa 95401, 545-8888 (Coral or Laura).
   Enjoy Life, Box 2593, Santa Rosa 95405, 575-1006. Monthly seminars and social get-togethers. Also matchmaking service. Violet Young. Publishes magazine that lists singles events for Sonoma County.
   40-60 Singles, 25 Chapala, Santa Rosa 95403, 525-0587 (Margaret) or 579-4995 (Pat). 40+. Dances, lectures, & discussions.
   Parents Without Partners, Box 6267, Santa Rosa 95406, (707) 664-1308.
   Presbyterian Church of the Roses Simply Friends, 2500 Patio, Santa Rosa 95405, 542-4272. Thursdays, 7:30pm. Dining out, card nights, Sunday brunches, weekend retreats. Wayne Johnson, Director.
   Resurrection Life Ctr Singles Outreach, 50 Mark West Springs Rd., Santa Rosa 95403, (707) 526-7752.
   Sierra Singles Network, Box 466, Santa Rosa 95402, 538-2991 (Susan). Walks, theater, rafting, etc. 21+.
   Singles Connection, Box 2593, Santa Rosa 95405, 575-1006. Guest speaker & dance to live music, Tuesdays, 8pm, El Rancho Tropicana Hotel, $2.
   Singles Outdoor Activities & Recreation (SOAR), Box 5196, Santa Rosa 95402, (707) 539-3795 (Gladys) or 539-5016 (Carolyn). 30+.
   Single Outdoor Living Experience (SOLE), Box 6374, Santa Rosa 95406, (707) 576-7442 or 538-8271 (Carl).
   Singularity Benefit Events, Box 5462, Santa Rosa 95402, 578-4707 (Carol Walsh). Large fundraising events for local charities. 21+. Wednesday evenings.
   Social Singles, Box 511, Santa Rosa 95402, 528-8632. Ballroom dancing to live music, 3rd Saturdays, 9pm, Veterans Memorial Bldg. 40+.
   Sonoma County Jewish Singles, 523-1700 (Nancy Leibowitz, days).
   Sonoma County Singles, Box 6897, Santa Rosa 95406, (707) 544-9101 (Mel). Potlucks, Friday nights. Also picnics. Mainly 40+.
   St. Eugene's Catholic Church 2325 Montgomery, Santa Rosa 95405, 542-6984. 2 groups: 1. New Dawnings Support Group, Box 14272, Santa Rosa 95405, 578-4116 (Kathy). Wednesdays, 7:30pm, free. All faiths. 2. Widow's Club meets at Hall.
   Widowed Person's Association, Box 5014, Santa Rosa 95402, 763-3360 (Bobbie). Dining, socials. Mainly 40-65.

Singles Clubs

SARATOGA
  Congregation Beth David Singles, 19700 Prospect, Saratoga 95070, (408) 257-3333 (Lynda Weiss) or 866-0365. Shabbat services/socials, 1st Fridays, 9pm.
  Mormon Singles Hotline, (408) 867-5267
  Parents Without Partners, Box 442, Saratoga, (408) 866-0800.
SCOTTS VALLEY
  1st Baptist Church Singles, 5000 Granite Creek Rd., Scotts Valley 95066.
  Singular Focus, 1050 Lockhart Gulch Rd., Scotts Valley 95066.
SOLANO COUNTY
  The Professionals Guild, (800) 992-1166. Mixers occasionally in Solano County. Coat & tie.
SONOMA COUNTY
  Singles Information Line, (707) 575-1006.
SONOMA
  Young Widows-Widowers Group, 938-4483. Frances Freewater, MFCC.
SUNNYVALE
  Apres Singles Ski Club, Box 1027, Mountain View 94042, 377-5966 or 259-5142. Even Thursdays, 8pm, Sunnyvale Elks Club, 375 N. Pastoria.
  Community Singles Shabbat Services (Jewish), 1537 Bedford, Sunnyvale 94087, (408) 968-0736 (Arnie Benowitz). Quarterly Shabbat services at various synagogues.
  1st Baptist Church Singles, 445 S. Mary, Sunnyvale 94086, 736-3120.
  Parents Without Partners, Box 60791, Sunnyvale 94088, (408) 245-3127.
  Snow Drifters Ski Club, Box 396, Mountain View 94042, 265-4206 (Bill Turner). Odd Wednesdays, 8pm, at The Bold Knight, 769 N. Mathilda Ave.
  Sunnyvale Presbyterian Church Singles in Touch, 728 W. Fremont, Sunnyvale 94087, 739-1892. Dinners, brunches, camping, lectures. 35+.
  Sunnyvale Singles, 837 Mulberry, 739-6862 (F. Lorimer). Square dancing, Thursdays.
  Sunnyvale Singles Squares, (480) 997-2653 (Jim) or 227-2162 (Gary). Thursdays, 8-10:30pm, Blackford Ave., San Jose. 30+.
TIBURON
  Tiburon Baptist Church Singles & Co, 445 Greenwood Beach, Tiburon 94920, 388-5403. Bible study, Sundays, 9am, Strawberry Joe's, Mill Valley. Also canoeing, trips, seminars, potlucks, parties, lectures, & discussions. Mainly 18-40. David Gragg, Singles Minister,
VACAVILLE
  Bereavement Recovery Club, Vacaville Community Ctr, 1100 Alamo, 448-6620 (Olga Chanda) or 642-7148 (Stanley Cornils).
  1st Baptist Church Singles, 1127 Davis, Vacaville 95688, 448-6209 or 447-0273. Fridays, 7pm. Aerobics, diet, nutrition, bowling. Bob Sorensen.

Singles Clubs

VACAVILLE (continued)

New Beginnings, (707) 446-2184. 1st & 3rd Fridays, 8pm, at 480 Buck St., Vacaville. For mature singles.

Valley Evangelical Free Church Singles, 5063 Maple Rd., Vacaville 95688.

Widow's Support Group, Vacaville Senior Ctr, 411 Kendall St., Vacaville 95688, (707) 446-6777. 2nd & 4th Wednesday, 1:30pm.

VALLEJO

1st Assembly of God Singles on a Rock (SOAR), 21 Locust, Vallejo 94542, 644-4451. Bible study & fellowship, Tuesdays, 7pm. Also potlucks, parties, cruises, and rafting.

1st Baptist Church Bereavement Recovery Club, 2025 Sonoma Bl., 644-4064 or 642-7148 (Stanley Cornils).

Friendly Singles, 644-0734/648-4630 (Mary Smith). Ballroom dancing, Mondays, 7:30pm, Dan Foley Park in Vallejo.

N. Bay Connection, Jerry Lipkin, 55 Valle Vista #912, Vallejo 94590, (707) 747-6407. Singles & couples.

Open Door Church Singles, 1004 Marin, Vallejo 94590, 648-8888. Brunches, socials.

Parents Without Partners, Box 144, Vallejo 94590, (707) 644-6407.

Singles Outdoor Activities & Recreation (SOAR), 643-0489.

Vallejo Revival Ctr Singles, 324 Mini, Vallejo 94589, (707) 642-2010. Singles lead church service 1st/2nd Fridays, 8pm. Socials. Mainly black singles, 25-35.

Widows in Christian Svc (WICS), 643-8190 (Hazel Carr). 2nd Wednesdays, 1pm, Community Room, Homestead S&L, 440 Santa Clara.

WALNUT CREEK

Ballroom Dance Classes for Singles, 687-5270. Classes are held at Veterans Hall in Walnut Creek. Monthly dance party.

B'Nai Shalom Jewish Singles, 74 Eckley, 934-9446. 21-39.

Cancer Society Singles League, 1250 Springbrook, Walnut Creek 94596, 934-7640. Fund-raising & socials. Mainly 40+.

Community Presbyterian Church Christian Singles, 1450 Creekside Dr. #18, Walnut Creek 94596.

Contra Costa Jewish Comm Ctr Singles, 2071 Tice Valley, Walnut Creek 94595, 938-7800. Lectures, Mondays, 7:45pm, $2. Also dinners, dances. 1. Jewish Singles, 40+. 2. Singles Chavarim, 21-40.

Diablo Singles, Box 5067, Walnut Creek 94596, 820-4299. Ballroom dancing to live music, 3rd Saturdays, Civic Park Community Ctr. 40+.

Divorce Classes, Patricia Padgett, M.F.C.C., 1844 San Miguel Dr. #317, Walnut Creek 94596, (415) 937-5131.

Evangelical Free Church, 2303 Ygnacio Valley, Walnut Creek 94598, 934-1273. 4 groups: 1. The Carpenter's Union (college-age). 2. Single Adult Fellowship (50s & 60s). 3. Thirst Quenchers (20s). 4. New Joy (30s and 40s.)

Singles Clubs

WALNUT CREEK (continued)

5th Wheelers, Box 4569, Walnut Creek 94596, 676-7129. Ballroom dancing to live music, even Saturdays, Veteran's Hall, 1250 Locust, $4. Bowling, 1st Mondays. Also potlucks, brunches. 40+.

Mormon Singles Hotline, (415) 935-0128 or 932-2903.

New Orinda Club, Box 31642, Walnut Creek 94598, 946-1313. Promotes arts. Also tennis, water skiing, travel, parties, dinners. Mainly 30s & 40s.

Parents Without Partners, Box 5693, Walnut Creek 94596, (415) 820-5160.

Personal Growth Groups for Single Men & Women, 2940 Camino Diablo, #250, Walnut Creek, 94596, 946-9449. Led by Tom Grimm.

Rusty Bindings Ski Club, Box 3096, Walnut Creek 94598, 724-3093 (Mariell Jaren). Tuesdays, El Papagallo Rest., 2995 Ygnacio Valley.

Single Adults, Dorothy Mitchell, 146 The Trees, Concord 94518, 689-9329, 932-5151. Coffee, fellowship, Bible study, Sundays, 9am, Mr. Steaks, 313 N. Civic Dr., Walnut Creek.

Single Again Workshops, 1200 Mt. Diablo Blvd., #107, Walnut Creek, 94596, (415) 254-5754. Led by Jean Wight.

Solutions, 2224 A Oakgrove Rd., #183, Walnut Creek, 94598. Offers to help you discover what you want in a relationship.

St. Paul's Episcopal Church Singles, 1924 Trinity, Walnut Creek 94596, (415) 934-2326.

Unity Ctr of Walnut Creek Singles, 1871 Geary, Walnut Creek 94596, 937-2191 or 938-2836 (Hank Visscher). Personal growth discussions followed by coffee and/or dancing, Sundays, 7-9pm.

Walnut Creek Presbyterian Church Singles, 1720 Oakland Bl, Walnut Creek 94596, 935-1574 or Katherine & Scott Anthony, 686-3251. Dinners, volleyball, special events, plays, picnics, beach parties, water skiing. 2 groups: 1. Kayaks (30+). 2. College/Career (20s).

Widowed Person Support Group, John Muir Hospital, 1601 Ygnacio Valley Rd., Walnut Creek 94598, 939-3000 x 20372 or 938-5246. Counselors from JFK Univ.

Widow-Widowers Socials, Box 5113, Walnut Creek 94596. Champagne brunches, dinners.

Winners, Box 195, Walnut Creek 94596. Mainly 24-47. Lee Kimball.

Ygnacio Valley Baptist Church Singles, 535 Walnut, Walnut Creek 94596, 939-2333.

Young Unattached Professionals, Box 31533, Walnut Creek 94598, 947-6700. Tom Coop, Director. Large coat & tie dances at elegant hotels.

WATSONVILLE

Beginning Experience, Monterey Bay Chapter, 144 Holm Rd. #20, Watsonville 95076, (408) 728-1177 or Tom Tanner at (408) 424-1458.

Corralitos Methodist Church Singles, 26 Browns Valley, Watsonville 95076, 722-4363.

Monterey Bay Singles, 724-9406 (Marty). Coffee, discussion, Tuesdays.

SINGLES PUBLICATIONS

The **Singles Clubs** chapter of this book lists publications that provide a calendar of events for singles. The **Personal Ad Romance** chapter features publications that accept personal ads. This chapter list publications that have articles of interest to singles, as well as full-length books.

National Periodicals for Singles

Christian Single, 127 9th Ave. N., Nashville, TN 37234, (615) 251-2289.
Concerned Singles Newsletter, Box 555, Stockbridge, MA 01262. Monthly newsletter for peace-oriented singles.
Jewish Singles Magazine, Box 247, Newton, MA 02159, (617) 244-5677.
Miss Mom, Box 547, Moab, UT 84532, (801) 259-5090. Monthly. Free.
News & Views, Single Life Institute, 810 Milford, Abilene, TX 79601, (915) 673-8687. Monthly newsletter for singles ministries.
Single Adult Ministry Information, Box 11394, Kansas City, MO 64112. Monthly newsletter for coordinators of Christian singles clubs.
Single Adult Ministries Journal, Colorado Springs, (303) 579-6471. Monthly newsletter for coordinators of Christian singles clubs.
Single Impact, 7245 College, Lima, NY 14485. Christian Quarterly.
The Single Parent, Parents Without Partners (P.W.P.). 8807 Colesville Rd., Silver Spring, MD 20910, (301) 588-9354. Monthly.
Singles Scene, Box 454, Crossville, TN 38557, (615) 456-0021. Christian.
Today's Single, 1933 Wisconsin, Milwaukee WI 53233, (414) 344-7300.

Local Periodicals for Singles

Enjoy Life Singles Magazine, Box 2593, Santa Rosa 95405, (707) 575-1006. Bimonthly. Violet Young, Editor.

In the Know, 634 Broderick, San Francisco 94117, (415) 346-7783. Juliette Smith, Editor.

Lifestyle, 421 W. MacArthur Blvd., Oakland 94609, (415) 420-1381. Bimonthly. Dave Sawle, Publisher.

Single Again, Box 384, Union City 94587, (415) 793-6315. Monthly magazine for divorced, separated, and widowed. Len Harris, Publisher.

Books for Singles

Brief Encounters, E. Coleman & B. Edwards. Garden City, NY: Anchor Books, 1979.

The Challenge of Being Single, M. Edwards & E. Hoover, NY: New American Library, Inc., 1975.

Cohabitation Agreement & Guide, designed to protect both individuals who are living together. Singular Approaches, Box 1045, Tres Pinos, CA 95075.

Coming Apart: Why Relationships End and How to Live Through the Ending of Yours, Kingma, Daphne Rose, Berkeley: Conari Press, 1987. To order a copy send $8.43 per copy to Conari Press, 713 Euclid Ave., Berkeley, CA 94708.

Catholic Singles Book Club, Box 1920, Evanston, IL 60204.

The Dance-Away Lover, Daniel Goldstine. NY: William Morrow & Co., 1977.

The Divorce Book, Gosse, Richard, et al, New Harbinger Publications, 1984. Send $11.66 to Singles, 4 Highland Ave., San Rafael, CA 94901.

Finding Love, Dr. Margaret O'Connor & Dr. Jane Silverman. NY: Crown Publishers, 1989.

First Person Singular: Living the Good Life Alone, S.M. Johnson. NY: New American Library, Inc., 1978.

Game Free: The Meaning of Intimacy, Thomas Oden. NY: Harper & Row, 1974.

The Great American Man Shortage, William Novak. NY: Rawson Associates, 1983.

How to Find a Lasting Relationship, Richard Gosse, Marin Publications, 1988. $11.66 to 4 Highland Ave., San Rafael, CA 94901. (415) 459-3817.

How to Pick Up a Man, Dian Hanscn. NY: G.P. Putnam's Sons, 1982.

How to Pick Up Girls, Eric Weber. NY: Symphony Press, 1970.

Singles Publications

Books for Singles (continued)

If I'm So Wonderful Why Am I Still Single?, Susan Page. Grafton Books, 1988.

Launching & Sustaining Successful Singles Ministry, Dick Dunn. $37.75 to Singles Ministry Resources, Box 1472, Roswell,GA 30077,587-1691.

Letting Go: A 12 Week Personal Action Program to Overcome a Broken Heart. Zev Wanderer & Tracy Cabot. NY: Warner Books, 1981.

The Little Black Party Book, Juliette Smith. Singles clubs and other social organizations. $7 to In the Know, 634 Broderick, San Francisco 94117.

Looking for Love Through the Personals, Judy Knoll. $9.95 to Personal Connections, Box 880004, San Diego, CA 92108.

Lover Shopping: How to Be Married One Year from Today, Dr. Martin V. Gallatin. Send $14.95 to Shapolsky Publishers, 56 E. 11th St.f, New York, NY 10003 or call (212) 505-2505.

Making Contact, A. Wassmer. NY: The Dial Press, 1978.

National Single Adult Ministries Resource Directory, Box 730, Redmond, OR 97756, (800) 452-1104, x76. $11.95. Jerry Jones, Editor.

National Square Dance Directory, Box 54055, Jackson, MS 39208, (601) 825-6831. Gordon Goss. $9. Includes many singles square dance clubs.

101 Creative & Effective Ways to Meet Worthwhile Men, Betsy Reifman. Singles Calendar, Box 3044, Laguna Hills 92654, (714) 855-2347.

Pairing, G.R. Bach & R.M. Deutzch, NY: Avon Books, 1970.

Passive Men; Wild Women, Pierre Mornell. NY: Ballantine Books, 1979.

Personal ADventures, Jay Wiseman. Send $6.29 to Gentle Persuasion Press, 2966 Diamond St., #212, San Francisco, CA 94131.

Professional Singles Manual, Renee Namaste, Ph.D. Also known as Solo Power. ARC Publications, 3142 Cork Ln, Costa Mesa 92626.

The Psychology of Romantic Love, Nathaniel Branden. NY: Bantam Books, 1981.

Single File: How to Live Happily Forever After With or Without Prince Charming, Susan Deitz. NY: St. Martin's Press, 1989.

Singles Ministry Handbook, Douglas L. Fagerstrom, National Assoc. of Christian Singles, 1933 W. Wisconsin Ave., Milwaukee, WI 53233. The

Single Mother's Survival Manual, Barbara Duncan. Send $14.45 to R & E Publishers, Box 2008, Saratoga, CA 95070.

Single, Straight Men: 106 Guaranteed Places to Find Them, Dr. Diana Sommerfield. St. Martin's Press, $9.95.

Singles: The New Americans, Simenauer, J. & Caroll, D. NY: Simon and Schuster, 1982.

Starting a Singles Ministry Kit. $34.95 to Mobilized to Serve, Elim Fellowship, 7245 College, Lima, NY 14485, (716) 582-2790.

Too Close, Too Soon, Jim Talley & Bobbie Reed. Nashville: Thomas Nelson Publishers, 1982.

The Whole Single Person's Catalog, E. Collins. NY: Peebles Press, 1979.

Singles Publications

SINGLES RESOURCES
with Rich Gosse

Rich Gosse is Chairman of American Singles, a nationwide, non-profit organization. He teaches classes for singles at more than 50 American colleges. Now you can experience the wit and wisdom of Rich Gosse in the privacy of your home or car with audio cassette tapes of his most popular college classes. These tapes, together with his informative and entertaining books, will give you all the resources you need to enjoy your single lifestyle.

ORDER FORM

Please mail me the following items:

___ Looking for Love in All the Right Places (tape)
___ How to Be Happily Single (tape)
___ Romantic Charisma (tape)
___ Initiating Contact & the Art of Flirting (tape)
___ How to Select the Right Partner/Eliminating the Competition (tape)
___ Self-Esteem for Singles (tape)
___ How to Find a Lasting Relationship (book)
___ Singles Guide to the San Francisco Bay Area (book)
___ Singles Guide to the L.A. Area (book)
___ The Divorce Book

$9.95 + $1.71 shipping & handling = **$11.66 per book or tape**.

Enclosed is my check for $_____.
Please charge my VISA or MC # _____
Name _____
Address _____
City, State, Zip, Phone _____

Mail to: Richard Gosse & Associates, 4 Highland Ave., San Rafael, CA 94901 or order over the phone, (415) 459-3817.